Putting the Horse before Descartes

In the series **Animals and Ethics,**
edited by Marc Bekoff

ALSO IN THIS SERIES:

Leslie Irvine, *Filling the Ark: Animal Welfare in Disasters*

Marc Bekoff, *Animals at Play*

BERNARD E. ROLLIN

Putting the Horse before Descartes

My Life's Work on Behalf of Animals

TEMPLE UNIVERSITY PRESS
Philadelphia

TEMPLE UNIVERSITY PRESS
Philadelphia, Pennsylvania 19122
www.temple.edu/tempress

Published 2011

Illustration on p. xii: Courtesy of M. Lynne Kesel

Library of Congress Cataloging-in-Publication Data

Rollin, Bernard E.
Putting the horse before Descartes : my life's work on behalf of animals / Bernard E. Rollin.
p. cm. — (Animals and ethics)
Includes bibliographical references and index.
ISBN 978-1-59213-825-8 (cloth : alk. paper)
ISBN 978-1-59213-827-2 (electronic)
1. Rollin, Bernard E. 2. Animal welfare—Moral and ethical aspects. 3. Ethicists—United States—Biography. I. Title.

HV4716.R66A3 2011
179'.3092—dc22
[B] 2010030142

♾ The paper used in this publication meets the requirements of the American National Standard for Information Sciences—Permanence of Paper for Printed Library Materials, ANSI Z39.48-1992

Printed in the United States of America

2 4 6 8 9 7 5 3 1

To *my mother, who died during the writing of this book at age 101 and who believed, as did many Catholic theologians who opposed Descartes and St. Thomas Aquinas, that "heaven would not be heaven without animals"*

Morality is not a single-shot shotgun.

—Cowgirl student in animal sciences, CSU, responding to the question "How can we worry about animals when people are starving?"

Contents

Preface

My work for animals spans more than three decades. During that period, I have lectured more than a thousand times in thirty countries on six continents and in forty-five U.S. states. I have written hundreds of papers and popular articles and seventeen books, and I have consulted for industry and government all over the world. I have been called both a lab trasher and the salvation of biomedicine by the research community, both a sellout and an angel for the animals by animal advocates, a Jew-bastard philosopher, an itinerant preacher preaching the gospel of kindness for the animals, a cross between a rabbi and a biker, the father of veterinary ethics, and a motherfucker. I have been blessed by having powerful enemies and wonderful teachers and friends. In observing human interactions with the most powerless and defenseless among us, I have seen goodness and courage, and I have seen evil sanctified by tradition—what the farm-animal behaviorist Temple Grandin calls bad becoming normal. Most sobering, perhaps, is that I have seen ideology enslave the most intelligent of people to patent nonsense.

When my good friend Marc Bekoff, a tireless fighter for animals, asked me to write my autobiography, I laughed. Yet as I thought about it, I came to realize that perhaps it is a story better told rather than untold, if for no other reason than to show that even in today's regimented and immensely complex world, individuals can effect meaningful change and perhaps inspire others to do so. There is no better legacy than diminishing the suffering one confronts.

Prologue

The Beginning

I was six years old, nagging my mother incessantly to get me a dog. The response was always the same: "You can't have a dog; we live in an apartment, and you have ellegies" (Brooklynese for "allergies," as I discovered later). One Saturday, she agreed to take me to an animal shelter to look at the animals. I recall my unbounded joy—all those beautiful dogs!

"What happens to them?" I asked the attendant.

"We put most of 'em to sleep."

"No," I said. "I mean when they wake up. Do people take them home?"

"No, sonny. We put them to sleep, and they don't wake up. They're killed. Nobody wants them."

I didn't understand.

I still don't.

Putting the Horse before Descartes

1

Life in New York

My academic career path gave little if any early indication of what was later to become my passion: moral concern for animals. Through college at City College of New York, I slavishly followed the stereotyped New York Jewish yellow brick road—hard academic grubbing resulting in a straight-A average after my first year, majoring in literature and philosophy. Except for my long hair, remarkably similar to Angela Davis's, I was my Jewish mother's ideal. The only deviation from this trite script was my insistence that I work summers in Coney Island, both because I could work eighty hours a week (at a dollar an hour) and because Coney Island was a dangerous, rough, intimidating "Sodom by the sea" as one book put it, thereby leading me to believe (with some justification) that I could learn street smarts there. It was in Coney Island that I developed some "real world at its worst" sense and honed the wisecracking, tough-guy persona that would later inform my teaching and lecturing.

There I got to interact with thugs, hookers, street cops, grifters, sideshow "freaks," mafiosi, bikers, kid gangs, drunks, disbarred lawyers, at least one murderer, and lunatics. I befriended a Cherokee Indian paratrooper who saved me from mayhem on a number of occasions, and we became blood brothers. Despite hours of practicing cold, deadeye stares in front of the mirror, I remained a 150-pound former yeshiva boy who didn't shave yet and from whose eyes, as a rabbi cuttingly put it years later, "the light of Judaism shines." Nonetheless, over the eight years I worked there, a bit of what I aspired to be began to emerge. I had acquired skills that would serve me well in combat on behalf of animals.

One additional summer job had major implications for my career. When I was twenty, I needed a job during the week, as Coney Island offered me only weekend work that year. My uncle Oscar was traffic manager for a giant Lily-Tulip paper cup warehouse in the Bronx, and I asked him for a job. He informed me that he did not hire relatives and that the people who worked in the warehouse were roughnecks, hooligans, racists, and anti-Semites. I explained that I needed the money for school, and he relented, but with the proviso that no one know we were related and with the understanding that he would treat me as he treated everyone else—badly, it turned out. I agreed.

The first couple of weeks were rough. I had to join the Teamsters, and the workers were very large, very bigoted, and disparaging of "college boys." They were Italian, German, Polish, Irish, Hungarian, a living museum of the history of anti-Semitism. The worst was an alcoholic German who kept baiting me about being Jewish. One day, I'd had enough. The next time he made a crack about my being Jewish, I said, "[I'll] cut your fucking liver out, if you have a liver left." Amazed, he gave me a wide berth; I had earned some respect. Gradually, the men started asking me what I was studying. When I told them philosophy, I elicited hoots of derision, along with "What the fuck is that?" So I started teaching them philosophy in plain language during breaks and lunch, introducing numerous paradoxes and classic questions. Sure enough, they bit, and I learned how to translate esoteric philosophy into plain talk that piqued their interest. I thus developed, contrary to most philosophers, a healthy respect for regular people. I found them willing to engage issues if I didn't patronize them and if I conducted the discussion in ordinary language, a skill essential to my later work with farmers and ranchers. This experience, of course, fit perfectly with the respect for the Common Sense philosophy that would also inform my subsequent career.

In fact, I was so successful in these discussions that Oscar deemed them subversive and ordered me to desist, particularly during smoke breaks, since I did not smoke. Since our relationship was employee to employer, I solicited the help of the Teamster shop steward, "Uncle Louie" Bongiorno, who rolled into the warehouse in a cream-colored Caddy convertible with red leather seats ("Hey, kid, have a cigar!"). Uncle Louie assured me of my right to lecture on philosophy and so informed Oscar, who cussed me out to my mother for half an hour on the phone but who left me alone thereafter.

At City College of New York, I fell in love with Linda, the brightest, most beautiful woman I had ever met, and throughout college we dated each other exclusively. (Why I loved her was clear; why she loved me was more perplexing. As a colleague uncharitably expressed it in later years, "How did a gargoyle like you land a world-class beauty like her?")

In my senior year, I was awarded a Woodrow Wilson fellowship and a Fulbright fellowship to Edinburgh to study David Hume, Immanuel Kant, and Scottish Common Sense philosophy. I had also applied to the Harvard doctoral program in philosophy, at that time the best in the United States. To my delight, I was accepted with a full four-year fellowship. I traveled to Harvard to determine whether I could defer my enrollment until after the year in Britain. The department head affirmed that I could but handed me my first academic disappointment when he commented, "Your application was very controversial." "Why?" I asked. "Because you have expressed interest in the history of philosophy—in Hume, Kant, Plato—what about *real* philosophy?" "Real philosophy?" I echoed. "Yes! British philosophy after World War I." He explained that analytic philosophy ruled Harvard, and I had shown no special interest in it. To me, it was yet another approach with no special status, and I told him so. "Well," he replied, "if you want to study hard and be thought of as a philosopher, not a historian, you'd best spend the year in Britain getting up to snuff on analytic philosophy." Shocked at his smug attitude, I blurted out that the Scholastics thought they had the ultimate method, too, and where were they today? He replied, "Well, we will take you next year, because *we think you can be saved,* but perhaps you'd best think about going to Columbia unless your attitude changes."

Many years later, I realized that he had done me multiple favors. I *did* master much analytic philosophy during my year in Scotland and learned its great value. And I did go to Columbia. But most important, I learned very early about arbitrary academic bias even in the best of places, determining almost as a matter of fashion what was legitimate to work on and what was not. Without that lesson, I probably would never have found the courage to buck the academic philosophical community's universal bias against philosophy that had anything to do with real-world issues, derisively dismissed as "applied philosophy," and to write in non-jargon, developing a style accessible to and even fun for interested people.

Edinburgh was unforgettable: physically beautiful, civilized, safe, with no need for street smarts. I got to work with George E. Davie, the great Hume and Scottish Common Sense philosophy scholar, and with W. H. Walsh, Kant scholar and analytic philosopher. This combination of influences imprinted me with a strong belief in common sense as a basis for philosophy, a position even the greatest of all skeptics, David Hume, espoused in his ordinary life moments. Linda and I hitchhiked across Europe over three months, encountering hospitality and kindness everywhere and mitigating considerably my New York–based belief that society was "a war of each against all," in Hobbes's immortal phrase, and that one always needed to lock one's doors. Absent the Edinburgh experience, I probably never would have left New York.

I returned to Columbia to earn my doctorate. It turned out that Columbia was an extremely cold, unfriendly, bureaucratic place. Though there were more than three hundred active graduate students in the doctoral program in philosophy, there was only one faculty adviser for all the students who were not yet ready to write their dissertations. One seminar I took had more than fifty enrolled students; the room held only twenty. It is arguable that the Columbia "student riots" of spring 1967 were not about the Vietnam War or about Columbia's racist policies toward its black neighbors (the ostensible reason for the insurrections) but, rather, about the total indifference of the university toward students' well-being. For example, although I had arrived with a Woodrow Wilson fellowship that was presumed to be renewed for a second year if I did not flunk out, in practice Columbia would appropriate the money, informing me that, since I had already invested a year, I would "find the money somewhere."

To qualify to write the dissertation, one needed to pass comprehensive exams on some fifteen thousand pages of philosophical material, which often did not overlap at all with courses offered. In addition, the highly competitive graduate students waged psychological warfare on each other, usually by invoking legends regarding the comprehensive exams. Example: "Oh, you're taking the metaphysics exam? I hope you've read Whitehead." "No—it's not on the reading list." "Doesn't matter. They often ask about Whitehead." Since Whitehead was utterly incomprehensible, fear and paranoia were the order of the day.

I doubt I could have gotten through the program without my wife, then doing a quickie master's degree so she could teach elementary school and help support us. Being far brighter than I am, she was invaluable—teaching me and my fellow graduate students logic, reading my papers, blunting paranoia. (She has an IQ of over 170 and got a Ph.D. in math at Colorado State University [CSU] for *fun,* never opening a math book after her oral exam.) Besides her love and friendship, animals were my salvation. New York air was such that one could slice it, producing beautiful sunsets, filthy white shirts, and, in me, chronic asthma leading to visits to the emergency room five times a week and more. Between the pressure of the program and the asthma working synergistically, I experienced the worst four years of my life.

Mao was an Abyssinian kitten I had acquired from Bideawee, a pioneering no-kill shelter. Linda and I spent hours playing with her; I even carried her on my shoulder to the park. Tough, smart, wisecracking—a paradigmatic New York cat—Mao later survived the move to Colorado, learned to negotiate the rural outdoors, had a litter of kittens, fished for carp, and eventually disappeared on one of her forays, presumably killed by coyotes. Helga was a 150-pound black Great Dane who accompanied me everywhere and whom I guard trained sufficiently for her to growl and snarl whenever my wife and I coughed in a certain way. On at least one occasion, she saved my wife from being mugged. As Linda left our building, she saw five teenage no-goodniks entering our building. Aware that we had no teenagers in the building, my wife coughed and alerted Helga. The kids obligingly held the door for Linda, wished her a good morning, and mugged the next tenant at knifepoint.

Helga was probably the sweetest dog I have ever known. I would walk her to Linda's school at 3:00 P.M. to pick her up. Hordes of schoolchildren would sit on Helga, hang from her ears and neck, and hug her, and she greeted them with gentle delight. I realized then—and even more so now—that the dog and cat were my salvation. The only thing that relieved the constant, nagging fear of the next asthma attack was playing with my animals, and their silent affection was a source of constant joy (except when the downstairs neighbors complained about my chasing the cat around the apartment at 3:00 A.M. or when the ineffectual Park Avenue allergist pumping me full of cortisone recited his weekly mantra, "Get rid of the dog and cat").

Anyone who has lived in New York is well aware of the coldness and callousness of people there. Mind your own business, don't get involved, don't make eye contact, and don't talk to strangers. Watch New Yorkers on an elevator: Each person unerringly finds a spot as far away from everyone else as possible and develops a great interest in examining the ceiling. When I later moved to Colorado, I suspected the entire city of Fort Collins of being populated by hookers, because women smiled at you in the street and said, "Good morning."

Life in New York, as I realized after moving west, can be far lonelier than living in rural Wyoming. The Wyoming cowboy, whose nearest neighbor may be eighty miles away, is separated from companionship only by geographic distance. The New York apartment dweller may be separated by two inches of plasterboard and never exchange a greeting. Shorn of physical distance from others, people create unbridgeable psychic distance.

Helga was, as she taught me, not only a source of unqualified love and companionship but also a bridge across that psychic distance and a social lubricant. The one exception to the "never talk to strangers" rule is if they or you or both of you are walking a dog. A dog—preferably a puppy or an exotic dog—is a license to approach another. "Wuh kina dawg is dat?" is a password for accessing other minds, or, alternatively, "Bewful dawg!" (Ice-breaking hint: All large Dobermans walked by Italian men are named Diablo, pronounced "De-ah-bull-o.")

I recall walking Helga at 4:00 A.M. on Broadway, a dangerous time, but I was unafraid. I was approached by a young black woman. "Sir," she said. "I was heading for Harlem, but I got off at the wrong subway station. You need a token to get back on at this hour, and I don't have one. I'm scared on the street. Would you walk me to Harlem with that big dog?" I did, wondering how she knew I wasn't a monster with a big dog.

I would usually work all day, take the dog to the park in the late afternoon, work until midnight or so, then take a long walk with the dog before going to bed from 6:00 A.M. to noon. On one occasion, I was about to enter Riverside Park, a beautiful two-mile-long park abutting the Hudson River, about which I will say more shortly. As I started to descend the stairs, a patrol car came screaming up. "Hey, you can't go in there," a cop shouted. "Why not?" I asked. Thinking me a simpleton, he said, "Because the park is full of bad people at night, and it's dangerous." "If that's the case," I replied, "why aren't you in the park getting the bad people, instead of giving me a hard time?" "Don't be stupid, buddy," he said. "We don't have that big dog to protect us." (He had only a day stick, a nightstick, mace, and a pistol, as well as, very likely, a throwaway gun and knife.) In fact, research has shown that a man-and-dog police team is far more effective in park patrol and crime deterrence than either cars or foot patrols. (Dogs were not used because of pressure from the black community. The dog was a symbol of white oppression, *vide* Bull Connor's use of dogs in Alabama. Some of my police friends told me they would rather have a dog than their weapons: "Bad guys know you can't bullshit a dog.")

My meanderings often took me three miles to the theater district. At an all-night doughnut shop, the prostitutes would assemble at 4:00 A.M. after work. My arrival—or, more accurately, Helga's arrival—was greeted with joyous cries of "Hilda, Hilda!" (as they had come to call her), as they dropped to their knees and hugged and kissed her. (I was addressed only for permission to buy her a doughnut.) These cynical, guarded, hard-bitten women would allow the little girl in them to emerge for the brief moments of pleasure and genuine affection toward the dog. I cannot recall those times without emotion.

Strangest of all, Helga introduced me to the "dog people," a subculture of people who walk their dogs at the same times in the morning or after work, year-round. The dogs, not knowing New York etiquette, would interact and romp while we watched. Eventually, we began to communicate with each other and, *mirabile dictu,* to care for each other. (Eventually, some would visit me in Colorado.) One story epitomizes that phenomenon for me: Red was a huge German Shepherd owned by Phil (I don't know his last name), a former British commando. Though aggressive with male dogs (Phil put Red in a pen alone to run or let him run with female dogs), he was an obedient angel with people. When Phil had surgery, we all took turns walking Red for the two weeks Phil was in the hospital. We had a key to Phil's apartment we passed around; though Phil did not know our last names or addresses, he seemed to assume we were worthy of trust. Through the animals, *Gesellschaft* was replaced by *Gemeinschaft.*

Perhaps two years after Phil's operation, I was suffering from chronic asthma, experiencing attacks every night, sometimes multiply in a night. My physician was preparing to hospitalize me indefinitely until the cycle was broken. I mentioned this to Phil one evening. He nodded and said nothing. The next evening he handed me an envelope. "What is this?" I asked. "The key to my cabin in Thunder Bay, Ontario, and a map. Stay there until you can breathe. The air is clean, and there's no reason for stress. It beats a hospital."

For more old people than I care to recall, the dog (or cat) was a reason to get up in the morning, to go out, to bundle up and go to the park ("Fluffy misses her friends, you know"), to shop, to fuss, to feel responsible for a life and needed.

Although I had various opportunities to remain in New York after finishing my qualifying exams for the doctorate, it began to dawn on Linda and me that New York was no longer the wonderland we recalled from our childhood. The air was polluted; the streets were paved with junkies; my skin erupted in giant weals, which the doctor assured me were "just the effect of acid rain"; a professor at Columbia was killed for refusing to surrender his wedding ring; I was forced to escort Linda everywhere, even to the basement to do laundry, for predators often sought victims there. The year in Edinburgh had taught us that there were nice places to live. We resolved to get out of New York as soon as I had finished my exams and was ready to write my dissertation. In 1968, I began applying for jobs, but only at places whose whereabouts I was unsure of, on the assumption that if I did not know where they were, they were probably not like New York. I still have a file of letters of application to Alaska, Calgary, Edmonton, Wyoming, Iceland, and the Faroe Islands.

In January 1969, we attended the American Philosophical Association's annual meeting in Washington, D.C. Since there were then still more jobs than applicants, the convention was not yet the "slave auction" or "meat market" peopled by desperate graduate students and academic wimps brimming with self-importance and lording jobs over the job-seeking students that it would become a few short years later, and remain until today. I had a number of interviews lined up, and was brightly optimistic. As we exited the elevator in the convention hotel, we literally bumped into a rube-ish elderly gentleman, shiningly bald and dressed in white socks and a manure-colored shiny brown suit that complemented his head. He peered at my convention name badge. "Columbia, huh?" he intoned in what I would later learn was a rural Hoosier accent. "Motty good school." I smiled and nodded. "Looking for a job?" I looked at his badge: "Willard Eddy, Colorado State University, Fort Collins, Colorado." "We need a man in History of Philosophy," he intoned. That was, indeed, what I wanted to teach. Furthermore, though I had vaguely heard of Colorado, I had never heard of Fort Collins. "Come for an interview at 1:30," he said. What the hell. I went to chat with him. He rocked dangerously in the chair as he told me about CSU. "It's just an old cow town," he intoned. "No fancy stores or anything like what you're used to. Bunch of retired ranchers. An ag school. Cowboy country."

My mind wandered out and began to create mental pictures. Elevated wooden sidewalks. A general store. Tumbleweeds. Indians. The Philosophy Department holding forth behind a cracker barrel. "I see you read Hé-brew. You a Jew?" "Umm, I came from that background but have no religion." "Never had a Jew in the department before," he exclaimed. "Got a Korean though." "I will have a friend ready-made," I said archly. "Got a woman, too," he continued. "Another friend," I countered. "Mott be nahss to have a Jew. Mott ask you to teach some religion." "I'm not interested in religion," I said, unheard. "You could teach some Judaism. But I gotta warn you: There's a Colorado state law against proselytizing." He apparently liked me, because he invited Linda and me to join him and a couple of department members for dinner. When I told Linda about our conversations, she said, "Don't waste our time." But we went, expecting little except a good story. I was later to learn that Willard was doing his "interviewing easterners" shtick, intended to turn off anyone from a city who was not interested in going to a small town. I never saw the brown suit again, and was to come to know Willard as one of three men I ever met who, if they asked me to jump, I would ask, "How high?" He was to exert an unmatched influence on my career. Absent his influence, my life would have been vastly different and impoverished.

We went to dinner and met Don Crosby and Dan Lyons, who had doctorates from Columbia and the University of Chicago, respectively. They made it plain that they would consider hiring me to get Linda. They also let me know that, while everyone else at CSU was hiring from the Midwest, Willard was hiring from Princeton, Yale, Stanford, and Edinburgh, seeking mavericks or people with respiratory problems looking for fresh air. I was both, as well as the first Jew. I ended up with offers from Wyoming and CSU and took the CSU job because the department had fifteen members and Wyoming's had three and because CSU offered me $10,500 to Wyoming's paltry $10,000. In July 1969, we rented a U-Haul truck, took the dog and cat, and, accompanied by my brother, drove west of New Jersey for the first time in my life to a job I had accepted, sight unseen.

As we loaded the truck for Colorado on our last day in New York, an old lady approached me with tears in her eyes. “You’re leaving?” she queried in a refugee accent. “Yes,” I said, thinking, “How can she be upset at my leaving when we’ve never even exchanged hellos?” “I will never feel safe again,” she declared. I stared uncomprehendingly. “I will never feel safe again without that wonderful dog watching over the building.”

2

Coming to CSU

The Start of My Animal Career

In the late 1960s, Fort Collins was a town of twenty-nine thousand, economically based in the university, retired ranchers, and a small group of light industries. As we drove our U-Haul into town, I was reminded of a booklet sent to me at Columbia titled "This Is CSU." My New York colleagues and I had been vastly amused by the document. First of all, one photo showed a lecture hall full of students with a cow standing in front and no professor apparent. This photo provoked the predictable jokes about "cow college." Even more amusing was a section titled "Your Car, Your Bike, Your Horse," in which students were advised that, while many students brought their horses with them to college, "there [were] no hitching posts on campus." The hilarity this occasioned in the Philosophy Department's office at Columbia generated a real sense of irony in the following year, when I wished to ride my horse to campus but was forestalled by the absence of hitching posts.

In any event, seeing the mountains and vast open fields surrounding the town, Linda and I resolved not to live in town (even then blighted by ugly subdivisions). Instead, we would pick a rural domicile.

In a week, we had rented it—twelve acres on a lake with a barn and silo and a pasture that I would be responsible for "irrigating." I thought "irrigating" meant turning on a water tap. I was soon to discover that it meant standing up to my crotch in cold, filthy ditch water that one would direct through sluices with "tarps." Oh, boy! There was even a horse—Halfmoon—that the man living in a second house and taking care of the property for the owner assured me I could ride. We moved in, and I bought a pair of cowboy boots and a black Stetson that, unfortunately, made me look like a Chassid.

René, the caretaker, was a Hungarian refugee of questionable reputation. He claimed to have been machine-gunned by Russians while escaping from Hungary and insisted on showing off his bullet wounds. An instrument technician for the Department of Atmospheric Science, he could repair any machine, tapped into the phone company's line for his service, and later spliced into my electricity, yielding a twelve-hundred-dollar electric bill and a bemused rural electric company that knew he had done it but could not figure out how. He also illegally hatched Canada goose eggs and imprinted the goslings on his boot so that a Conga line of them followed him everywhere. He was known to "borrow" the university's airplane on weekends for joyriding (naturally without a license) and set his own leg when he broke it in seven places while skiing and the doctor had detected only six. Highly athletic, he climbed a tree in a walking cast a month later and today, at seventy-five, sailboards nude on the lake, according to my students.

I arrived in July 1969 and spent a pleasant summer preparing my courses in the history of philosophy and beginning to write my doctoral dissertation. I also realized what an immense cultural change Linda and I were experiencing. Two examples illustrate. Near us was a rural liquor store patronized almost exclusively by cowboys. One day we went in and were greeted by a great display of Mogen David sweet kosher wine. Perplexed, I asked the proprietor if he served a large Jewish population. He looked at me without comprehension. I tried again. "How come all this kosher wine?" I queried. "Oh," he said, "the cowboys love it. It's sweet and even cheaper than Ripple." And in my third week in Fort Collins, I received a phone call from an engineering professor referred to me by Willard Eddy. In a western drawl, he asked if I could help resolve a debate in his church. "Why me?" I asked. "Willard tells me you're a Jew," he said. "So you should know: Aren't Jews a kind of Christian?" "No, sir," I replied. "Christians are a kind of Jew." He hung up and never spoke to me again.

I got to know Willard Eddy well. A benevolent despot ruling a department of fifteen people, all at least thirty years younger than he was, he had been at CSU for decades. As he coached me on the nature of the university and the students, he gently informed me that, while I was free to pursue whatever intellectual interests I had, since CSU was a land-grant agricultural school it would be good if I could devote some of my efforts to integrating philosophy into the university in a way that served the people of the state. That seed, planted by Willard, was to blossom into my subsequent work with animals. It had in turn been implanted into Willard when he was a graduate student at the University of Chicago by Professor Charner Perry, who despised the ivory-tower nature of twentieth-century philosophy and urged making it meaningful to real things.

Many of my colleagues heeded that call—brilliant young people all. Holmes Rolston would go on to establish the field of environmental ethics; Pat McKee, the field of philosophy of aging; Dick Kitchener, the philosophy and ethics of psychology; Jim Boyd, the study of cross-cultural values while also becoming a leading Zoroastrian scholar. We read one another's papers, exulted in one another's publications, had reading groups and seminars, and even split our raises equally for a number of years. While all were first-rate thinkers from major doctoral programs, many had found these places stifling and had come to Colorado to seek more intellectual freedom. I was later to note that in the 1970s and 1980s, it was such people at state universities who established fields such as animal and environmental ethics.

I also received invaluable advice from Willard Eddy in my evaluation conference at the end of the first year. "Bernie," he told me, "there are two ways to be successful in academe. One is to suck up to people above you; the other is to publish your butt off. The first is closed to you." I took that message to heart and have felt its wisdom reverberating throughout my career. If one wishes to survive and be controversial, one needs to develop an international reputation by publishing and lecturing so that one puts the institution on the map and it, in turn, forgives your nonconformity.

I loved, and still love, the CSU students from the very first class I taught there. Unlike too many young people I had known in the East, they had no element of pseudo-intellectual posturing, no Nietzschean texts conspicuously sticking out of their pockets, no pretentiousness. In Socratic terms, they knew that they didn't know (a higher stage than thinking they did) and were eager to learn. Many had never known a New Yorker and were delighted with my teaching style, a strange mixture of Lenny Bruce and erudition, scholarship and vulgarity, hard work and high expectations leavened with humor. When I began teaching History of Philosophy, it was a three-hour class. I began offering an optional hour on Thursday afternoons; all attended, and it soon became three-plus hours on Thursday. I successfully petitioned to make it a five-hour class (it already occupied three quarters and, later, two semesters) and then added three more optional hours on Thursdays. At the end of the academic year in the early 1970s, one of my best students, Steve Hillard (later to become a successful lawyer who won compensation for the Eskimos for the land that Anchorage was built on), presented me with more than five hundred pages of handwritten notes on a legal pad ("I thought you'd like to know how much you taught me.").

I taught the history of philosophy from Thales through Hegel and made the students do unbelievable assignments by today's lax standards—for example, to summarize Aristotle's *Metaphysics* or Kant's *Critique of Pure Reason* paragraph by paragraph in their own words. But as I mastered more and more of the major figures in the history of philosophy, a thought kept emerging. Philosophers had asserted the unreality of the physical world (Plato and Parmenides), the impossibility of motion (Zeno), the unreality of time (McTaggart), the claim that matter was mind (Berkeley) and mind was matter (Smart), and so on. Yet nowhere in the great history of ideas had anyone raised the question of the moral status of animals and of what entitled us to use them as we see fit. If the issue did arise, it was "resolved" by affirming, as did Descartes, that animals had no minds (hence, the title of this book) and were just machines, a position that burgeoned in the twentieth century. Or else it was argued, as by both Descartes and Kant, that animals, lacking language, could not reason or even have a mental life.

As it happened, not so coincidentally, the doctoral dissertation that I wrote from 1969 until my defense of it in 1972 and that appeared as the book *Natural and Conventional Meaning: An Examination of the Distinction* in 1976 in the *Mouton Approaches to Semiotics* series seriously questioned the dualism of natural meaning and conventional meaning, dogma since antiquity. I claimed there that such natural-meaning vehicles as clouds meaning rain or smoke meaning fire differed only in degree, not in kind, from the meaning of words and sentences. If I was correct, it dawned on me, then a major way to create a metaphysical chasm between humans and animals—the possession of language by the former but not the latter that had been a mainstay of Descartes—might not be tenable and, in any case, could not justify the neglect of animals' moral status. I received succor from the eighteenth-century philosopher David Hume, the greatest skeptic who ever lived and whom I had studied in Edinburgh, who, despite denying mind, body, God, causation, and science, opined that the fact that animals experienced thought and feelings was so obvious that it could fail to escape only the "most stupid," meaning Descartes.

The dissertation, incidentally, was written under Professor Arthur Danto, arguably the greatest living philosopher, eclectic in his interests, an artist and art critic and a great friend and adviser. It was Danto who later encouraged me to get involved in animal issues and who, in 2002, assuaged my self-doubts by saying, "You have accomplished the most of any of my graduate students."

While these ideas kicked around in my mind, I was not sure what to do with them. In 1970, I drew up a plan for an anthology dealing with human moral obligations to the non-human world—animals and the natural environment—and sent it to a dozen publishers, who rejected it with a

"Don't be silly. Who is interested in that?" letter. Chastened, I abandoned the project.

At the same time, my connection with animals deepened. As I mentioned earlier, René gave me permission to ride the horse he was boarding. In fact, he saddled Halfmoon and helped me climb on her back, whereupon she ran me through the trees, splitting my head open, eliciting an offer from René to "sew it mit dental floss." I got back on. Halfmoon scraped me along the barn and shortly thereafter dumped me in a mud puddle. René assured me that it was a matter of practice and to keep trying. Some weeks later, I could more or less stay on at a variety of gaits. One day, a pickup truck drove up, and a man jumped out, shouting, "What the hell are you doing on Halfmoon?" I explained that René had told me I could ride her. "Oh, you can ride her," he said, "if you want to get killed. She's here because she broke my son's arm." "She seems fine now," I said. "Doggone, you done broke her," he said. "Thanks!" The next week, he sold her.

Now established (in my own mind) as a rider and trainer, I bought a "killer horse," Raszam, half-Arabian, half-Standardbred, who had belonged to a woman who was afraid of him. It turned out that she simply got off whenever he acted up, so she had trained him to act up. Too dumb to be afraid, I worked with him constantly, even setting up an illuminated ring for night riding. After a few months, I could control him by just shifting my weight, and he was totally reliable. In fact, he would follow me like a dog, much to the delight of novice riders who thought they were controlling him. One of my colleagues had a child with cerebral palsy who needed to wear heavy leg braces. One day when they came to visit, I asked her if she wanted to sit on the horse. (This was well before anyone had thought up riding for disabled people.) Her face broke into the sweetest smile I had ever seen, and she nodded enthusiastically. With her parents' permission, I put her on the saddle, admonishing her to hold the reins and the saddle horn. I then walked all over the property with Raszam behind me. As I walked, he walked on eggs, as if sensing the child's vulnerability. We walked for hours, the smile never leaving Beth's face. Unable to walk, she had sat high and seen the world from a point higher than others.

I loved the horse and the country life. My only regret was that, although Linda also loved the horse and would pet him and walk with him, she refused to ride, claiming, "It's too high to fall from." Realizing that the horse was lonely on his own in the field, I had an inspiration: "I'll get Linda a donkey for Christmas, and he can keep the horse company." My rural friends directed me to one Pappy Spence (believe it or not), an old prospector who looked like Gabby Hayes and had a herd of donkeys. He agreed to sell me one for seventy-five dollars but cautioned me, "Come spring, he might get mean." "What do I do then?" I inquired. "You need to cut him." "Cut him?" I replied, envisioning some primitive domination ritual. "Yep. Castrate him." "Me?" "No, get the vet to do it." I put a red ribbon on the donkey and gave the animal to Linda for Christmas. "Very cute," she said, and never rode. But the horse and the donkey became inseparable friends.

Spring came, and the donkey launched a flying kick at my head, seemingly confirming Pappy's prediction. So I called CSU's equine ambulatory service and spoke to Jim Voss (who figures prominently later in this account). Voss asked me if he could bring an extra group of students, because "we don't get too many donkey castrations." I readily agreed, asking him if he minded my bringing some friends along, since "I don't do too many donkey castrations." All was set, and we agreed to meet at 4:00 P.M. two days later at my place.

Unfortunately, the freight train that bisected Fort Collins blocked me in, and I was late. I was greeted by a strange sight: a large group of students sitting stone-faced and a tall man who looked like James Garner (Voss) covered in mud, body tense. "Well," I said heartily, "I'm here. We can get started." The Garner-looking man said, tight-lipped, "We're done." I remonstrated. "You were supposed to wait for me!" "That your donkey?" he said. "Yes." "That your only donkey." "Yes." "That donkey is female," he spat with barely controlled rage, turned on his heel, and drove off. I grabbed one of the students. "What happened?" "Well," he said, "your donkey isn't trained and wouldn't let Dr. Voss catch her. So he roped her, and she took off dragging him around the pasture and eventually dumped him in the mud." "He's very pissed off," he added, unnecessarily. My excuses sounded lame, even to me. "Pappy Spence told me it was male. It had shaggy hair—I didn't know what donkey genitalia looked like." I later examined a male donkey and learned just how stupid I had been.

Linda stood there staring at me long after all the students had left. She finally spoke, with a lack of emotion far worse than anger or amusement or ridicule. "I wonder what they'll bill you for?" The answer arrived a week later: a bill for twenty-five dollars labeled "examination for castration." I consoled myself by thinking I would never see Voss again. I was very wrong, as I shall shortly describe. The donkey, whom we had named Edward R. Burro, remained in our household as a constant testimony to my stupidity.

At about this time, I was finally able to get the asthma that had plagued me in check. Instrumental in this process was a student, Perry Smith, a black football player recruited from Froggy Bottom, South Carolina, who took my introductory philosophy class and fell overwhelmingly in love with philosophy. He proceeded to enroll in my History of Philosophy class, and we became friends. (Perry was later to anger his teammates at the Oakland

Raiders by deluging them with philosophical paradoxes demonstrating the unreality of motion and time.) At the end of the academic year, after I had asked him to run a session of this class, he approached me and asked, since he had "done my thing" for an academic year, would I return the favor by doing "his thing"? "What?" I asked suspiciously. "Come work out with the football team," he replied. "Work out?" I said. "What's that?"

This was the early 1970s, before fitness was "in," and I was a product of New York Jewish culture that viewed the body as merely a taxi for moving the mind from place to place. I had absurdly taken Ping-Pong to fulfill my physical education requirement in college and pursued no athletic activities. When Perry explained "working out," I told him rather smugly that I could not do this because I had bad asthma. "So do I," he replied. "Working out makes it better." I agreed to go "work out" with him.

My introduction turned out to be a four-hour marathon session of running, lifting for every muscle group, all cleverly designed to show me what wretched shape I was in and how weak I was and, I realized later, to awaken the competitive spark Perry had astutely recognized in me. As he half-carried me to my car, Perry looked at me with artful contempt and sneered, "Too much for you. You'll never be back." "Like hell," I said. "When do we go next?" Until Perry went off to play for the Raiders in the early summer, we worked out together, he doing his natural athletic moves and I pathetically and ludicrously pushing tiny weights and "running" like a ruptured duck. When Perry went off to training camp, he left me in the custody of a giant lineman—six-foot, six-inch, 300-pound Gerald Caswell. An amiable giant from Texas, Cas cheered my pathetic efforts and even had me spot him as he bench-pressed mammoth weights. Tired of being an object of ridicule to myself (though never to the athletes, who were kindness personified), I vowed that I would bench as much as Perry—225 pounds—by the time he returned from the pros in January. I kept that promise and, incidentally, my asthma waned significantly.

Within a year, I was hooked and obsessed. I soon coached Perry and other athletes and lift weights to this day. At my best (around age thirty-five), I could bench-press 505 pounds and squat 600. Always a New York smart-ass, I now had the muscle to back it up. It turned out that my newfound strength was as important for gaining ingression into the macho culture of veterinarians and cowboys as were my intellectual gifts.

3

Veterinary Medicine

Following Willard Eddy's admonition, I published extensively in Philosophy of Language and History of Philosophy and continued my quest to bring philosophy to the provinces. The problem was I had published two books and an impressive list of articles, and I had been invited to lecture on a number of occasions internationally. I should have been happy, but I was plagued with doubts. Could I really do the same sort of thing for the rest of my life? Though I had not been a student activist in the 1960s, those years had left in me a yearning to make a difference in the "real world." However, academic philosophy did not seem a promising vehicle for doing that.

Enter my newfound passion for working out. As every academic knows, the best place to get anything done in the university was in the locker room, where all stand naked together and artificial barriers are removed. In one of those life-changing accidents that seem to pepper one's life, the locker next to me was occupied by a gregarious, amiable, extroverted gentleman named Harold Breen. Dr. Breen was a veterinary pathologist, an air force officer, and a genuine intellectual. We exchanged pleasantries for months. One day, he asked me, "You teach medical ethics for the pre-meds, right?" I did, indeed, as part of my service load. "Well," he said, "could you do the same sort of thing for veterinary students?" Brashly, I said yes, assuming someone had written a book on the subject. Breen continued, "I have a strong sense that the world is changing rapidly, particularly with regard to animals in society. Our students need to be prepared for such changes. Could you do that?" "Sure," I said from a vantage point of total ignorance. "Great! Could you draft a course syllabus?" "Sure." Over the next few weeks, in dialogue with Breen, I prepared the document. He then submitted it to the curriculum committee. Predictably, I now realize, fourteen months later we received a terse memo from that committee: "proposal rejected."

I now understand the absurdity of our suggestion. In veterinary school, as in medical, dental, law, and all professional schools, space in the curriculum is highly contested. With knowledge relevant to veterinary medicine growing exponentially, every field sought to expand its share in a curriculum that was already absurdly full. I later realized that proposing a philosophy class to a vet school was as ludicrous as proposing a veterinary class to a doctoral program in philosophy. Oh, well. I didn't need extra work, particularly as I was already planning a freshman honors biology course, eventually funded by the National Science Foundation, in which philosophy would be taught in tandem with biology as one unit. (That course ran for more than twenty years and was, according to students, a great success. Many are now physicians, scientists, and professors and still express appreciation for being taught to think and for having their vistas expanded.)

I suspect that the course would have languished in the trash heap of good ideas but for a serendipitous event a few months later. While I was lecturing in Europe, my beloved Helga developed an ear hematoma (blood blister) in the pinna of one ear. My wife took her to CSU, where a surgeon I will call Dr. Nott told her that surgery under general anesthesia needed to be done immediately. My wife was suspicious, knew that an aging Great Dane was a surgical risk, and asked another vet what to do. "You can leave it alone if you don't mind a little crumpling from scar tissue." My wife went back to the surgeon and told him no general surgery. As she left, she heard him say to the students, "We lost that one; we'll find you another." When I returned home and she told me the story, I was furious and sought out Nott in the clinic. I waited for him and introduced myself. "I have nothing to say to you. Your wife would not heed my advice." I exploded: This son of a bitch would have subjected my dog to unnecessary surgery that might have killed her for his convenience. I picked him up by his shirtfront and carried him to a wall. "What do you want to talk about?" he asked ingratiatingly. "Whether you're left- or right-handed, so I know which hand to break," I snarled, "so you will never do unnecessary surgery on an animal again." Unsettled, he confessed that he was only doing what he was taught. "They teach us to say whatever is necessary to get the client off our back so we can do whatever we want," he whined. Furious, I released him and marched to the office of the Dean of Veterinary Medicine.

At the time, the dean was Bill Tietz, a liberal-arts graduate from Swarthmore (a rarity among veterinarians) who later became the spectacularly successful and beloved president of Montana State University. I told him the story, leaving out the surgeon's name. "Is that what you teach them?" I asked. "Well, I wouldn't have thought so," he mused, "but I'm not sure. Last week, after leaving a cage door open and losing a client's black cat, one of our clinicians tried to pass off another black cat on the client." "It probably won't help," I said, "but why not allow me to teach the ethics class we proposed? It might at least raise awareness of ethical issues." "Fair enough," he said and committed to allowing me to teach a ten-week, one-hour-a-week experimental course the next spring. "If it goes well, we'll expand it to the full semester."

I ran out of his office over to the library to find the veterinary ethics books. There were, of course, none. I realized the enormous stupidity of what I had done. How could I teach the class? I knew nothing of veterinary medicine. However, I did have the conceptual syllabus we had submitted. I called Breen and, through his good offices, began to network with clinicians at the hospital who graciously began to educate me. I spent many hours talking to them and even accompanying them as they dealt with cases. I will always be indebted to Wally Morrison, then a resident and now a prominent oncologist, and Mary Lee Keating, one of the few female clinicians then at CSU, for hours of guidance and dialogue. The picture they painted was not promising: atrocious laboratory exercises, regard for animals only as people's property, a widespread macho attitude toward animals, contempt for animal welfare, a predominance of cowboy students who sheared hippies with sheep sheers, and the like.

From Wally I learned of trouble he had incurred by doing a research project for the American Humane Association on rodeo injuries. As he did pathology on a roping calf with a broken neck, he was startled by being lifted off his feet by a world-renowned equine surgeon, who told him such research was unacceptable since the surgeon received research money from rodeo interests. The surgeon in question, a man of enormous physical strength, enjoyed legendary status (I will call him Dr. Eaves): Eaves punching out a rambunctious bull; Eaves spending lunch hours lifting massive weights and climbing a rope to the top of the gym ceiling using just his hands; Eaves taking on the whole senior class in hand-to-hand combat; Eaves blocking women from admission to veterinary school; Eaves throwing students out of his surgery physically if they had beards, long hair, or mustaches (I, of course, had all of the above). In my increasingly paranoid mind, Eaves assumed Satanic proportions.

I did not feel much better when Dr. Keating allowed me to accompany her at the clinic. She told me to wear a clinical smock and a stethoscope and keep my mouth shut. My first day, she could find only a size 38 smock. Since

I was a size 48, the effect was ludicrous. I watched silently as she worked up a dog whose entire family was anxiously present. After four hours, she delivered her diagnosis—a grim one. The entire family turned to me, a man, albeit a ridiculous one: "Is there any hope, Doctor?" Under her baleful gaze, I muttered, "There is always hope."

On another occasion, she told me to come early and observe as a clinician told a woman that her bitch and entire litter of puppies had died on the operating table. The woman fell forward in a semi-faint, her arms extended with the need for solace. The clinician back-pedaled like a cornerback, stopping only when he slammed into the wall, and the woman grabbed him. "Promise me you will fix that sort of thing if you ever can. We are terrible about dealing with grief," said Dr. Keating. I remembered that promise, and kept it.

All of this did not ease my mind about my course, which was rapidly approaching. I was, in fact, so nervous that on Christmas Eve before the spring semester I was to teach the class, I had gotten a key to the library and was frantically—and futilely—searching archived veterinary journals for *anything* about ethics. Nor was I reassured when I received a phone call from Voss's secretary—he was now head of the Clinical Sciences Department—asking me to meet with him. Voss was widely seen as a redneck, and I dreaded the meeting, particularly given our history. When I entered his office, he said, "I know you." Squirming and stammering, I said, "I have changed. I do know a male donkey from a female. I have been reading veterinary . . ." He cut me short.

"What do you expect our students to get out of your class?" Aha—this I could answer. "I want to teach them that there are many conceptual and ethical questions in veterinary medicine." "You going to give them answers?" he snapped. (OK—I get it. He's worried about my laying my New York Jewish hippie urban answers on cowboys.) "No," I said, "of course not. I will teach them the tools to derive their own answers." "You must give them answers," he intoned. "What answers?" I asked. "The answers of the Professional Veterinarian." I warmed to the subject. "But I'm not a professional veterinarian. You are. Why don't we team-teach?" "No way," he said. "Why not?" "Because you will make me look bad. I don't care about that—I have often looked bad. No, the major reason is we will confuse the students—two full professors saying opposite things." "That's the point," I said. "We will create dialogue, which, as Plato pointed out, is the essence of thought." "Well that's your mistake," he said. "You want to produce thinking men; we want to produce Professional Veterinarians."

Ironically, I would come to know Voss as one of the brightest veterinarians at CSU or anywhere else, as a man of honor, as a person who could change, and as my greatest supporter in changing atrocious practices. I never guessed then that six years later he would authorize me to speak for him and the veterinary school on animal-welfare issues when he became dean and that I would move heaven and earth to get the veterinary hospital named after him on his retirement. Jim Voss was the second of only three people in my life who, if they asked me to jump, I would ask, "How high?"

Willard Eddy was the first; the third was Harry Gorman. While planning the ethics course, I asked the dean for a veterinary co-teacher for the sake of credibility and as a resource on veterinary issues. After a few weeks, he announced that he was assigning Harry Gorman to me. "Who is he?" I asked. "He's our associate dean for professional liaison and retired colonel in the air force." I exploded. "You're giving me a colonel? Some reactionary? That will sabotage . . ." He cut me short. "Why don't you meet him before you blow up?" Good point. Expecting little, I made an appointment and, in the interim, did a bit of research.

Harry's résumé read like a who's who for veterinary medicine. He had invented the artificial hip joint used in humans; was a world-renowned experimental surgeon; had run the aerospace program's animal use; founded the School of Aerospace Medicine at Lackland Air Force Base in Texas; was president of the American Veterinary Medical Association; had been raised on a ranch; and was a tough, salty, warm man I liked on sight. When we met in his office, he pulled out a bottle of Blackjack (my brand, as well) and poured two large drinks. We chatted for three hours. It turned out that he had always been concerned about animals and agreed that an ethics and animal-welfare class was essential. He had a fine sense of humor. Example: He pointed to my chest and remarked that he had once had such a chest, but that it had migrated down, patting his belly and grinning with his charismatic smile. In the ensuing years we taught together, I learned as much from Harry about veterinary medicine as I ever learned from anyone. I still keep a picture of Harry in my living room, and his memory still inspires me. I was to learn later, after his death, that his relationship with me hurt him in the eyes of conservative, old-guard veterinarians, a fact he never shared with me. On one occasion, four years after we began to teach together, we "debated" veterinary ethics at a national conference. At Harry's suggestion, we traded roles and costumes. I wore a suit and took a conservative veterinarian's line; he dressed as a "hippie" espousing radical animal-rights dogma. A quarter-century later, older veterinarians recall that day with smiles and chuckles.

With Harry's help, I came to know what until then passed as "veterinary ethics"—intra-professional etiquette on how large one's sign could be and whether sending Christmas cards was "ethical" or a form of "ethically forbidden" advertising. The American Veterinary Medical Association's Code of Ethics contained dozens of references to advertising but not one mention of euthanasia of a healthy animal for an owner's convenience, as I was later to write in "Updating Veterinary Ethics," my first, and critical, piece in the *Journal of the American Veterinary Medical Association.* I had bet Harry a bottle of Blackjack that the journal would not publish it, and when it was, in fact, accepted, I paid up and we drank it together. I always suspected, and still do, that Harry pulled strings to get the article published in the staunchly conservative journal that shunned controversy and criticism. He always denied it.

Given the centrality of ethics to the veterinary profession, it is surprising how little attention veterinary medicine has devoted to ethical issues. A study of veterinary practice conducted in the early 1980s showed that veterinarians spent more time managing ethical issues than in any other single activity. It is also arguable that the major challenges facing veterinary medicine in North America are societal ethical questions: What should be done about the welfare of food animals raised in intensive confinement systems? Ought the legal status of animals as property be modified, and if so, how? Given the strength of the human–companion animal bond, graphically illustrated during Hurricane Katrina, ought the value of companion animals be raised from mere market value? How should veterinarians respond to the "magic thinking" that underlies increasing public demand for non-evidentially based "alternative medicine"? How does one determine and weigh considerations of an animal's quality of life in medical decision making?

Organized veterinary medicine and veterinary educational institutions have demonstrated little understanding of, or formal training in, dealing with ethics. Indeed, veterinary ethics historically amounted to little more than veterinary etiquette with "ethical" codes addressing issues like advertising (the size of one's sign and the sending of Christmas cards) and totally ignored issues such as the teaching of surgery by multiple use of animals in sequential procedures, or the regulation of the use of animals in research, or the lack of analgesia use in veterinary teaching and practice.

This cavalier disregard of genuine ethical issues came from a variety of sources, including the historical subordination of veterinary medicine to agriculture and the general failure of science and medicine to embrace ethics, captured in the mantra that science is "value-free." But as society has become more concerned about animal-welfare issues and the treatment of animals, and has grown more litigious, ethics is ignored by professions at their own peril. It is thus imperative for nascent veterinarians to enjoy at least a rudimentary understanding of the "logical geography" of ethics.

We may speculate that the failure of veterinary medicine to engage or teach ethics (even today, only a few veterinary schools have full courses in ethics) comes from the scientific ideology discussed later. Correlatively, organized veterinary medicine does not deal with ethics well. The *Journal of the American Veterinary Medical Association* has always rejected the idea of an ethics column as "too controversial."

One extreme incident that illustrates all of this is worth recounting. I received a call from a U.S. veterinary school asking me to speak at an ethics conference on very short notice. The person I was dealing with, the administrative assistant to the dean, explained that a couple of years earlier the dean had taken money from a local foundation to conduct a conference on ethics. But he was fearful that ethics was "too controversial" and did not arrange the meeting. Finally, he was visited by a battery of foundation lawyers who insisted that he either hold the conference or return the money. Since no dean *ever* gives money back, he reluctantly authorized his assistant to invite me. He did not, however, attend the conference for fear of being seen as radical.

As the administrative assistant drove me to the hotel from the airport, she remarked that this was her last day after more than twenty years in the dean's office, though she had spent only a short time with this particular dean. "Why are you leaving?" I inquired. Her reply: "I will not work for a man who considers talking about ethics to be 'too controversial.'" This is a classic case of scientific ideology clashing with ordinary common sense.

In any case, the course I started in 1978 was taught to the sophomore veterinary students. Harry, who had chaired the Admissions Committee, assured me that the students were wonderful. The group was peppered with military veterans of Vietnam and the largest group of women ever admitted, including numerous older, highly accomplished women who had been professors, business executives, documentary filmmakers, artists, and so on and who all seemed to have climbed Everest on weekends. And, said Harry, the majority were a great bunch of cowboys. "Cowboys?" I thought. "The guys who shear the hippies with sheep shears? The people who ride bucking horses and bulls? The guys who wear thirty-two-inch waist and forty-inch-length jeans? The ultimate hostile *goyim*?" "They will test you out," said Harry gnomically, leaving it to my imagination to define. My mind raced. Would I need to slug it out with them, stripped to the waist? Or worse, a *High Noon* reprise, with me shooting it out with a gang of them? I began to fantasize about abandoning this whole endeavor and fleeing to the safety of courses on Kant, where I did not have to deal with "cowboys."

With 138 veterinary students in the sophomore class, I elected to teach them in three back-to-back groups of 46, knowing there would be no way to generate discussion with all of them at once. And so I walked in the first day with a prepared lecture on "the importance of ethics to the veterinarian" or some such schmucky title, attired in my suit, absurdly feeling like a Bar

Mitzvah boy. As I entered the room, my worst fears materialized. In the back of the room, caps emblazoned with incomprehensible logos such as "King Ropes—Sheridan Wyoming" and "Dally Up" pulled over their eyes, feet up on the seats in front of them, chewing tobacco in their mouths, was a group of cowboys insolently grinning what I dubbed the "shit-kicker smirk" and wearing an expression that said to me, "Go ahead—teach me something, urban hippie Jew boy."

"Be cool," I said to myself as I launched into my lecture, a resolve that lasted three minutes as they whispered and nudged one another with elbows. All the weeks of angst burst forth. "Hey, you shit kickers in the back: Get your damn feet on the floor, take off those hats, stop talking, and listen up. If I remember to speak in words of one syllable, you might learn something. And if you don't wipe off those smirks, I'll take you out in the hall and do it for you." (Jesus, what did I say?) The effect was instantaneous: Twelve or so pairs of cowboy boots hit the floor at once; twelve hats came off; twelve smirks disappeared. "That's better," I said and coolly continued.

Two days later, I was in the football weight room preparing to bench-press when I was surrounded by a group of cowboys grinning at me. "Don't pay us much mind, Doc. We're just here to see if you could make what you said stick." I proceeded to bench four hundred or so pounds, and we were friends. I have since discovered repeatedly, as I later illustrate, that cowboys, collectively, are the best people I have ever known and wonderful, open, serious, moral people.

The course proceeded beautifully. These were extraordinary bright people (vet school was harder to get into than medical school) who loved the chance to reason about issues close to their hearts, particularly the moral status of animals. Being only thirty-five, I made friends with a number of them. They asked the dean to extend the course to an entire semester, and he did. Then a shadow fell over our happy discussions. "We've heard some unsettling rumor about how they teach us surgery next year. Could you help us find out the truth?" I appealed to Harry, and with his help we brought in senior students who had been through it, and some instructors. Both the students and I were shocked and horrified. They were to do eight successive surgeries on the same dog, spaced Monday, Wednesday, Friday; Monday, Wednesday, Friday; Monday, Wednesday, and the dog was killed in a last procedure on Friday. The students were graded on the carpentry. If they wished to provide any aftercare, they had to cut class. One overworked technician cared for the animals the best she could.

I rushed over to the veterinary hospital and will never forget those dogs. That was a tipping point in my life, creating an anger and sorrow and righteous indignation that has fueled my efforts for thirty-plus years.

I was in a state. My root assumption had been that people went into veterinary medicine because they cared about animals. If so, how could such a situation occur? I discussed it with the students in terms of common decency; it was clearly morally outrageous. Harry suggested that I talk to the surgeons. I knew one, whom I will call Pete, from the gym (naturally). I visited him in his office. "Pete," I said, "is that the only way to teach surgery?" His response surprised me. "Of course not. Do you think I like cutting on an animal over and over to save money? Do you think I went sixty thousand dollars in debt to do that just because the dog has no owner?" "I don't know, Pete. Tell me." "I hate it. It's awful. It is wrong. You're the ethics guy—fix it." "Yeah, right," I said. "With my exalted status? But do the other surgeons feel that way?" "Of course," he said. "Well, if you guys join me, maybe we can do something."

This meeting was a watershed for me. I suddenly realized the truth of Plato's doctrine: When dealing with ethics and adults, one cannot teach, one can only remind. Had I walked in and yelled at Pete, "You sadistic bastard. How can you do that to innocent dogs?" his hackles would have risen; he would have become dismissive and defensive. As it was, by *asking,* I opened his moral floodgates; I caused him to recollect the moral basics that drove him as a veterinarian. Unwittingly, I had used judo rather than sumo. I return to this concept shortly.

The next week, matters came to a head. As I entered the 8:00 A.M. section of my vet course, I was greeted by an older student, a graduate of the Air Force Academy and a student leader. "Sir," he barked, "I have something to give you," and he handed me a document. "What is it?" I asked. "A petition, sir, signed by fifty-eight members of our class saying that we will not do the multiple surgery. If they try to make us, we will over-anesthetize the animals after the first procedure." I was touched and incredulous. "They won't let you get away with that," I said. "You made us think about it. That is where we stand," he said quietly. I asked Harry what to do. "Well," he shrugged, "the dean put us in here to raise their consciousness and consciences. We've done that. The ball is in his court." I ran to see the new dean, a decent and fair-minded man. Surprisingly, his initial response was anger. "I won't have the sixties sort of revolution in the seventies in vet school. The faculty creates curriculum, not the students. If they don't do what they're ordered, we'll expel them and find others."

I was terrified. "But wait a minute," I shouted. "I did what I was supposed to do. The kids responded appropriately with great courage. If you mess with those kids, you mess with me." "And?" he said. Indeed, I thought, what can I deter him with? Suddenly I spotted a copy of the *New York Times* on his side table. I was desperate. I turned to him and yelled, "If you mess with me, you mess with the *New York Times*." (I knew he knew I was from New York, though my only actual, and tenuous, connection to the *Times* was that my doctoral adviser's daughter delivered it in her building.) He was instantly chastened. "The *Times*?" he said, suddenly quiet. That was all I needed. I leapt from the chair. "That's right. The *New York Times.* Great story: Dean expels students for refusal to cut eight times on dogs. OK—so be it. I'm calling the *Times*!" He pursued me to the door. "Wait. We can work this out," he said. "We'll appoint a committee." By the start of fall semester, a policy had been hammered out mandating single survival surgery, a single surgical procedure with the dog allowed to recover once. The students would be graded on aftercare as well as carpentry and allowed to do such care, and then a terminal procedure would be performed. As CSU had the best veterinary-surgery program in America, the policy spread to numerous other schools, and my work as an animal advocate was launched.

The surgeon in charge of the labs, however, was furious. He stormed into Harry's office, ignoring me completely, and dramatically threw a letter of resignation down on Harry's desk. "If I can't do what I want with my own damn animals, I quit," he said. Harry fingered the envelope and shrugged: "Plenty of surgeons." The surgeon snatched his letter and walked out. Shortly thereafter, he assembled the students and demanded their view of the new policy in a public vote. The fifty-eight stood their ground. "Hah! Majority rules!" he shouted and marched over to the office of Jim Voss, who was now head of the Department of Clinical Sciences, demanding that the policy be revoked. "It's not a student decision," said Voss. "It's an administrative decision. You want to change it, go through channels." The surgeon next approached the dean, who was now solidly behind the policy. With inspired sagacity, he affirmed Voss's comments and added, "You could debate Bernie on the issue in front of the whole vet school." Verbal facility not being his long suit, the matter was done.

A year later, the students informed me of another atrocity: In a laboratory exercise in the *third week* of the freshman year of veterinary school, the students were asked to feed cream to young cats, "anesthetize" the animals with ketamine, and do exploratory visceral surgery, allegedly to watch the transport of cream through the intestinal villi. The instructor took great pride in the lab and invited me to watch it. I did and was horrified, as were the students. They watched as the animals squirmed when the intestines were touched, vocalized, and showed signs of visceral pain. Upset, I researched ketamine and found that it was not a visceral analgesic (i.e., it did not control gut pain), though it was somatically analgesic (i.e., it controlled skeletomuscular pain). It was a dissociative, essentially scrambling the cat's brain and making it hold still while not controlling the pain. (I later learned that the failure to control pain in animals was ubiquitous in veterinary medicine and research. I explain this in detail in a separate chapter.) I was horrified and approached the instructor. Ironically, he had been highly supportive of my class, even asking me to find out why students came into the program idealistic and emerged cynical. I asked him the point of the lab, and he replied, "It is to teach these students they're in vet school now, and if they're soft, get the hell out early." When I pointed out that his own lab was part of the reason students got cynical, he stopped talking to me except through a go-between and told the go-between that "no fucking Jew bastard philosopher was going to tell him what to do with his animals." Since he was too old and feeble to hit, I merely responded in kind. A full year went by with my informing the dean of an impasse. At one point the dean asked me how the issue was being resolved. I told him that communication had "broken down." When he asked what I meant, I said that I preferred not to discuss, but when he pressed for an answer, I replied that he had said "no fucking Jew . . ." "What?" shouted the dean. "If that's how he defends his activity, I'm canceling that lab." And he did.

Needless to say, both the surgeon in charge of the multiple surgery and the cat-lab teacher were furious at me. However, both cases saw excellent closure. Some years later, the cat-lab individual called my secretary to make an appointment. When he came, he shook my hand and said, "The years have proven you correct and me wrong. I apologize." The surgeon had moved on to another school, as he had threatened. Some years later, I visited that school, ignorant of his presence. The student who picked me up at the airport said that a faculty member in surgery wished to talk to me. Perplexed, I said I knew no one there. "Ah, but he knows you—his name is Dr. X." "X wants to see me?" I shouted. "He hates me." I went on to explain why. "It can't be the same Dr. X," said the student. "When this guy took over as our chief of small-animal surgery, the first thing he did was to stop multiple procedures." Intensely curious, I agreed to meet him before we went on to the motel, while I entertained fantasies of a surgeon committing the perfect murder—an air embolism perhaps. Sure enough, it was the same surgeon. Resolved to be a gentleman, I held out my hand and said, "Dr. X, regardless of what disagreements we may have had in the past, I thank you for what you've done for animals here." He clapped me on the shoulder in what would today be called a male-bonding way and said, "No big deal—same thing we did at CSU." "We did at CSU?" I was quite angry when I called my wife that evening and told her about it. "Schmuck," she said (one of her terms of endearment), "don't you realize what was accomplished? Not only does he no longer believe in multiple surgery; he now thinks he never believed in it."

One more improvement in animal use I helped birth is worth mentioning. The students informed me that all veterinary students, whether they were agriculturally oriented or not, were required to learn pregnancy palpation. This entailed inserting an arm up a cow's rectum (affectionately known as "greensleeves") and feeling for the fetus. What upset the students was that only a dozen cows were used to teach this to 138 students. Since many of the students were not from agricultural backgrounds, they didn't know what they were doing, and at the end of the labs the cows were torn and bleeding. I entered into the dialogue with the faculty, again doing a good deal of learning about the procedure. I pointed out that it was questionable whether potential poodle doctors needed to learn to palpate. Assuming they did, surely the experience should be emblematic of what they would encounter in the real world. The faculty agreed. Well, I continued, the ordinary cow would be assaulted by 138 students, and such insults, in fact, have a cumulative effect on the rectal mucosa, causing a radical change in how it feels when palpated. Fair enough, they said. The lab was radically modified and then eliminated.

All of these cases illustrate what should be obvious to those attempting to effect change—but isn't. That is, one should know all aspects of what one is criticizing before shooting off one's mouth. Any critic is by nature on thin ice with those being criticized, and it is in their interest to dismiss or blow off the criticism. The best way to do that is to impeach the critic's credibility, and the best way to do that is to catch him or her in a major (or minor) error. Had I not known about rectal mucosa, or ketamine in the case of the cat lab, I would have had no credibility and people would not have listened to what I had to say.

Too many animal advocates have a "don't bother me with the facts" attitude. On one occasion, a radical group asked me to look at a protocol involving delivering electroshocks to the brain of a kitten. They told me they had paid for a full-page ad in the *New York Times* to promulgate knowledge of this atrocity. It was the worst piece of research they could find. I was to tell them how much pain the procedure caused the kittens. They were speechless when I pointed out that (1) there are no pain sensors in brains and (2) even if there were, the electroshock was so minute as to be undetectable. (Unfazed, they went ahead with their ad.) Incidentally, all of these cases illustrate an aphorism that I share with people who ask me how I have the nerve to take on powerful figures in fields of animal use I am new to: "The bad news is that God has given me powerful enemies. The good news is that he made them stupid."

In the ensuing years, we went on to abolish all of the invasive labs at CSU, including the infamous hemorrhagic shock lab that is still required at some human medical schools in the first decade of the twenty-first century, which involved bleeding out a dog, and had been used to cull sensitive students. (Why would medicine want sensitive people?) Since CSU had the best veterinary surgery department in the world, our actions spread to other schools. And showing how ethical thought is self-proliferating, the surgeons at CSU agreed in 1980 to end survival surgery (i.e., surgery in which the teaching animal awakens from anesthesia) altogether. "We can teach recovery on client animals," they said. The local humane society, amazed at what had occurred, offered us the unadoptable animals they were going to euthanize, since terminal surgery (i.e., surgery where the animal does not awaken from anesthesia) caused no additional pain and some good came of it. This agreement was unique in the country and persisted for almost a decade, until it was brought to a halt in a manner I relate later.

On the strength of all these changes—and, even more important, thanks to the dean's belief that we need to publicize the changes we had made—our reputation began to grow. By 1982, we had been written up in *Nature,* the British science journal, as the best school in the United States vis-à-vis animal welfare.

Soon after I started teaching the veterinary ethics course at CSU, I began to receive invitations from veterinary colleges and veterinary practitioner organizations to lecture on veterinary ethics. Veterinary ethics thus became a major concern of mine, potentiated in 1990 by a request from the *Canadian Veterinary Journal* that I undertake a monthly column discussing cases involving ethical issues submitted by readers. As of 2008, I had written about two hundred such columns. The column in turn spurred me to embody both my theoretical thinking and my analyses of the cases in the book *An Introduction to Veterinary Ethics: Theory and Cases* (Rollin 2006a), which is in its second edition and serves as a standard textbook in many schools. In 2005, I received the Henry Spira Award from Johns Hopkins for being "the father of veterinary medical ethics."

4

Ethics, Veterinary Medical Ethics, and Emerging Animal Ethics

What are we talking about when we talk about "ethics"? We are talking about two related but different concepts—$Ethics_1$ and $Ethics_2$. $Ethics_1$ is the set of beliefs about right and wrong, good and bad, just and unjust, fair and unfair that all persons acquire in society as they grow up. One learns $Ethics_1$ from a multiplicity of sources—parents, friends, church, media, teachers, and so on. For most people, these diverse teachings are haphazardly stuffed into one's mental hall closet and are not critically examined or much discussed. The chances of their forming a coherent whole are negligible. Consider, for example, what parents teach about sexual ethics versus what one learns from friends and college roommates and films.

$Ethics_2$, by contrast, is the systematic study and examination of $Ethics_1$, addressing such questions as whether the beliefs in question are consistent, why and whether one must have ethics, whether there is a coherent way to affirm that some ethics views are better than others, how one justifies $Ethics_1$ statements, and so on. One learns to do $Ethics_2$ from philosophers, since philosophy is the branch of knowledge whose purpose is to examine critically what we take for granted.

Some further distinctions must be made. Under $Ethics_1$, we can distinguish three subclasses: social ethics, personal ethics, and professional ethics. A moment's reflection makes one realize that, if we wish to avoid a life of chaos and anarchy in which, as Hobbes put it, life is "nasty, brutish, and short," ethical notions must bind everyone in society. That is what I call the social consensus ethic, and it is most clearly found reflected in the legal system. Imagine a Martian graduate student in anthropology assigned to write a paper about the Canadian or U.S. social consensus ethic and having only enough methane in his space suit to visit for six hours. Where would he look? I submit that his wisest course would be to examine the U.S. legal system and the U.S. Constitution on which it is based. He would emerge with a fairly good overview of what the society saw as right and wrong.

But fortunately for the freedom humans seem to love, the social consensus ethic does not dictate all ethical decisions. Much is left to an individual's personal ethic, his or her own beliefs about right and wrong, good and bad. Such ethically charged issues as what one eats, what one reads, and what charities one chooses to support are, in Western democracies, left to the personal ethic, with the proviso that the societal ethic trumps the personal on matters of general interest.

The purview of both social and personal ethics evolves over time. In the 1950s, in the United States, for example, the social ethic forbade abortion, homosexuality, and pornography; it allowed institutionalized discrimination against black people, and it allowed parents to discipline children pretty much as they saw fit. To whom one rented or sold one's property was a matter of personal ethics. All this, of course, has changed, with abortion and sexual behavior reverting to personal ethics (with the exception of rape or child molestation) and renting and selling of property governed by the social ethic. (In general, things move from personal ethics to social ethics when leaving them to individuals is seen as generating widespread injustice and unfairness.) As we shall see, animal treatment, once paradigmatically the purview of personal ethics, is increasingly falling under a societal umbrella.

What is professional ethics? A profession is a subgroup of society entrusted with work that society considers essential and that requires specialized skills and knowledge, such as law, medicine, veterinary medicine, accounting. Loath to prescribe the methods by which a profession fulfills its function, society, in essence, says to professions, "You regulate yourselves the way we would regulate you if we understood in detail what you do. If you fail to do so, we will hammer you with draconian regulation." Not to respect this charge is to risk losing autonomy, as has occurred in the United States with accounting.

Some years ago, Congress became concerned about the excessive use of antibiotics in animal agriculture both to promote growth and to mask poor husbandry, since such overuse led to the evolution of dangerous antibiotic-resistant pathogens. When it became clear that veterinary medicine was partly responsible for this practice, Congress considered withdrawing the privilege of extra-label drug use from veterinarians (i.e., using drugs in a way not indicated on the label). Had this transpired, veterinary medicine as we know it would have been dealt a mortal blow, since veterinary medicine relies on human drugs used in an extra-label fashion.

Every area of ethics is subject to being rationally criticized or else one could make no moral progress. For example, as we saw earlier, U.S societal ethics was criticized during the civil-rights era for segregation's being logically inconsistent with fundamental principles of American democracy. In particular, Martin Luther King Jr. and Lyndon Johnson used Plato's dictum that, in dealing with ethics in adults, one could not teach; one needed to remind. Thus, Johnson realized that the vast majority of Americans, even southerners, would accept the following two premises: (1) All humans should be treated equally and (2) black people are human. But they did not draw the logical conclusion that black people should be treated equally, and only when it was "writ large" in law did they acquiesce to it.

Similarly, though most people don't realize it, personal ethics is also subject to rational criticism. For example, I sometimes ask my lecture audiences how many of them are Christians and for Christians to hold up their right hands. I then ask the same audience how many of them are ethical relativists, people who believe that good and bad vary from society to society or individual to individual, and for the relativists to hold up their left hands. I am faced with many people waving both hands, due to their failure to realize that one cannot logically be a Christian and a relativist, as being a Christian commits one to some moral absolutes, and being a relativist denies any such absolutes.

Finally, professional ethics can be rationally criticized, as when Congress was about to spank veterinary medicine for indiscriminate dispensing of antibiotics despite its commitment to ensuring public health.

Both individual veterinarians in all areas of practice and organized veterinary medicine face countless ethical issues that must be adjudicated and resolved. But before one can deal with an ethical issue, one must realize that it is an issue and identify all relevant ethical components, even as in medicine one must diagnose before one can treat. However, identifying all ethically relevant components of a situation is not always easy, as we perceive not only with our sense organs but also with our prejudices, beliefs, theories, and expectation.

When I teach this idea to my students, I begin with the following child's trick. I ask them to give me a single word for each thing I describe:

Me: What is a cola beverage that comes in a red can?
Them: Coke.
Me: If I tell a funny story, we call that a . . . ?
Them: Joke.
Me: What is the white of an egg called?

Most will automatically say, "Yolk."

Among the serious examples of the ways that background, theory, and expectation can determine perception is the famous Rosenthal effect in psychology. Researchers studying rats' behavior were told that one of the groups of white rats they would be working with was a special strain that was highly intelligent. In subsequent studies, the researchers found that the bright rats did better than the ordinary rats in learning trials. In fact, they were all "ordinary" rats—the "brightness" came from the researchers' expectations. Often we experience the same "halo" effect with students in our classes when we are told by other instructors about a particular student's brightness. Furthermore, learning itself enables subsequent learning.

Consider the first time one looks at a radiograph. The radiologist points to what he says is a fracture, but a novice sees only dark and light, even though the same stimuli impinged on our retinas as on his. As one's knowledge of radiography broadens, however, one *sees* differently, though once again the retinal stimulation is unchanged.

Similarly, exposure to some ethical considerations enables us to be more attuned to ethical matters generally. An excellent example of a case where veterinarians were blind to many ethical dimensions of a situation occurred some years ago. A man brought a small comatose dog with a head injury into our veterinary school clinic. He freely admitted, and even boasted, that he had struck the dog in the head with a frying pan because it barked too much. When the dog did not regain consciousness, and the man's wife became upset, he took the dog to his regular practitioner. The veterinarian advised him to take the dog to the veterinary school hospital. The dog died there, and the animal's body was brought to necropsy and presented as a case to a group of students by a pathology instructor.

Coincidentally, one of the veterinary students in that class was an animal-control officer, among whose duties was investigating complaints of cruelty. With the instructor's permission, the student took the client's name from the file and began to investigate the case, phoning the client's home and speaking with his wife. The client became irate and complained to both the referring veterinarian and to the veterinary-school clinician who had taken his case that his right to privacy had been violated. The private practitioner and the veterinary school's referral clinician in turn were furious with the student. The student was frightened, worried about the effect of the incident on his academic and subsequent career, and sought help.

What moral conflicts and problems does this case raise? Initially, the referring practitioner, the veterinary-school clinician, and some administrators saw only one issue: the betrayal of client confidentiality by the student. As the case evolved, administrators were also troubled by the involvement of the pathologist who had "betrayed" the identity of the client. Only after much dialogue with an ethicist, the pathologist, and the student did the parties begin to realize that there were many other concurrent issues.

First, there was an animal-welfare issue: The client should not be allowed to fatally beat an animal with impunity. In addition, there was a social or moral obligation to report the occurrence of a crime, the same sort of moral obligation (now also a legal one in human medicine) that exists for health-care professionals to report suspected child abuse. Furthermore, there was the moral (and legal) question of whether one could invoke confidentiality in a public teaching hospital, where it is implicit that cases will be discussed with students as part of their learning process. Finally, the pathologist argued that, as a veterinary teaching institution, the school had a high moral obligation not to condone that which society as a whole has recognized as immoral and illegal.

Some veterinarians argued that the pathologist was within his rights to reveal the name but that the student ought not to have acted on the information. To this point, the student replied that, as a law officer, he had a sworn duty (a moral obligation) to enforce the law. Some veterinarians hypothesized that if confidentiality isn't strictly observed, abusers of animals will not bring animals in for treatment. A controversy also arose over the fact that the school's clinician had at least obliquely threatened the student with recriminations when he came to the clinic. Others worried that the information about the case and these issues had not been sent back to the referring veterinarian for that party to handle. The issue of a conflict of interest between being a veterinary student and serving with animal control was also raised.

Ultimately, the situation was resolved, at least for future cases, by the university's drafting a formal policy that suspected abuse cases of this sort would automatically be reported to the school and government authorities. One of the noteworthy features of the case was its dramatic teaching value in demonstrating just how complex a single ethical problem or case can be.

How does a veterinarian ensure that he or she does not miss morally relevant dimensions of a situation? One excellent approach is to maintain a diverse array of conversational partners with whom to discuss situations that seem to be "ethics laden." For example, suppose you encounter a situation in which you worry that an animal-welfare issue might be present that you are unable to articulate. Having an animal liberationist as someone to engage in dialogue with will help ensure that the issue emerges with clarity. The fact is that most of us tend to seek friends who share our views, and this is particularly true of veterinarians who, as students, are physically isolated from the rest of the university where they are educated. An extreme example of such a situation occurred when a veterinarian friend confessed that he was socially comfortable only with fellow veterinarians who had attended veterinary school in the U.S. Midwest between 1964 and 1968.

Nonetheless, dialogue with others who do not share one's views is a fine way to keep oneself honest. When I wrote a book on the ethics of genetic engineering, I gave the manuscript to some of my genetic-engineering colleagues to garner criticism, which they were collegial enough to provide, particularly since they tended to see ethics as only peripherally relevant, if at all, to science. In that way, I made sure that I would get a researcher's perspective on my ideas. Ideal though such dialogue may be, most people will not seek it out. I have therefore developed a heuristic device to help veterinarians home in on all ethical aspects of a case. This involves reflecting on the ethical vectors relevant to veterinary practice and applying the ensuing template to new situations.

Veterinarians have moral obligations to animals, to clients, to peers and the profession, to society in general, to themselves, and to their employees. Ethically charged situations present themselves where any or all or various combinations of these obligations occur and must be weighed. In every new situation, the veterinarian should consider each of these ethical vectors and see whether they apply to the case at hand. In this way, he or she can maximize the chances of not missing some morally relevant factor through the sort of blindness we witnessed in the case of the dog struck with the frying pan. In addition, some veterinary associations meet regularly to discuss difficult ethical issues. The columns I write for the *Canadian Veterinary Journal* are an excellent resource in this area. In the two hundred or so columns we have done so far, one can find virtually any combination of these ethical vectors. The astute reader has probably realized that, far and away, the most difficult cases one encounters concern moral obligations to animals, since the social consensus ethic or societal ethic is virtually silent on animal treatment, with the exception of proscribing deliberate deviant cruelty. Yet the question of a veterinarian's moral obligation to animals is so important to veterinary medicine that I have called it the "Fundamental Question of Veterinary Ethics." The issue, of course, is to whom does the veterinarian owe primary obligation: owner or animal? On the garage mechanic model, the animal is like a car: The mechanic owes nothing to the car and fixes it or not depending on the owner's wishes. On the pediatrician model, the clinician owes primary obligation to the animal, just as a pediatrician does to a child, even though the client (usually the parent in the case of a child and an owner in the case of an animal) pays the bills. When I pose this dichotomy to veterinarians, the vast majority profess adherence to the pediatrician model as a moral ideal. Happily, as we shall see, though animals are property, society's ever increasing concern with animal welfare is putting increasing limitations on what one can do with animals, as in recent research laws that restrict the treatment of animals in the United States and other laws for research and agricultural animals in Europe.

Leaving obligations to animals aside for the moment, how does one deal with ethical questions regarding people, assuming one has "diagnosed" all the relevant ethical components? In the simplest cases, of course, the answer is dictated by the social consensus ethic, which, for example, prohibits stealing, assault, murder, and so on. So, for example, throttling an obnoxious client, however tempting, is not a real option. In most cases, of course, the ethical issues confronting the veterinarian are not so simple.

Other cases are also simple, wherein the answer flows from principles one holds dear in one's personal ethic. Most of us, for example, needing a new pair of saddlebags for the Harley, might be fleetingly tempted to overcharge or pad the bill of a vastly wealthy client. But most of us, too, would quickly quash that thought as unfair and violative of basic principles we hold, even as we would return a diamond earring dropped by a client in our office.

We all, of course, grow up with a toolbox of moral principles in our Ethics_1: Don't lie, don't steal, give to charity, help others, keep your word, don't hurt other people's feelings, and so forth. In easy situations, we just deploy them, but difficulties arise when a given case evokes two contradictory principles. For example, the principle affirming "don't lie" may often conflict with the principle "don't hurt people's feelings"—as when a friend gets a new dress, nose, or husband and asks, "How do you like it (or him)?" or when one is approached by a beggar and feels a conflict between "help the needy" and "don't encourage shiftlessness." In such cases of competing principles, one needs to appeal to a higher-order principle to weight them. Therein lies a major role for ethical theory.

Construction of such ethical theories has occupied philosophers from Plato to the present. Rather than survey the many diverse theories that have been advanced, let us look at two significantly different systems that nicely represent extremes in ethical theory and that, more important, have been synthesized in the theory underlying our own consensus social ethic.

Ethical theories tend to fall into two major groups. *Consequentialist,* or *teleological,* theories stress goodness and badness—that is, the results of actions. *Deontological* theories stress rightness and wrongness, or duty—that is, the intrinsic properties of actions or what one is obliged to do. The most common deontological theories are theologically based, wherein action is obligatory because commanded by God. The best-known consequentialist theory is *utilitarianism,* most famously associated with the nineteenth-century philosophers Jeremy Bentham and John Stuart Mill. In its simplest version, utilitarianism holds that one acts in given situations according to what produces the greatest happiness for the greatest number, wherein "happiness" is defined in terms of presence of pleasure and absence of pain. Principles of utilitarianism would be generalizations about courses of action that tend to produce more happiness than unhappiness. In situations wherein principles conflict, one decides by calculating which course of action is likeliest to produce the greatest happiness. Thus, in the trivial case of an ugly hairstyle, telling a "little white lie" will likely produce no harm, whereas telling the truth will result in hostility and bad feeling, so one ought to choose the former course of action. There are many problems with this sort of theory. The only point for our present purpose is that adherence to such a theory resolves conflict among principles by providing a higher-order rule for decision making.

Suppose you approach a very liberal friend in a quandary. You are thinking of entering into an adulterous relationship with a married woman who is terminally ill—despised and abandoned by her vile, abusive husband who does not care what she does but who nonetheless sadistically blocks a divorce—and she is attempting to snatch a brief period of happiness before her demise. Embracing a utilitarian approach, the friend might well say, "Adultery is generally wrong, as it usually results in great unhappiness. But in this case, perhaps you both deserve the joy you can have together. . . . No one will be hurt." A German Lutheran friend, however, would be very likely to say, "I don't care what the results will be. Adultery is always wrong, period." This is, of course, a strongly deontological position. The most famous rational reconstruction of such a position is found historically in the writings of the German philosopher Immanuel Kant. According to Kant, ethics is unique to rational beings who are capable of formulating universal truths of mathematics, sciences, and so on. As rational beings, humans are bound to strive for rationality in all areas of life and subject any proposed action to the test of *universality* by thinking through what the world would be like if everyone behaved the way you are considering behaving. Kant called this requirement the "categorical imperative"—that is, the requirement of all rational beings to judge their intended actions by the test of universality. In a world in which everyone told "white lies" for the sake of convenience, the notion of telling the truth would cease to have meaning; thus, so, too, would the notion of telling a lie. In other words, no one would trust anyone.

Thus, universalizing a lie leads to a situation that destroys the possibility of the very act you are contemplating and therefore becomes rationally indefensible, *regardless of the good or bad consequences in the given case.* By the same token, subjecting your act of adultery to the same test shows that if one universalizes adultery, one destroys the institution of marriage and would thereby in turn render adultery impossible. Thus, in a situation of conflicting principles, one rejects the choice that cannot possibly be universalized.

Of course, there is much more to say about Kant's theories, but not here. My point is that both personal and social ethics must be based in some theory that prioritizes principles to ensure consistency in behavior and action. Having such a theory helps prevent arbitrary and capricious actions. Whatever theory we adhere to as individuals, we must be careful to ensure that it fits the requirements demanded of morality in general: It must treat people who are relevantly equal equally; it must treat relevantly similar cases the same way; it must avoid favoring some individuals for morally irrelevant reasons (such as hair color); it must be fair and not subject to whimsical change.

Obviously, a society needs some higher-order theory underlying its social consensus ethic. Indeed, such a need is immediately obvious as soon as one realizes that every society faces a fundamental conflict of moral concerns—the good of the group or state or society versus the good of the individual. This conflict is obvious in almost all social decision making, be it the military demanding life-threatening service from citizens or the legislature redistributing wealth through taxation. It is in society's interest to send you to war—it may not be in yours, as you risk being killed or maimed. It is in society's interest to take money from the wealthy to support social programs or, more simply, to improve quality of life for the impoverished, but it arguably doesn't do the wealthy individual much good.

Different societies have, of course, constructed different theories to resolve this conflict. Totalitarian societies have taken the position that the group, or state, or Reich, or however they formulate the corporate entity, must unequivocally and always take precedence over the individual. The behavior of the Soviet Union under Stalin, Germany under Hitler, China under Mao, and Japan under the emperors all bespeak the primacy of the social body over individuals. On the other end of the spectrum are anarchistic communes, such as those of the 1960s, that give total primacy to individual wills and see the social body as nothing more than an amalgam of individuals. Obviously, societies along the spectrum are driven by different higher-order theories.

In my view, Western democratic societies have developed the best mechanism in human history for maximizing both the interests of the social body and the interests of the individual. Although we make most of our social decisions by considering what will produce the greatest benefit for the greatest number, a Utilitarian/teleological/consequentialist ethical approach, we skillfully avoid the "tyranny of the majority" or the submersion of the individual under the weight of the general good. We do this by considering the individual as, in some sense, inviolable. Specifically, we consider those traits of an individual that we believe are constitutive of his or her *human nature* to be worth protecting at almost all costs. We believe that individual humans are by nature thinking, speaking, social beings who do not wish to be tortured, want to believe as they see fit, desire to speak their minds freely, have a need to congregate with others of their choice, seek to retain their property, and so forth. We take the human interests flowing from this view of human nature as embodied in individuals and build protective legal/moral fences around them that insulate those interests even from the powerful, coercive effect of the general welfare. These protective fences guarding individual, fundamental human interests even against the social interest are called "rights." Not only do we as a society respect individual rights; we do our best to sanction other societies that ride roughshod over individuals' rights.

In essence, then, the theory behind our social ethic represents a middle ground or synthesis between utilitarian and deontological theories. On the one hand, social decisions are made and conflicts are resolved by appealing to the greatest good for the greatest number. But in cases wherein maximizing the general welfare could oppress the basic interests constituting the humanness of individuals, general welfare is checked by a deontological theoretical component—namely, respect for the individual human's nature and the interests flowing therefrom, which, in turn, are guaranteed by rights.

The practical implications of this theory are manifest. Consider some examples. Suppose a terrorist has planted a time bomb in an elementary school, placing the lives of innocent children in jeopardy. Suppose further that there is no way to defuse the bomb without setting it off unless the terrorist, whom we have in custody, tells us how to do so. But he refuses to speak. Most of us would advocate torturing the terrorist to find out how to neutralize the bomb; after all, many innocent lives are at stake. Yet despite the enormous utilitarian costs, our social ethic would not allow it, because the right not to be tortured is so fundamental to human nature that we protect that right at whatever cost.

Similarly, suppose I wish to give a speech advocating atheistic, satanic bestiality as a religion in a small ranching community in Wyoming. The citizens do not wish me to speak—they fear heart attacks, enormous expenses for police protection, harm to children exposed to these ideas, and other evils. No one in the community wishes to hear me. Despite all this, I could call the American Civil Liberties Union or some such organization, and eventually federal marshals would be dispatched at enormous taxpayer expense to ensure my being permitted to speak, even if no one, in fact, attended my speech.

This, then, is a sketch of our underlying social ethical theory. One may choose any personal ethical theory, but it must not conflict with the precedence of the social ethical theory. Thus, I may choose to limit what I read by virtue of my adherence to some theological ethical theory, but if I am a librarian, I cannot restrict what *you* read. We shall shortly return to the consensus social theory just discussed, as it is highly relevant to the new ethic emerging in society about animal treatment, an ethic that in turn is highly relevant to veterinary ethics.

Thus, societal ethical theory and personal ethical theory function to resolve conflict of principles. If one wishes to be morally consistent, it is valuable to articulate one's personal ethical theory and apply it uniformly.

None of this, however, helps us with resolving the Fundamental Question of Veterinary Ethics, since the societal ethic historically has been silent with regard to the moral status of animals and our obligations to them. And few people have bothered to develop a consistent personal ethical theory for animal treatment.

However, as society has developed increasing concern for animal treatment, a characterizable ethic has begun to emerge. Anyone attending to cultural history over the past three decades cannot have failed to note a crescendo of societal concern about animal treatment across the Western world. This is clearly demonstrated in multiple ways. During that period, laws and regulations constraining the use of animals in a variety of areas, including biomedical research and agriculture, have proliferated worldwide. In the United States, two pieces of landmark laboratory-animal legislation passed in 1995, despite vigorous and powerful opposition from the research community, who also publicized the claim that such laws would threaten human health. In the European Union, increasingly stringent regulations pertaining to both toxicological testing and animal agriculture have been promulgated (e.g., that sow stalls must be abandoned within a decade and that in vitro cosmetic testing must replace animal testing). And in 1988, the Swedish Parliament passed—"virtually unopposed," according to the *New York Times* of October 25, 1988—a law eliminating confinement agriculture (what is colloquially known as "factory farming"). Recent years in the United States have witnessed numerous examples of federal bills floated in Congress pertaining to animal welfare in areas as diverse as protecting marine mammals from tuna nets to preventing duplication in research, and in 2004, some twenty-one hundred bills were introduced in state legislatures relevant to animal treatment. Most notable, perhaps, in dramatic terms, was the successful California law making shipping horses for slaughter or knowingly selling a horse to someone who will ship the animal for slaughter a felony, a bill later pursued federally, with horse slaughter in the United States abolished before the law passed. Animal laws continue to proliferate, now focusing on agriculture.

Historically, both the laws protecting animals and the societal ethic informing them were extremely minimalist, in essence forbidding "outrageous neglect" and deliberate, willful, sadistic, deviant, extraordinary, unnecessary cruelty not essential for "ministering to the necessities of man." This ethic is found in the Bible and in the Middle Ages, when St. Thomas Aquinas, while affirming that although animals were not direct objects of moral concern, nevertheless presciently forbade cruelty to them on the grounds that those who would be cruel to animals would inexorably "graduate" to people, an insight buttressed by decades of contemporary research. Beginning in roughly 1800, the anti-cruelty laws were codified in the legal systems of most Western societies.

The question naturally arises as to why, if the anti-cruelty ethic and laws sufficed for most of human history, did the past three decades call forth a demand for a new ethics and new laws? In contract research I undertook for the U.S. Department of Agriculture, I identified five factors:

1. Changing demographics have resulted in consequent changes in the paradigm for animals. Whereas at the turn of the century, more than half the population was engaged in producing food for the rest, today only some 1.5 percent of the U.S. public is engaged in production agriculture. One hundred years ago, if one were to ask a person on the street, urban or rural, to state the words that came into his or her mind when one said, "animal," the answer would doubtless have been "horse," "cow," "food," "work," and the like. Today, however, for the majority of the population, the answer is "dog," "cat," or "pet." Repeated studies show that almost 100 percent of the pet-owning population views animals as "members of the family." Virtually no one views them as a source of income. Divorce lawyers note that custody of the dog can be as thorny an issue as custody of the children.
2. We have lived through a long period of ethical soul searching. For almost fifty years, society has turned its "ethical searchlight" on

humans traditionally ignored or even oppressed by the consensus ethic—black people, women, disabled people, minorities. The same ethical imperative has focused attention on our treatment of the non-human world: the environment and animals. Many leaders of the activist animal movement, in fact, have roots in earlier movements, such as civil rights, feminism, homosexual rights, children's rights, and labor.

3. The media have discovered that "animals sell papers." One cannot channel surf across normal television service without being bombarded with animal stories, real and fictional. (A *New York Times* reporter recently told me that more time on cable television in New York City is devoted to animals than to any other subject.) Recall, for example, the extensive media coverage a decade ago of some whales trapped in an ice floe and freed by a Russian icebreaker. It seems that someone in the Kremlin realized that liberating the whales was a cheap way to win credit with the Western public.
4. Strong and visible arguments have been advanced in favor of raising the status of animals by philosophers, scientists, and celebrities.
5. The most significant reason, however, is the precipitous change in animal use occurring in the mid-twentieth century.

Traditionally, society's major use of animals was agriculture—for food, fiber, locomotion, and power. The key to agricultural success, in turn, was good husbandry, which meant taking great pains to put one's animals into the best possible environment one could find to meet their physical and psychological natures (which, following Aristotle, I call *telos*), then augmenting their ability to survive and thrive by providing them with food during famine, protection from predation, water during drought, medical attention, help in birthing, and so on. Thus, traditional agriculture was roughly a fair contract between humans and animals, with both sides being better off in virtue of the relationship. Husbandry agriculture was about placing square pegs into square holes, round pegs into round holes, and creating as little friction as possible in doing so. Welfare was thus ensured by the strongest of sanctions, self-interest, with the anti-cruelty ethic needed only to deal with sadists and psychopaths unmoved by self-interest.

The rise of confinement agriculture, based in applying industrial methods to animal production, broke this "ancient contract." With technological "sanders"—hormones, vaccines, antibiotics, air-handling systems, mechanization—we could force square pegs into round holes and place animals into environments where they suffered in ways irrelevant to productivity. If a nineteenth-century agriculturalist had tried to put one hundred thousand egg-laying hens in cages in a building, they all would have died of disease in a month. Today, such systems dominate. At the same historical moment, animals began to be used on a large scale in research and testing, again causing new and unprecedented degrees of suffering.

The amount of suffering arising from these sources far outweighs what is produced by deliberate cruelty. Further, the anti-cruelty laws do not cover these new uses and cannot be twisted to fit anything like steel-jaw trapping, sow stalls, or toxicology, since these exemplify "ministering to human necessity." Thus, a demand was called forth for a new ethic.

In Western societies, as we saw, human ethics balances utilitarian considerations—greatest good for the greatest number—against concern for individuals by building "protective fences" around essential features of human nature. These fences are called rights. Rights are a moral/legal notion designed to save essential features of individuals' human nature—for example, the desire for free speech—from being submerged for the general welfare. The logic of this notion is being exported to animals. Society wishes to ensure that their basic interests, flowing from their *telos,* are not submerged and that farm animals live decent lives and laboratory animals have pain controlled.

Direct rights for animals are, of course, legally impossible, given the legal status of animals as property, the changing of which would require a constitutional amendment in the United States. (Many legal scholars are working to elevate the legal status of animals.) But the same functional goal can be accomplished by restricting how animal property can be used. Thus, the laboratory-animal laws require pain and distress control, forbid repeated invasive uses, require exercise for dogs, and so on. Some European laws have forbidden sow stalls. This mechanism is the root of what I have called "animal rights as a mainstream phenomenon." This also explains the proliferation of laws pertaining to animals as an effort to ensure their welfare in the face of historically unprecedented uses. I elaborate on this new ethic in the next chapter.

This new ethic is good news for veterinarians, as they can now expect more and increasing social backing for their commitment to animals, what I have called the pediatrician model. Veterinary medicine must engage and lead in providing rational answers and laws protecting animals' well-being in all areas of animal use. Not only will job satisfaction increase, but, as the status of animals rises in society, so, too, will the status of those who care for them.

5

The New Social Ethic for Animals

A Philosophical Approach to Animal Ethics

When I first agreed to teach the veterinary ethics class, I realized that the biggest challenge to my thinking—and thence to my teaching—was understanding the moral status of animals. Even before I had ever dreamed of being involved with veterinary medicine, in teaching the history of philosophy I had been curious about the neglect of the question of animals' moral status by philosophers or by their cavalier dismissal of the issues, as one found in the writing of Descartes and Kant. Since the moral status of animals seemed to me to be the chief question of veterinary ethics, I was obliged to provide a satisfactory answer.

In 1975, Peter Singer's pioneering *Animal Liberation* appeared. While Singer's book was well written and well argued, I did not find it satisfying as a theory for grounding animal ethics. In the first place, it was based in utilitarian ethical theory, the view that *good* is that which maximizes pleasure and minimizes pain in beings—including animals—capable of feeling pleasure and pain. Singer's philosophical ancestor, Jeremy Bentham had declared, contrary to Descartes and Kant, that the key feature for being in the scope of moral concern (i.e., being an object of moral attention) was not the ability to reason but the ability to suffer (i.e., to experience pleasure and pain) and thus that the effect of our actions on animals deserved to be part of our moral deliberations and applied to our uses of animals in research and agriculture.

But I was troubled by Singer's approach. In the first place, utilitarianism, in my view, was logically flawed, even with regard to humans. For one thing, any action producing more benefit than cost (i.e., more pleasure than pain) was morally acceptable. Thus, on utilitarian grounds, it would be morally acceptable to do invasive research, even very painful research, on people if it benefited more people than it hurt, and this seemed to me to be totalitarian in nature. Given this logic, it would be morally acceptable to mistreat, silence, seize the property of, or otherwise harm some people to benefit most people. Yet we reject such behavior as paradigmatically immoral. By the same logic, Singer's own blanket condemnation of animal research seemed inconsistent. For example, I knew of terrible animal research that had produced great benefit, such as burning pigs with blowtorches to study burn healing, which had, in fact, much improved the treatment of human burn victims. In addition, much Nazi research on prisoners, contrary to the mass media, had not been demented efforts to make everyone blue-eyed but, in fact, had generated valuable results in the fields of toxicology, high-altitude medicine, and hypothermia. If utilitarianism were correct, we should applaud, not condemn, such research. (Recently, Singer has admitted this point regarding some invasive animal research.)

Further, while Singer's method of influencing people garnered some followers—for example, he tried to convert people to vegetarianism, even supplying vegetarian recipes—it did not strike me as likely to work for the average person. As one person said to me, if Singer's ethic requires me to give up meat, I can't accept it. Even more dramatically, one Australian animal researcher told me, "OK! Singer got my attention, but if I go any further, I'd have to give up my research career to be a morally sound person, and I am not prepared to do that."

I thus felt that, first of all, Singer's ethic did not capture all of what was needed in an animal ethic and, equally important, it provided no way to move animal ethics forward short of abolishing animal use, something most people would not accept. Finally, it could not persuade a non-utilitarian and did not seem to me an adequate fulcrum for moving the society. But what could better accomplish these goals?

I knew, and even joked about, the fact that anyone could start a movement or cult and attract a few hundred or even a few thousand adherents: witness the Maharishi, Jim Jones, the Raëlians, and so forth. But what would convince ordinary people? And more particularly, what moral-theoretical base would convince such people or even putatively hostile people to augment the status of animals and provide a method to do so?

In a previous chapter, I related the story of my dialogue with Pete, the surgeon, and how I unwittingly touched him morally on the issue of multiple survival surgery. As mentioned earlier, Plato had pointed out, in a rather different context, that when one is attempting to draw ethical truth out of a partner in dialogue, one needs to remind, not to teach, as illustrated in

Plato's *Meno.* One does not need to buy into Plato's elaborate metaphysics and epistemology to see the value of such an approach. Think of a parent trying to convince a teenage child not to date a given individual. The more one preaches (teaches) at the youngster, the more obdurate he or she gets. When I reminded the surgeon of his root ethical commitment to animals, by contrast, he could understand for himself why multiple surgery was abhorrent.

From this modest root flowed many implications for my work. First, I assumed that however reprehensible veterinarians' behavior toward animals might be, surely it was by and large moral concern for animals that drove their choice of career. People did not enter veterinary medicine, particularly at that point in time, to get rich. Human medicine paid *much* better, and anyone who qualified for veterinary school could typically get into medical school. Indeed, having lectured to many veterinarians, I knew for a fact that the vast majority chose the field because they believed animals to be worth caring about.

Furthermore, I had lived through the 1960s and 1970s and seen the progress made by the Civil Rights Movement and various others to raise the status of the historically disenfranchised—black people, women, children, disabled people, minorities. The logic operative in these movements was, of course, not a demand for new moral ideas but, rather, the demand that the logic of our consensus societal ethical system be extended to those previously excluded on the basis of morally irrelevant characteristics such as gender, skin color, and ethnic origin. Indeed, it dawned on me that the history of the United States was a history of gradually discarding morally irrelevant differences as a basis for excluding people from the full scope of moral concern. After all, the original rights-bearers under the U.S. Constitution were white, male, adult, native-born property owners. And the history of enfranchisement was the history of reminding the society that certain differences were morally irrelevant.

At that time, I was studying martial arts with an interesting older student, a man who had been a Golden Gloves boxing champion, had a black belt in karate and one in judo, and had trained the U.S. Navy Seals in the hand-to-hand fighting at the Holy Loch in Scotland. Since my right eye was black for the better part of two years ("I have to train you to protect that eye"), and since what he taught me was highly eclectic, ranging from boxing to protecting against the garrote (the reader is duly warned not to attack me with a garrote), I tended to think in fighting terms. Plato's admonition to remind as opposed to teach was transmuted in my mind, when facing a stronger opponent, to use judo, not sumo. Sumo is a contest between two large men in an eight-foot circle. Generally, as with two football linemen, the larger, heavier, stronger protagonist prevails.

In judo, by contrast, one uses an opponent's superior force against him (or her) by redirecting it. To this day, as I lecture around the world,

I demonstrate the difference by choosing a small woman, putting her in a chokehold from the rear, and asking her to escape by force. (Generally she ends up hanging from my arm, feet dangling and kicking.) I then teach her how to shift her weight and throw me over her shoulder. The more force I am exerting, the more easily and farther I will fly.

Both of these approaches can be easily illustrated in twentieth-century U.S. history. Prohibition was a sumo attempt by a small group to change an unwilling majority. Not only did it not work; it resulted in people drinking more and gangsters getting a foothold in legitimate business that we have not yet escaped. The Civil Rights Movement, however, was classic judo. As noted in the previous chapter, Martin Luther King Jr. and Lyndon Johnson both realized that most Americans, even southern rednecks, would accept that all humans should enjoy equal treatment and that black people were human. They had just not bothered to draw the conclusion. Johnson bet his political reputation when he "wrote the principle large" in law, in Plato's felicitous phrase, that people would acquiesce to it. Had he and King been wrong, civil rights would have been as irrelevant as Prohibition.

This is the logic I applied to animals. First, rather than construct my own ethic and try to convince others, I attempted to *remind* people of the logic of the societal ethics they already accept for humans if it were to be extended to animals. Second, I tried to show that there was no solid reason to withhold those ethical notions from animals. Third, I tried to articulate explicitly the results of the foregoing. Thus could I use judo, or remind.

I have always been blessed with the ability to teach, lecture, and write clearly and entertainingly, using stories and humor. (I once kept 150 ranchers in Montana interested and engaged for nine hours.) This infused my lectures and writings on animal ethics. I deliberately worked hard to encode that approach in my first book on animal ethics, *Animal Rights and Human Morality* (Rollin 1981), which is in its third edition and, incidentally, makes a wonderful gift for Bar Mitzvahs, weddings, or any occasion. Amusingly, when the book was about to be published—indeed, the night before the printing—the publisher called and said he was having second thoughts. "Why?" I cried. "Because the book is full of stories and humor and is fun to read. I fear loss of credibility with the philosophical community." Thanks to the protests of the copy editor, he went ahead with the book, and it, in fact, garnered multiple reviews in many quarters praising its readability. It ended up being designated one of the Outstanding Academic Books of the Year by the American Association of University Libraries, and it won other awards. I have always tried to write in the same way, even angering Oxford University Press when I used an off-color joke as a frontispiece to the book I published there.

In any event, the logic of the book may be summarized as follows: Our societal ethic implicit in our Constitution, our laws, and our political system is neither wholly utilitarian nor wholly its opposite, deontological. (Deontological ethics focuses not on good but on the rightness and wrongness of actions independent of their results.) Every society faces a conflict between two goods: the good of the group and the good of individuals. Many of our social decisions are, indeed, made by appeal to utilitarian considerations—the greatest happiness for the greatest number (i.e., maximization of pleasure and minimization of pain). But, as we saw, exclusively utilitarian ethical considerations inevitably lead to oppression of the minority in the name of the general welfare. While some totalitarian societies indeed function in a putatively utilitarian way and worry about only the general good or the good of the state, Reich, *Volk,* church, and so forth, that is not the only possible moral approach. As noted earlier, one can imagine anarchistic communes in which every social decision is unanimous and no one is the oppressed minority, but these don't exist—or, if they are tried, as in the Hippie era, they don't last. Western democracies, most notably U.S. democracy, strike a Solomonic balance between group oppression and anarchism. While we make most of our social decisions by utilitarian reference to the general welfare, we protect individuals *even* from the general welfare by building protective fences around fundamental human interests seen as essential to one's human nature. The Bill of Rights essentially embodies a theory of human nature and the interests flowing therefrom: Humans are beings who wish to believe (or not believe) in religion freely, hold on to their property, not be tortured, speak freely, and so on. Rights such as freedom of speech are a check against excessive utilitarianism. Hence, we allow Nazis to speak and march even if it upsets a community such as Skokie and costs millions in police protection and lost business. Rights are thus a deontological moral notion that serve as a check on using general welfare as a sole moral criterion, and so rights have legal implications.

My idea was to plug animals into the logic of our societal ethical system and thus provide a basis for protecting animals beyond the very limited protection the law provided to them. In the eyes of the law up to that time (the late 1970s), animals were property (and are still property); domestic animals were private property, and "wild animals" were communal property. The only protection provided to animals was in the form of anti-cruelty laws. These laws, first articulated in Britain in the eighteenth century, prohibit deliberate sadistic, deviant, intentional willful, purposeless infliction of suffering on an animal and outrageous neglect such as not providing food or water. As case law attests, and as St. Thomas Aquinas argued eight centuries ago, such laws exist more to ferret out sadists and psychopaths who begin with animals and graduate to people than to protect the animals. Modern psychosocial research has confirmed that insight: Animal abuse is sentinel behavior for psychopathic behavior and foreshadows spousal and child abuse. Eighty percent of the violent offenders in Leavenworth Federal Penitentiary have early histories of animal abuse, as do many serial killers and children who have shot up their schools.

No behavior "ministering to the necessities of man," as one judge put it, can count as cruelty, regardless of how much pain and suffering it causes. Agricultural castration of cattle and pigs without anesthesia; the use of steel-jaw traps; the crating of veal calves, which keeps them immobile and anemic—all of these practices and a slew of others were and are invisible to the cruelty laws. People in the hundreds of audiences I have spoken to about these issues realize this. If I draw a pie chart representing all the pain and suffering animals experience at human hands and ask people how much is the result of deliberate, sadistic cruelty, almost everyone says "1 percent," meaning only a small amount. For example, the United States alone raises some ten billion broiler chickens per year, and up to 40 percent are bruised or fractured by the time they go to market—four billion chickens. Obviously, there is nothing like that amount of sadistic cruelty or else we would be surrounded by it.

This, then, is the meager moral/legal status traditionally enjoyed by animals in society. I realized that moral/legal protection for animals needed to be significantly extended beyond cruelty. Since the law is the social ethic "writ large," the logic of my argument involved increased legal protection. The vehicle by which I made this argument was the notion of "morally relevant differences" and "morally relevant similarities." If one wished to exclude animals from the moral arena or the scope of moral concern, one needed to adduce a difference between humans and animals that would bear the moral weight of exclusion. I argued that, just as we had come to realize that skin color, gender, religion, national origin, and property-holding status were not sufficient to bear the moral weight of excluding certain humans from being morally considerable by our moral/legal machinery, so, too, would fall the standard historical reasons for excluding animals. For example, it was historically claimed that animals lacked a soul and thus were morally excluded. Aside from the obvious point that one can't know who has or lacks a soul, or even what a "soul" is, this way to distinguish humans morally from animals is open to a more subtle objection, first articulated by Cardinal Robert Bellarmine. He pointed out that, if animals lack a soul, unlike the case of humans, wrongs on them will not be redressed in the afterlife. Thus, we are obliged to treat them better.

Other criteria for exclusion also do not stand up to rational scrutiny. It has been argued that since we are more powerful than animals, we may use them as we see fit. By that logic, of course, the mugger or rapist or murderer who is stronger than his victims may do as he wishes with them. Furthermore, this view entails "might makes right," a major notion morality exists to counter.

Sometimes it is claimed that animals are excluded from the moral circle because they are not rational beings. Even if that is true, it wouldn't exclude them from the moral circle, since many non-rational humans—the insane, the senile, the comatose, children, the mentally retarded—are also not rational but are included in the moral circle. Also, we worry about aspects of human nature that are independent of rationality, such as pleasure and pain, which are aspects animals share. Nor can we cavalierly hurt people to make them more rational, showing that rationality is the sine qua non for moral considerability.

Not only are we unable to define morally relevant differences between people and animals; we are able to easily identify a fundamentally relevant similarity—what we do to animals *matters* to them. They are conscious; they can feel pain, fear, anxiety, boredom, loneliness, pleasure, grief, happiness. It is therefore no surprise that people—particularly scientists from Descartes to the present day—attempt to deny consciousness and even pain to animals, an issue so significant that I discuss it separately.

I also had the major insight that nowhere in society's use of animals are they given the best treatment possible, even consonant with their use. Indeed, sometimes the way they are treated is *inimical* to their use, as when scientists have failed to control pain and distress, variables that, as we shall see, skewed their results.

In any case, putting all of the foregoing components together, I argued that animals were entitled to the full application of our moral machinery for people, full entry into the moral arena, and legal protection commensurate with their moral status. The obvious moral/legal concept to encapsulate these points was the concept of *rights,* which, as we saw, provides a bulwark against oppression of fundamental aspects of individual humans' natures for the sake of the general welfare.

I was also unhappy with Peter Singer's account of basing our moral obligations to animals solely on maximizing pleasure and minimizing pain. It seemed to me that there were many morally relevant ways we could behave toward animals that could not be called pleasure and pain. To me, the key to an animal's welfare is what it experiences, its subjective "take on what happens to it," a position espoused at roughly the same time (circa 1980) by Marion Dawkins and Ian Duncan. What we do to animals matters to them in ways beyond pleasure and pain: Animals can be frightened or fearful, lonely, bored, hungry, anxious, depressed, frustrated, thirsty, restricted in mobility, sexually restricted, excited (in a positive way, as when horses are turned out to pasture after months in a confined space), lonesome for a friend or person, happy to be reunited with that friend, comfortable, joyful, happy, contented, and so forth. The question became how to express all this in ethical terms.

After much reflection, I realized that if humans had natures, and their moral/legal rights were based on our view of human nature, animals also had natures, the fulfillment or thwarting of which mattered to them. If anything, animal nature was easier to comprehend than human nature, being simpler and more consistent across a species or type of animal. Deriving this notion from Aristotle and his functionalist view of nature, I borrowed his concept of *telos,* or a unique set of functions, needs, and interests specific to each kind of animal—the "pigness" of a pig, the "dogness" of a dog. Though Aristotle was out of fashion, I saw the concept as completely in harmony with common sense's view of animals, as well as with modern biology, which sees *telos* as determined by an animal's genes and expressed in the environment in which the animal lives. As I characterized it, "Fish gotta swim; birds gotta fly."

Some critics saw *telos* as a mystical notion, mistakenly equating it with supernatural purpose. I completely disagree. I never said, as did the Bible and Aristotle, that species were eternally fixed and immutable. Insofar as we recognize kinds of animals—dogs, cats, horses, tigers, elephants—it makes perfect sense to characterize their ubiquitous essential features even while acknowledging that, metaphysically, species are stop-action photos of a dynamic evolutionary process. Even if birds eventually evolve in some unexpected way, it is still clear that birds as they exist today "gotta fly."

If human nature determines human rights (i.e., the aspects of humanity that are protected by our legal/moral system), I reasoned that animal *telos,* and the fundamental aspects of the animal's life flowing from that nature, should determine the features of an animal's nature we protect. Much of this is evident to those who ordinarily engage with a kind of animal. One need not be an animal behaviorist like Konrad Lorenz to see that keeping a veal calf isolated in a tiny crate, anemic and unable to move, is a violation of its *telos,* as is the situation I once witnessed of a giraffe in a cage in which he could not stand up, or social monkeys such as baboons kept singly in small cages, as I was to encounter in primate research.

The concept of *telos* closed the loop of my argument. To recapitulate, what we do to animals matters to them and ramifies in their subjective life. What matters most to them is what their nature or *telos* dictates. Violation of *telos* thus harms the animal in ways that go beyond simple pleasure and pain. (As I would later realize, satisfaction of *telos* results in *happiness* for an animal.) Since we protect fundamental aspects of human nature from intrusion even for the sake of the general welfare (e.g., freedom of speech), in our legal system, we should also protect the fundamental interests of animals as dictated by their *telos* even as we use them.[1] I could see that we systematically violated animals' natures in all our uses of them—zoos, agriculture, research. I thus predicted that if society continued to be concerned about animals, it would move toward greater and greater legal codification of rights for them.

At that time, I argued for increasing the legal status of animals from their position in the law as property, and in *Animal Rights and Human Morality* I outlined some jurisprudential strategies for doing so. Over the ensuing years, I realized that this is a monumental legal task, and although many legal scholars have tried to figure out how to carry it out, it seems doubtful it will happen. After all, we never passed the equal rights amendment, and making animals something other than property would probably require a constitutional amendment. But as I watched societal change in favor of animals, it occurred to me that greater animal protection could be generated indirectly simply by limiting the use of animal property, as we did in the laboratory laws discussed later. With more than twenty-one hundred bills intended to benefit animal welfare floated in state legislatures in just one recent year (2004), that is precisely what society is doing.

Incidentally, people often ask me, only somewhat facetiously, if I have the gift of prophecy, since so much of what I discuss in *Animal Rights and Human Morality* came to pass. My answer is simple: If prophecy is construed in the crystal-gazing Nostradamus sense, of course, I do not have it. If, however, one thinks of prophecy in the Old Testament sense, I do. Old Testament prophets were careful to articulate their predictions in hypothetical, if–then ways: "If Israel keeps challenging the authority of Babylon, it will be destroyed militarily." In the same way, I "prophesied" that if societal concerns for animal treatment and the moral status of animals continue to grow, then what we have described is the form it is likely to take, given the logic of our societal moral/legal machinery.

I discuss other aspects of my ethical thinking as we proceed through this book. But the stage is now set for how we approached such issues as animal research and animal agriculture.

---

[1]As ministers of Canadian government agencies concerned with animals said at a full-day seminar I ran on these issues in 1980, this really calls for a Bill of Rights for animals protecting their various natures. Gratifyingly, some years later, an anonymous source in Canada sent me a copy of a letter written by the Canadian Ministry of Fisheries and Oceans to a Canadian aquarium that had requested permission to capture killer whales in Canadian waters. The minister responded that this would not be allowed until the aquarium demonstrated that the facility could accommodate the animals' *telos*.

6

Companion Animals and Animal Advocates

Given that I, like most people, had my first connection with animals through pets, it was appropriate that I gave my first public speech on animal issues to the annual general meeting of the American Humane Association (AHA). It was on companion animal issues. I found AHA people to be kind, warm, and very dedicated to dogs and cats but completely naïve about such issues as research and agriculture, pretty much replicating what I had found in local humane societies.[1] Moral thought about our obligations to animals was essentially absent; emotion was believed to be both necessary and sufficient for a good humane-movement member. A veterinarian colleague, Dave Neil, confirmed my perception, and I decided to talk about ethics.

In my talk, which was the first time a philosopher had ever addressed the AHA, I spoke about the need for a rational ethic for animals (as sketched out in Chapter 5). I then turned specifically to dog and cat issues, something I

[1]The AHA's long history goes back to the nineteenth century. It is particularly interesting that it consists of two divisions—an animal division and a child division—that are quite separate even though they are housed in the same building. In any event, Dave Neil told the AHA that I was a good speaker, and I was invited to keynote the conference in Miami in 1978. The AHA historically has been largely made up of dog and cat people and is strongly motivated by emotion rather than rational ethics. In fact, the much larger Humane Society of the United States broke off from AHA in 1954 to form a separate organization because some members were of the opinion that the parent organization was insufficiently progressive.

have always felt strong emotions about. I berated the AHA members for passively accepting society's dirty work—killing healthy companion animals. I criticized the more-than-fifty-year-old mantra of spay and neuter, which was ineffective in stemming the endless flow of animals relinquished to humane societies for adoption that were often "put to sleep"—that is, killed. I pointed out that if stray animals were the issue, it would have been solved long ago with the efficiency of animal control. I listed the reasons animals are relinquished. The following is a passage from the first edition of *Animal Rights and Human Morality* (1981, 158–159), and it is very similar to what I said in my talk:

> People bring animals in to be killed because they are moving and do not want the trouble of traveling with a pet. People kill animals because they are moving to a place where it will be difficult to keep an animal or where animals are not allowed. People kill animals because they are going on vacation and do not want to pay for boarding and, anyway, can always get another one. People kill animals because their son or daughter is going away to college and can't take care of [them]. People kill animals because they are getting divorced or separated and cannot agree on who will keep the animal. People kill animals, rather than attempt to place them in other homes, because "the animal could not bear to live without me." People kill animals because they cannot house-break them, or train them not to jump up on the furniture, or not to chew on it, or not to bark. People kill animals because they have moved or redecorated and the animals no longer match the color scheme. People kill animals because they bark at strangers or don't bark at strangers. People kill animals because the animal is getting old and can no longer jog with them. People kill animals because they feel themselves getting old and are afraid of dying before the animal. People kill animals because the semester is over and Mom and Dad would not appreciate a new dog. People kill animals because they only wanted their children to witness the "miracle of birth" and have no use for the puppies or kittens. People kill animals because they have heard that when Doberman Pinschers get old, their brains get too big for their skulls and they go crazy. People kill animals because they have heard that when Great Danes get old, they get mean. People kill animals because they are tired of them or because they want a new one. People kill animals because they are no longer puppies and kittens and are no longer cute, or are too big. People kill animals because they cannot run fast enough to win a race, or because their color is wrong for winning a dog show.

The foregoing catalogue sounds grossly exaggerated and overly dramatic. Once again, let the reader visit a pound or a veterinarian and find out for himself or herself. And the animals who are killed represent pets of people who are at least willing to handle the matter forthrightly or who delude themselves into thinking that the animal will be adopted. Countless others simply abandon the animals, leaving them in an apartment or turning them loose on public roads. A favorite place to abandon them is on country roads. I know this personally because I live on one. I have ended up with three dogs and twelve cats who were abandoned at my place. Any farmer will confirm this. On one occasion, I saw a car stop, a German Shepherd was thrown out, and the car sped away. I will always remember watching the dog chase the car down the road until it could run no more.

I talked to the AHA members about the euphemistic phrase "putting animals to sleep" and how it sugarcoats reality. I reminded them that, as Neil had put it, the AHA practiced "preventive death—killing the animals so that nothing bad would happen to them." I finished up by saying that "shelter" was another euphemism—the only thing being sheltered were irresponsible people, sheltered from the true consequences of their actions. My last remark concerned the bitter jest society played on those who care most deeply about companion animals, putting them in a position of killing and burying these beautiful creatures and burying the issue of social irresponsibility.

The applause was thunderous, and many people were in tears. In a very long question period, we explored options for changing all this. As I was ready to leave, a young man named Richard Avenzino approached me. He was an attorney who had just taken over as executive director of the San Francisco Humane Society, and the organization was seriously in debt. We talked a fair amount, there and later by phone, and he pledged to end the killing of animals. I knew about a shelter named Bideawee in New York that had such a policy but also knew it was very well funded. I applauded Avenzino for his idealism and hoped he would succeed. He did. A few years ago, the San Francisco Humane Society was solidly in the black and had more than four hundred volunteers to foster animals until they were adopted. Some measure of Avenzino's degree of class came when the media whined that the society's facilities were better than those for the homeless. Quick as a flash, Avenzino announced that he would welcome homeless people in his facility. At a meeting a couple of years ago, Avenzino warmly thanked me for inspiration and support and mainly for setting his career off on the right path. I could have gotten no better reward.

In the ensuing years, I talked to many humane societies locally, nationally, and internationally about pet-related issues and moral global issues in animal ethics. Some of these are discussed as we proceed. At the moment, however, I would like to follow up on the remark regarding the stress associated with hurting or killing animals. Three pivotal anecdotes will help the reader understand how my thinking developed in this area.

The first incident took place in the early 1980s during a conference for veterinarians on dealing with clients' grief that I had arranged with the Animal Medical Center and Columbia Medical School. At the end of the first day, the participants made it clear that they by and large believed that they knew how to manage clients' grief or they could not have stayed in practice. They asked instead for help with managing their own grief, based on a constant demand to do "convenience euthanasia" (euthanasia done for the convenience of the animal's owner). Indeed, that phenomenon has been shown to lead to a high suicide rate for young veterinarians in a number of countries. We organized a second conference for the next year with the same sponsoring groups on the issues of veterinarians' grief.

At the end of the first day, I was approached by a woman in uniform who asked me what I was doing that evening. She said she really needed to talk to me. I had ninety minutes before a dinner engagement, so I sat down with her. She was evidently very stressed and explained that she was a board-certified laboratory animal veterinarian for the military—a major, I believe—who had gone to veterinary school to help animals, had become convinced that laboratory animals were the most neglected, had become board-certified, and had joined the military. Now fighting back tears, she said that despite all of her training, she was powerless to alleviate the suffering of research animals. (This was around 1982, before the laws we discussed passed.) She felt trapped, frustrated, and impotent. We spoke for a long time; I was, in fact, late for my dinner appointment. I sensed that she was more affected than she showed, and I phoned her to chat a few times. Six months later, she was dead by her own hand.

The second story is similar, although it took place a decade later. I was at an annual meeting of the American Association for Laboratory Animal Science (AALAS) in Denver. (These are meetings for the laboratory animal science industry.) Each year, Charles River, the world's largest supplier of laboratory animals, throws a lavish party with food, drink, and a band at the AALAS meeting. I had given a talk and was having a snack before going home. The band was playing, and people were dancing. I spotted an acquaintance waving at me, and we moved closer. He was a laboratory-animal veterinarian colleague from a major medical school, and I noted that he was slightly high on alcohol. He remarked that it was his anniversary. "Congratulations—how long are you married?" I asked. "Not that anniversary," he answered. "A much more important one. . . . The day I left the Green Berets, after some years in Cambodia." I was at a loss. His face fell. "I did terrible things there, and I'm still doing them, only to animals," he continued, and began to sob—great whooping sobs from deep within. I moved him over to a corner and let him talk. After a time, I put my hand on his shoulder and said, "You need to get another job." A few days later, he phoned me and apologized for his behavior. "I was drunk," he said. I replied, "The only thing to apologize for is this call. There is nothing wrong with being overwhelmed and human. Get another job." A few months later, he did.

The last story goes back again to the early 1980s. Humane shelters had won some legislative battles to allow them to euthanize animals with sodium pentobarbital, a barbiturate that provides an easy death if done properly, replacing many hideous methods. CSU, through Dave Neil and Lynne Kesel, put on a "euthanasia school" to ensure that shelter workers learned proper techniques; if it is not administered correctly, pentobarbital is caustic and can cause pain. We lined up an excellent program, including a forensic pathologist to explain the physiology of death, a lab for the demonstration of proper procedure, me to talk about ethics, and a psychologist to talk about stress issues. All went well until the psychologist began to speak. Naïve about animal matters, he assumed that stress was stress—indeed, he gave examples of newspaper editors putting out newspapers against a deadline and flagpole sitters. He advised the attendees to relax while plunging the needle in and imagine a happy scene, such as a beach they enjoyed.

The reaction from the audience was incredible. As he spoke, I could hear some people growling (seriously!). Others were looking daggers at him. We hustled him out, fearing mayhem. I threw away my talk and began a dialogue with them, asking them why they were angry. "Because he doesn't get it!" they said." "This isn't like other kinds of stress. His suggestions are as useful as putting a Band-Aid on a bullet wound." I began to understand that they were talking about a qualitatively different sort of stress—what I subsequently called "moral stress"—growing out of major tension between what one has chosen as a vocation, helping animals, and what one is, in fact, doing: hurting or killing them.

The groups most obviously susceptible to this sort of stress are veterinarians, humane-society workers, laboratory-animal veterinarians, and laboratory technicians. In my own experience, I have heard this form of stress described at length by members of each of these groups, illustrated in the preceding stories.

For veterinarians in pet practice, the demand that they kill healthy animals for the convenience of their owners is a constant source of stress.

No veterinarian in small-animal practice can escape this situation. In fact, euthanasia is the largest cause of pet-animal death in the United States, and the most common reasons for euthanasia are behavioral problems. Veterinarians cannot turn their backs on these cases, for they know that doing so simply pushes them on to a colleague or to a pound down the street. Even worse, veterinarians' failure to engage the issue can lead to abandonment of the animals or do-it-yourself "euthanasia," such as the time-honored gunny-sack-off-the-bridge technique or the release of animals onto the freeway. Exactly the same problem holds true for workers in humane societies. Among laboratory-animal veterinarians and technicians, the complaint is the same but compounded by the fact that they are often engaged in inflicting pain, disease, and injury on animals, for reasons that do not benefit the animals, before the final act of killing them.

There is probably no analogy to this sort of stress in people whose jobs require primary concern with humans. Although dentists are universally feared as inflictors of pain, even in the notoriously high-stress profession of dentistry, both patient and dentist at least know that there is good reason for the pain, that it is of ultimate benefit to the patient, and that it is, after all, an unfortunate consequence of a therapeutic modality. No such recourse exists for those who work with pet or laboratory animals. The death and pain they are required to inflict are not excused by the fact that they are benefiting the objects of their ministrations. In every case, there is another choice: The particular animals could conceivably live or not be used invasively or, as one vet bitterly told me, could be out chasing butterflies.

The stress on these workers is augmented by a bitter irony: the fact that these people care most deeply about the creatures they must hurt or kill. If one is totally insensitive, if one does not care deeply about animals, if one is hard or even sadistic, there need be no stress whatever in these occupations. But consider those who became veterinarians because they wanted to make things better for animals (75–85 percent of veterinarians, in my experience), those who became shelter workers because they wanted to help animals (more than 90 percent), or those who became laboratory-animal technicians because they liked to take care of animals (90 percent of the people in the field). For such people, the stress is unrelenting, unceasing, and unbearable because the source of stress is constant, overwhelming, and inescapable. It arises from a sense of discord and tension between what one is, in fact, doing and one's reason for choosing that field, between what one feels one ought to be and what one feels oneself to be, between ideal and reality. It is for this reason that I call this *moral stress.*

It is obvious to anyone who has experienced this sort of stress that it is qualitatively different from physical and mental stresses of other sorts.

Whereas other stresses impinge on the periphery of what one does, this sort of stress strikes at one's very core. It is equally obvious that no array of stress-management techniques can really help deal with this sort of stress. In actual fact, to apply these techniques to this sort of stress is roughly analogous to using amphetamine for exhaustion: Both may help individuals carry on, but ultimately the individuals are worse off.

In any case, in my presentation at the euthanasia school I raised serious questions about the relevance of such "Band-Aids" to performing euthanasia on healthy animals. As I described it, the source of stress for these people is based, in the final analysis, on their belief that it is wrong to kill healthy animals. Even though shelter workers, for example, could say they were saving the animals from something worse, that didn't really help, first because they couldn't know this for certain, and second because they were still killing healthy dogs and cats who they thought should not be killed but should, instead, be out doing doglike or catlike things. I also argued that their stress is based on the tragic self-awareness that those who cared most about animals had essentially been "conned" by society, as one person put it, into doing what they saw as one of the worst things to animals: taking their lives to clean up society's mess. Everything I said was fervently confirmed by the participants.

Furthermore, I continued, there is really only one way to deal with this stress, and that is to feel that one is expending every effort to make one's own job obsolete. In other words, these people had to feel that they were not merely society's hatchet men but, in addition, that they were doing something positive, whether by educating the public, attempting to pass legislation, or taking other action to eradicate the need to kill healthy animals in the future. Thus, I argued (and again, this was confirmed by the participants' responses) that the only way to control the stress of such a job was to be absolutely clear about why one was doing it, by having a plan to change the society that makes the job necessary, and by doing whatever one could to implement that strategy. Thus, in this case, the response to moral stress is the articulation of one's moral principles and the articulation of the manner in which one hopes to realize them.

I submit that a similar situation causes moral stress for pet-animal veterinarians, laboratory-animal veterinarians, and laboratory technicians who were drawn to these fields because they like, care about, and wish to help animals (or even partly for these reasons). The situation is, in fact, much worse for laboratory-animal people, not only because they must cause pain as well as death but also because of increasing attacks on the use of animals in research. The moral stress is not only internal but also external. With more and more people raising questions about the legitimacy of the research enterprise, it is difficult not to feel morally insecure about what one does. This is somewhat true of shelter workers, as well. Members of both groups have told me repeatedly that they hide the nature of their work from friends and even family and are often criticized for it by people close to them who know what they do. Such a situation is clearly untenable. It not only generates stress and makes job satisfaction increasingly difficult. It also isolates people in this field from one of the most basic mechanisms for alleviating stress: talking about it to anyone who will listen.

In summary, seven facts are the major sources of moral stress on people who must kill healthy animals:

1. These people have been drawn into their work partly by genuine moral concern for animals. (If one has no concern for animals except as tools for human benefit or scientific research, this sort of stress will not arise.)
2. Laboratory-animal veterinarians and technicians are required to inflict pain, disease, and suffering on healthy animals, as well as to kill healthy animals.
3. Except for those that are starving or suffering, animals themselves do not benefit from the killing.
4. Society often disapproves of or does not support these activities, even though their justification is often in their benefit to society. Pet owners and society in general prefer to believe that humane societies are able to find good homes for the vast majority of animals.
5. People in this field often feel compelled not to discuss their work with "outsiders."
6. These workers often feel that they must suppress their rage and moral indignation at owners and clients.
7. These people are reluctant—or unable—to discuss the stress at home.

Taken together, these facts seem formidable. It is not surprising that some people in these fields protect themselves by enclosing themselves in a carapace by abandoning the moral concern that is the chief source of the moral conflict that generates their stress, by thinking of themselves only as "scientists" or public servants, by taking the view that animals don't suffer or that their suffering doesn't matter. As protective devices, such moves are quite comprehensible. But do they represent the best answer to dealing with stress?

In my view, there is a way to deal with moral stress that is better for people in the field, for society, and for animals, even though it is far more difficult. This method requires that one not forget the reasons one was drawn to care for animals but, on the contrary, remember them in Plato's sense of remembrance—not only recall them but also systematize them into a rational and defensible moral position. All those drawn to pet practice, humane work, or laboratory-animal work either wholly or partly by feelings that the suffering, pain, and lives of animals matter must, first and foremost, articulate for themselves in rational terms their ideal ethical position regarding the moral status of animals in society. This idea is important in much the same way that we need ideals for science, ethics, and politics, not as blueprints for instant social change, but as yardsticks to tell us where we are deficient.

In my work with each of these groups, I have tried to develop that ethic in terms of the fundamental rights of animals. That need not be anyone else's ethic—for example, some people may simply believe that animals ought not to suffer or die unnecessarily or for trivial reasons. I know from experience that most people in each of these groups hold some notion like mine, that animals have value in themselves, not just as tools for us, and that aspects of their nature ought to be protected. However, the point is that these individuals need to have some rational and defensible articulation of their basic feelings of concern for animals. Having articulated to themselves a moral position, workers in this field must then ask themselves whether they are doing everything in their power, individually and collectively, to actualize that ethic. Few people in any of these fields have taken these steps. Until recently, few people in humane work had developed an ethic. Even though most of them had realized that something is wrong in a society that kills ten million to fifteen million healthy dogs and cats a year, few had gone beyond the tired old saw of "spay and neuter."

However, as progressive humane societies such as the one in San Francisco have shown, individuals armed with an ethic can dramatically raise the animal adoption rate and awaken the public to the realities of animal-related problems. One must not resign oneself to doing society's dirty work. As long as someone will do it, the dirty work will keep coming. It is essential to feel and to know that one is somehow striking at the sources of the problem, not merely at its symptoms, and working toward a world in which no one must do such a job. Meaningful public education directed at adults, not merely children, and efforts to legalize the rights of pet animals, perhaps by licensing pet owners, are major steps in the right direction.

There is also much positive work to be done by pet veterinarians. Organized veterinary medicine has tended to sidestep animal-welfare issues. A growing number of veterinary schools (but still a minority) are incorporating ethics courses into their curricula, and the key question in veterinary ethics is, of course, the moral status of animals. Ideally, no veterinarian should emerge from veterinary school without having formulated a clear picture of the value of animal life and suffering and of the hard realities of such ethical questions as the euthanizing of healthy animals. Furthermore, veterinarians who value animals in themselves, as the vast majority of veterinarians do, must emerge as animal advocates and educators. American veterinary medicine is culpable for its failure to use its Aesculapian authority (the powerful authority possessed by all medical professionals that comes with the title "Dr." and the white coat) on behalf of the welfare of animals in society; all too often, it has gone with the flow of social and economic pressure. But as society begins to engage the hard questions of the moral status of animals, veterinarians must inevitably provide leadership in this area. This means that veterinarians must be far more than medical practitioners. They must, for example, be counselors on behavioral problems because, as noted earlier, euthanasia for behavioral problems is the single largest cause of death among pet animals. This, in turn, means that behavior must loom large in veterinary curricula. At the moment, few veterinary schools have required courses on this subject. Veterinary education must adapt to the changing view of animals in society. Accordingly, curricula must highlight, not ignore, ethics, behavior, and the complex social dimensions of veterinary medicine.

Individual practice, too, can be changed dramatically to harmonize with veterinarians' view of themselves as animal advocates. Far too few veterinarians take seriously their role in educating clients on behalf of animals. With the Aesculapian authority they bear as medical professionals, such a role is natural. Assuming such a role need not mean financial loss. I know a veterinarian in California who has clients who do not yet own animals; these clients pay the veterinarian to advise them on the selection, training, and assimilation of a pet into the family even before they acquire an animal. Veterinarians must be trained, if possible, to do what good veterinarians have always done intuitively: to plead the cases of animals whose owners wish to receive euthanasia for bad reasons and to seek alternatives for such animals. Veterinary schools would profit greatly from having successful local practitioners as adjunct faculty. Too often, veterinary education is more concerned with teaching about laser surgery or monoclonal antibodies than with developing techniques for persuading clients to do the right thing.

Finally, organized veterinary medicine, beginning at the local level, must work to create social policy in the form of legislation or ordinances to elevate the status of animals and to make the acquisition and destruction of a pet animal at least as difficult as getting a driver's license. Initiating rational legislation in this area is in the veterinarian's, not merely the animals', self-interest. Not only would such action mitigate moral stress. It would also forestall the extreme legislation that can emerge from crisis situations—for example, the legislative banning or severe restriction of animals after a dramatic dog-bite case, after a crusade against dog feces, or after a zoonotic epidemic.

Precisely the same sort of strategy should be relevant to individuals in the laboratory-animal field. The situation for these people is more difficult, however, for there is virtually no hope of creating a society in which there will be no need to hurt or kill animals for scientific research. Therefore, the moral stress and the correlative tendency toward callousness is very great, although one must never minimize what pet veterinarians must feel when they are casually asked to kill animals they may have delivered or, on some prior occasion, fought to save from disease or injury. Laboratory-animal workers sometimes get to know their animals individually, as well, and give them names instead of numbers, a practice greatly discouraged by the culture of science. However, when such concern is divorced from a reasoned stance of animal advocacy, it can increase moral stress when the animals one has cared for so deeply must be hurt or killed. Doubtless it is for this sort of reason that many people choose to leave the field, ironically eliminating from it those who care the most. A better way, a more productive way, it seems to me, is to stay in the field and try to ensure that the interests of the animals are served as fully as possible even while the animals are being used. In essence, this, too, means becoming an animal advocate and seeking out ways in which conditions can be improved for animals within the context of scientific research.

Although moral stress differs markedly from ordinary stress in the ways noted, it can still have identically pernicious effects on physical and mental health. Cardiovascular health, blood pressure, susceptibility to infection, susceptibility to cancer, reproductive ability, gastrointestinal illness, ulcers, post-surgical or other wound recovery, migraine, headaches, colitis, irritable bowel syndrome, skin disease, intellectual abilities, arthritis, allergies, asthma, alcohol, and drug abuse are all directly tied to stress factors. In addition, a person's exposure to stress obviously can wreak havoc in his or her family life, sex life, career, social relations, self-image, life satisfaction, productivity, and so on. In short, no area of one's life is untouched by the effects of stress.

As my views on moral stress became known through speeches and papers, I received many invitations to speak, not only to veterinarians and humane societies but also to animal-control personnel. I had stereotyped the last as troglodytes. In fact, I could not have been more wrong. Like many lab-animal veterinarians and technicians, and many humane society workers, they suffered from moral stress. I will never forget their pointing out to me that they would love to be out of that job, that they would much prefer to be educators and resource persons, not dog catchers and dog killers.

A couple of psychologists picked up on my concept of moral stress and began to work with humane society workers, apparently successfully. I continued to talk at humane societies, but those invitations began to tail off. Eventually I heard why. At one humane society, a woman had told me, in tears, about a blind sixteen-year-old Labrador retriever brought in to be relinquished because the owner found him to be "too much trouble." She specified that he should be adopted only to a country home with acreage *and* a lake. The worker sobbed as she said, "There is no way that dog will ever be adopted. If his owner won't take the trouble to care, who will?" "What did you tell her?" I asked. "What I'm told to: 'We will do our best,'" she said and began crying anew. "Why didn't you tell her the truth?" I said. "Tell her the dog will be dead in five days and she's invited to watch the killing!" "We're not allowed to!" she answered. "Well no wonder you're stressed. They're telling you to lie to spare the feelings of the guilty and irresponsible. Screw her: Next time say what you feel and stop being a Sin-eater." That sort of advice certainly helped the morally stressed, but it upset the administrators who do the inviting and, but for a sporadic period, ended my counseling career.

Naturally, I was called on to lecture and provide advice to many major animal-welfare groups during my years of involvement with animal ethics. They included the American Humane Association, the Humane Society of the United States (HSUS), the Canadian Federation of Humane Societies, the Animal Protection Institute, and numerous other groups, such as the Universities Federation for Animal Welfare (UFAW) in Britain. The last is a very interesting group operating at a very high intellectual level and putting out valuable books and holding excellent conferences on all areas of animal use, including the first text on proper use of laboratory animals. There is nothing comparable in the United States in terms of membership: many British veterinarians, scientists, and physicians belong to UFAW. In 1982, I was honored to be the second UFAW C. W. Hume lecturer at the University of London. (C. W. Hume founded the UFAW.) The executive director of the UFAW, Roger Ewbank (who was later honored with an Order of the British Empire, the highest award given in Britain), and I became fast friends. My lecture was published by UFAW as the pamphlet "The Teaching of Responsibility." In the late 1980s, in the wake of a scandal in the use of research animals at the University of Cape Town, Roger and I went to South Africa to discuss our respective countries' regulation of animal research under the aegis of South Africa's Medical Research Council.

My most active involvement was probably with the HSUS, the richest animal-welfare organization in the United States. In the late 1970s, recognizing the need for an intellectual element in the humane movement, the HSUS hired Michael W. Fox, a British veterinarian and animal behaviorist, to develop the Institute for the Study of Animal Problems. Fox was and is a charismatic speaker and prolific writer who did pioneering work in the behavior of canids—dogs, wolves, and coyotes. We became friends in 1977, and I did a good deal of work with the institute, including speaking and writing for its excellent journal, the *International Journal for the Study of Animal Problems.* Fox was soon joined by Andrew Rowan, a South African Rhodes scholar who had received his doctorate from Oxford, with whom I also became friends. Whereas Fox was brilliant but eccentric, Rowan was brilliant and staid, and they made a wonderful unit, each complementing the other. Although both were solidly grounded in science, Fox increasingly gravitated toward New Age approaches and alternative medicine, an interest that eventually destroyed our friendship when I began to publish critiques of alternative medicine.

I did numerous talks for the HSUS, but the most memorable was in 1979 in Orlando. I had been invited by John Hoyt, executive director of the HSUS, and asked to do the keynote twenty-fifth anniversary address at the annual meeting. He asked me to avoid my usual tendency to elevate blood pressures and to do a low-key talk. I agreed and chose as my topic the need for reason and rational ethical thinking in the humane movement, rather than emotion, and showed how reason helps generate progress. Surely, I thought, such a truism could anger no one. I was seriously wrong. I gave my talk after a pleasant breakfast with John, who assured me that I had a great career ahead of me in animal-welfare work. I consequently felt warm and confident as I gave my talk. Indeed, the audience's response was highly positive, and I received a two-minute standing ovation. Perfect, I thought.

My bubble burst when a tall, well-dressed, WASPy looking man strode toward the podium with a look that was anything but laudatory. He grabbed the microphone and started to rave: "We don't need reason or science in the humane movement—all we need are emotion and Christian ethics!" I replied that Christian ethics had nothing to say about animal issues, and emotion had not accomplished much. That infuriated him further, and he shouted that I was lucky he "had not come up to the stage during my talk and removed me physically." I had enough. I grabbed the microphone back and said, "No, pal! You were lucky you didn't put a hand on me—I would mop up the floor with you!" The audience was dumbstruck, as was I.

It turned out, as I heard from others later that day, that he continued to rave at the next session, intoning that there was no need for "Jew logic" in the humane movement. John Hoyt was noticeably cold to me and walked away. I confronted him and asked why he and the other man were angry. "After all," I said, "I got a two-minute standing ovation." "No you didn't," he said factitiously. "It was only one minute and forty-five seconds. I looked at my watch." I gradually pieced together what had happened. The raving man was chairman of the HSUS board, and he was angry that I had been invited. In telling the story about using rational thought to bring about changes in the CSU vet school rodeo to the benefit of the animals, I had pointed out that, in Colorado, messing with rodeo was like "farting in church." Apparently, a Jew talking about farting in church was too much for him. When I left, I was snubbed by the upper echelon administrators but was greeted at the taxi stand by dozens of lower-level employees who braved their bosses' wrath to tell me how well I had spoken and who wanted to assure me that they had been educated and inspired.

It was years before I was again invited to an HSUS meeting, and then only because John Hoyt needed someone smart enough to refute a speaker he disagreed with. I asked him if he was still angry at me as he brought me an hors d'oeuvre. "Don't be silly," he said, embracing me, "Mr. [board member] was 'unwell' that day, and it was all a misunderstanding." The new leadership at HSUS, under Wayne Pacelle, has purged all that and is much more effective for animals, as I relate later.

I also enjoyed a checkered history with the radical organization People for the Ethical Treatment of Animals (PETA). PETA's release of the videotapes of the head injury studies done at the University of Pennsylvania in 1983 unquestionably helped get our laws passed. But PETA's founder and leader, Ingrid Newkirk, despised me. One day early in the 1980s I shared a lecture forum with her at the University of Colorado, Boulder. She began by saying she should not even be sharing the stage with me, as I "worked with *them*." In response, I mildly pointed out that if I were a dog being used for surgical research, I would rather have Bernie Rollin pressuring for the use of morphine than Ingrid Newkirk pressing for abolition.

Nonetheless, I have generally maintained cordial relations with PETA, and it has certainly done good for animals with its exposé of truly horrific situations in labs and slaughterhouses. A few years ago, PETA released videotape of an instance of horrific kosher slaughter at a slaughterhouse. Kosher slaughter was meant in antiquity to be a humane alternative to bludgeoning. It requires that the slaughterer be an expert in animal anatomy and cut the veins of the animal's throat with a razor-sharp knife, inducing fairly rapid unconsciousness. Though not as humane as non-kosher slaughter—where the animal is ideally rendered unconscious by a blow to the head from a captive bolt powered by compressed air (or, more archaically, by gunpowder) before being killed—kosher slaughter can be fairly humane if done perfectly. In the film PETA made, the animal was brought in an inverted Weinberg pen (a restraining cage), upside down, vocalizing and rolling its eyes in terror. The slaughterer's knife was so dull that even when he sawed at the throat, it took much effort to break the skin, whereupon he pulled out the trachea, turned the pen upright, and released the animal to stagger around and die of suffocation. In a letter regarding this incident, which appeared on PETA's Web site, I pointed out that such abuse made me ashamed to be of Jewish background and that, based on my understanding of Jewish law, the meat was not kosher. Many prominent rabbis agreed, and I received additional footage taken at another kosher slaughter facility, again demonstrating either sadism or gross incompetence. When I gave the keynote speech at the American Meat Institute (AMI) shortly after the film of the incident appeared, I challenged its members on why they did not speak out against this brutality. They explained that they were being threatened by rabbis with accusations of anti-Semitism, the same rabbis idiotically pointing out that *Hitler* had attacked kosher slaughter—playing the "persecution card." I told the AMI I would happily come to its aid if there was ever another incident of this sort, since I knew the Talmud and would be overjoyed to debate any and all rabbis trying to excuse animal abuse by invoking Jewish law.

PETA regularly asks me for letters regarding various atrocities toward animals in all areas of animal use, including the case of two inept policeman who Tasered a calf to death after it had escaped its enclosure. In that case, I wrote expert witness testimony for those bringing charges of cruelty. To CSU's immense credit, it does not share most universities' PETA phobia. It is happy to have me write for PETA when that organization's cause is just.

In fact, this discussion brings up a question I've gotten from both sides on animal issues: "Whose side are you on, anyway?" Both sides accuse me of working with the other side. My usual response is "I'm on the animals' side." As a result, I am credible to and respected by both sides and able to mediate compromise, though not loved, liked, or lionized. As I grow older, I realize that being liked is overrated and that I count my successes as much by having the right enemies as the right friends. I also work assiduously to keep both sides from demonizing each other, with some success. Emblematic of that success was a PETA worker's remark when I got a particular scientist to affirm that a piece of research that the group was criticizing was extremely poor. "Wow," she said. "There are good scientists?"

One of the most effective of animal advocacy groups is the Animal Legal Defense Fund (ALDF), formerly known as Attorneys for Animal Rights. This group was formed more than twenty-five years ago by a young lawyer and force of nature, Joyce Tischler, whose first campaign was to argue against the military's exterminating of wild burros at the China Lake military reserve. Joyce started the group by sheer force of will, and I keynoted its first meeting in California. I fully supported the group since, as the reader will recall, I saw the true force of "animal rights" as lying in increased legal status and protection for animals. Gratifyingly, twenty-five years after my first speech for the ALDF, I was invited to speak at its conference at Harvard Law School in 2007, with three hundred registered attendees and an almost equal number turned away for lack of facilities to seat them. More than ninety law schools have animal law programs; numerous young lawyers are choosing animal law as a career; and many first-rate, high-powered lawyers and legal scholars do pro bono litigation on behalf of animals. The ALDF has by far the best slogan of any organization: On its posters and T-shirts depicting baskets full of puppies and kittens is emblazed the powerful statement "We may be the only lawyers on earth whose clients are all innocent."

7

Creating Law for Animal Research

In 1975, when I read Peter Singer's newly published *Animal Liberation* and focused on the chapter chronicling animal research, mostly a litany of atrocities, I distinctly remember thinking, "Wow, worrying about rats and mice. That's not anything I'll ever get into." I recall my scornful amusement when my cousin became a laboratory-animal veterinarian. What subsequently developed was a clear instance of the old Hungarian proverb "God does not punish with a stick," for I was to become very knowledgeable about precisely those issues and even to write a two-volume reference book about them.

It all began when, in 1976, CSU hired a new laboratory-animal veterinarian, David Neil, to take charge of the research animals. I remember thinking (1) that he looked like Commander Whitehead in the Schweppes commercials and (2) that he was, as the British say, "a smarmy-looking bastard," wearing an ascot (!) and a very carefully groomed beard and moustache. I was as far from carefully groomed as was humanly possible and already suspicious of animal use, so I hated him on sight. "He's a sleazy type fronting for research, probably with an English accent that makes him seem smart to American ears even if he's merely reading the phone book," I thought, and forgot about him.

Some months later, my interest was renewed. David Neil, laboratory-animal veterinarian, had apparently moved into the presidency of the local humane society and was negotiating a deal for the humane society to sell the dogs they were going to kill as "unadoptable" to the veterinary school for surgical teaching. "Son of a bitch," I expostulated. "Sleazy bastard making blood money." The issue was to come to a vote at the humane society on Thursday evening. It was Monday. "By God," I thought, "I'll put a stop to this." Off I marched to Neil's office.

I was stopped by his secretary. "He's closed up in his office working on his speech to the humane society and is not to be disturbed," she said. "I'll bet," I growled and, to her amazement, strode around her and marched into his office. There he sat, looking even smarmier in person. Never one for moderation, I said, "I'm your worst nightmare, pal, and I want to talk about that deal you're brokering. I'm the vet school ethics person." "OK," he said, "sit down, and let's talk." We did—from 1:00 P.M. to 10:00 P.M., in his office and then over dinner. I raged about what I had heard about multiple surgery. (This was before Harry and I had had our fateful interaction with the students.) "That's what I'm trying to stop," he said. "The vet school is promising to use these animals only once." "And you trust them?" I asked. "How will you verify this? Apparently they see nothing wrong with the multiple use. You can't need the money that much." In the course of the conversation—which consisted mostly of my ranting—he listened carefully. After a couple of hours he interrupted me. "OK," he said, "you've convinced me. I'll withdraw the proposal. Come to the meeting Thursday night and see for yourself." At the risk of incurring the wrath of both the veterinary school and the humane society, he did, with me present.

The afternoon wore on. "Now that this is settled," he said, "can we talk about something else?" Dave went on to tell me that a group of citizens was proposing legislation at the state level to regulate animal research. He admired their good intentions but saw their bill as naïve and impracticable. He proposed working *with* them to create a viable law—a first in the United States. He had been trained in England and worked there, where researchers labored under a tight law, the Act of 1876, in part authored by Charles Darwin. He felt that that law, which used an inspector system, was inadequate and that better law could be written. When he had moved to Canada and worked for the Canadian Council on Animal Care, he had envisioned legislation but understood that the issue at root was an ethical one, and he needed a philosopher to help him think through the issues dialectically. None of the Canadian philosophers were willing to sully their hands with such a mundane issue, all being highly academic analytic philosophers. Suddenly there I was. Kismet.

Research, he continued, was basically unregulated. Although there was a growing body of knowledge in the field of laboratory animal science and medicine, veterinarians like him were powerless to impose anything on researchers, who typically ignored them. In research institutions, particularly at medical schools, the veterinarian was at best a "glorified shit cleaner" who was trotted out to assure the public that animal care was fine, even when it was not. Routine animal care was done by students, who often missed supplying food and water, especially on weekends and holidays. Stress variables were ignored. Disease control was minimal. And if the veterinarians in charge pushed too hard, they lost their jobs. Would I work with him? Would I help? He said it was a major uphill battle, but my rude entrance into his office had convinced him that I didn't mind—and even relished—a fight. He offered to pay a month of my salary in the summer beyond my nine-month appointment.

How could I say no? It was tailor-made for me. As pointed out in the Trevanian novel (and, later, movie) *The Eiger Sanction,* in which an art professor on a nine-month salary becomes a hit man for U.S. intelligence, professors will kill for summer money. Here also was a chance to work synergistically on what I had committed to with veterinary medicine. Best of all, it was a chance to do something never done before in the United States and a chance to fight. We worked closely together until Dave left CSU in 1987. The major effect was, indeed, legislation. But I also became a kind of hit man for Dave at CSU. When senior researchers refused to comply with proper care and use, I would pay them a visit. Because I enjoyed a reputation for being smart and intimidating and would challenge them on what they were doing and persistently engage them by demanding a rational basis for their atrocities or inaction, people began to comply. By 1982, CSU had gotten grants based on its reputation for good and humane animal care. Equally important, as I publicized our work and the vet school's improvements, we came to garner invaluable credibility with the public so that we were never picketed or attacked, and CSU's researchers were never threatened. All of this, in turn, motivated the researchers to do the right thing, increasing our reputation. In 1980, CSU voluntarily put itself under the provisions of the legislation I am about to describe, to give us ammunition to help convince Congress to pass it.

It further helped that, in 1981, Dave hired and trained one of my favorite veterinary students from the class of 1981, Lynne Kesel, to work with us. Lynne was a professional artist, a former English major, and a humanities-trained, somewhat bohemian free spirit who worked perfectly with Dave and me. From the two of them I learned enough never to get caught in an egregious error about animal research. I also taught them both about ethics and philosophy. Both also became close personal friends, with Lynne the closest thing to an aunt my son, Michael David Hume Rollin, born in 1979, had. Lynne could make anything with her hands, and through her skill he had his first sailor suit, business suit, Superman suit, and ninja suit; his first surgery lesson; and major exposure to animal medicine. Lynne was to become the teacher of surgery to every veterinary student at CSU for ten years after Dave left, the teacher of dentistry, and the person who taught experimental surgery to graduate students after a student complained about being told to do surgery on research animals with no training, before returning in 2004 to laboratory animal work. She has remained a close friend and mentor and virtually a member of our family.

In any case, Dave assembled our team to write legislation: Robert Welborn, a prominent lawyer in Denver and a member of the board of the Humane Society of the United States (HSUS), and Harry Gorman, a charter member of the American College of Laboratory Animal Medicine (ACLAM). Between Harry and Dave, our group had well over fifty years of experience in animal research, a senior partner from one of Colorado's foremost law firms, and me for ethics and comic relief.

Dave was an unparalleled influence on my subsequent career path. The first day we sat down to draft a model bill, he urged us to lay out our wish lists. I chattered about banning the LD50 and Draize rabbit eye irritancy test in Colorado and other absurd hopes.[1] When we were all done, he said, "OK, now that all of the fantasy is out of your system, let's work on something viable that could pass." Later he gave me an invaluable lesson: "Every few months, take stock of what you're doing. If the animals are no better off in virtue of your efforts, you have been engaged in a masturbatory exercise." I learned from that and have tried to chart my career by that compass. We worked on a practicable law (described later) until 1979, when we were to present it before the Colorado House of Representatives via the Subcommittee on Agriculture. Despite our hard collective efforts and political connections, we were trashed in the subcommittee. As one legislative member, Melba Tolliver (I will never forget that name), said, "Today you worry about the treatment of mice; tomorrow you will tell ranchers how often we can use a hotshot [electric prod]." We were thus summarily dispatched.

In the wake of that debacle, the *Denver Post* ran a beautiful story, the gist of which was "Something right and good was attempted today the Colorado legislature, and was killed by the know-nothings." We regrouped, bloody but unbowed.

Shortly thereafter, we received a phone call from the office of U.S. Representative Pat Schroeder (D-Colo.) asking whether we would take a

[1]The LD50 is an absurd toxicology test that tells how much of a test substance will kill 50 percent of the animal subjects during a specified time period. It provides legal protection for industry but has little scientific credibility.

shot at creating federal law. We went to Denver to meet with her. A charming and urbane, highly intelligent person, Representative Schroeder gently pointed out our naïveté. One could not legislate for laboratory animals on a state level; researchers and their research would simply move out of the state. She explained that we needed to try for federal law and offered to carry it for us. We eagerly agreed. A few weeks later, after the newspapers in Colorado reported on her involvement, I got a call from her. "I was mildly committed to your law," she said, "until I got a letter from the dean of the Medical School in Colorado. Now I am greatly committed." She explained that, in the first paragraph of the letter, the dean had said that there was no need for such legislation because "everything we stipulated was already being done at the medical school." She continued, "Then, in the second paragraph, the dean wrote that, if that law passed, all medical research at the medical school would have to stop." Punning execrably, she concluded, "I smell a rat."

We moved forward with the legislation and quickly learned the truth of the old adage that there are two things one should never watch being made: law and sausage. Deep truth. For one thing, the actual work is done by senators' or representatives' staffs, eager young people who know nothing about the issue. For another, the politics is unbelievable. For example, when I went before the U.S. House Committee on Health, Science, and the Environment to defend the legislation, I sat through a ten-minute mini-filibuster by an archconservative legislator from California who droned on in this vein: "Let the record show that this body spent hours on the pain of mice while millions of unborn children are being murdered."

Nonetheless, it was fascinating. After a couple of years, the bill was carried by Representative Doug Walgren (D-Penn.). In 1982, I was summoned to testify before Representative Henry Waxman's House Subcommittee on Health and the Environment on only one week's notice. Even worse, I found out that testifying against our bill would be Michael DeBakey, a pioneer in trauma surgery and open-heart surgery and the president of Baylor University, and Donald Kennedy, former commissioner of the U.S. Food and Drug Administration and, at that time, president of Stanford University. I confess to a period of panic: What could I possibly say to counter the testimony of such titanic figures?

The panic wore off and was replaced by a determination to kick ass and get the attention of Congress. I talked to many friends in the research community sympathetic to our law and was reassured. "Don't worry about DeBakey," they said. "The research community trots him out to do a 'research is important' speech. He very likely doesn't even know what's in your bill." When I made further inquires about Donald Kennedy, I was told that

Stanford had an awful record in animal care and was advised to request the record of U.S. Department of Agriculture citations against Stanford under the Animal Welfare Act of 1966, the weak law we were seeking to amend. I contacted friends in Washington and received that record, which numbered hundreds of pages. I phoned colleagues at Stanford and asked them to relay to Kennedy that, if he saw fit to testify against our bill, I would be "forced" to read Stanford's infractions into the *Congressional Record* when I testified. Kennedy withdrew.

In a more positive vein, I sought support and ended up with a variety of powerful endorsements. In 1980, I had convinced CSU to adopt the measures included in the legislation we proposed—most notably, protocol review through an Institutional Animal Care and Use Committee (IACUC) and inspection of facilities. By 1982, we knew that the system worked, and I was able to garner the enthusiastic support of Ralph Christofferson, the university's president, on behalf of CSU. (He came to his office on Sunday morning specifically to discuss this and provide me with the endorsement before I went to Washington.) I also had the endorsement of the powerful University of California system, also working voluntarily under a similar scheme, and that of the University of Florida. Most important, through the good offices of David Robertshaw, chairman of CSU's Physiology Department (in which I held an appointment) and a major figure in the American Physiological Society, I received the endorsement of that group, a traditional *opponent* of any intrusion into research process. I also found out hearteningly that testifying on behalf of the bill would be two senators: Bob Dole (later presidential candidate) and John Melcher, at the time the only veterinarian in the Senate. My anxiety diminished somewhat, from paralysis to simple hysteria. I felt that the fates of millions of animals rested on my testimony.

I also received a phone call from a good friend, Dr. Franklin Loew, then the dean of Tufts Veterinary School and a prominent scientist who was named to the National Academy of Medicine. (He is now deceased.) He was also very much animal welfare-oriented, having eliminated multiple surgery at his institution on becoming dean, and a true scholar who had published a history book. Famous for his humor and kindness, Frank called to let me know that, ironically, he had been called on by the research community to replace Donald Kennedy to testify before the committee, *against* the legislation. He was in a very difficult position. The chief contributor to Tufts Veterinary School was Henry Foster, owner of the Charles River breeding labs, the largest purveyor of laboratory animals in the United States. Foster asked Frank to speak against the bill. Further muddying the waters was the fact that Andrew Rowan was testifying for the bill as science vice-president for the HSUS. Dramatically, Frank had just hired Andrew to help him create an animal-welfare presence at Tufts, but Andrew had not yet informed the HSUS. Frank asked my advice. I said, "You know you support the bill. We've talked often about it. On the other hand, you can't come out staunchly in favor, given your situation. Further, I have the support of the American Physiological Society, and if you oppose the bill, you will greatly harm your progressive reputation. So do what a dean does best—double talk." Frank went on to testify that while he wasn't sure legislation was needed, this was the best legislation possible.

At the hearing, the revered DeBakey spoke first. He opined that the people behind the bill were well intentioned but scientifically and medically naïve. He went on to extoll the benefits produced by research, beginning with the hackneyed and ubiquitous example of the Banting and Best Institute's development of insulin via research on dogs.

When I entered the hearing room early in the morning, I distributed texts of the endorsements I carried. DeBakey had apparently not had time to read them. When I rose to testify, I pointed out that far from the naïve Pollyannas DeBakey posited as being behind the bill, we carried serious scientific and medical endorsements. To DeBakey's credit, he went to lunch with Representative Walgren and me and confessed that he had been "snockered," told by people in the research community that we were naïve radicals and had not even read the bill. Later in the hearing process, Representative Waxman gently suggested to DeBakey, "In the future, . . . restrict your activities to surgery."

Senators Dole and Melcher and a number of congressmen were magnificent. Dole pointed out that advocating for the welfare of research animals would win him no political kudos in Kansas but was "the right thing to do." When a representative of Agriculture Secretary John Block protested that Block didn't understand much of the bill, Dole remarked, in essence, that we would be meeting for years if we had to cover all that Block didn't understand. Dole's courage, brilliance, and wit remain a source of inspiration to me whenever anyone faults our system, and I deeply regretted his defeat when he ran for president.

In my testimony, I pointed out that what we were asking for not only would not hurt science but would help it, since uncontrolled pain and distress in research animals affected science in unpredictable ways. I illustrated this by referring to literature on cancer research that had to be discarded because of the conditions under which the animals were kept. I spoke also of the Good Laboratory Practices Act—what an influential scientist friend called "the shame of the biomedical research community"—because it mandated such practices as proper record keeping and separation of sick animals in toxicology studies, practices that were theoretically presuppositional to proper science. I provided documentation that the research community was fibbing when it said the bill would cost billions, by adducing a detailed account of what CSU spent on the system. I remarked acidly that, when the medical research community claimed it would cost billions, it must have been counting the revenue high-priced plastic surgeons lost when they couldn't do butt lifts, breast augmentation, and nose jobs during the time they served on an IACUC.

I will never forget the kindness of one of the members of the Waxman Committee, Representative Mickey Leland (D-Tex.). He called me aside and said that while the bill wouldn't pass this time—too many people were influenced by the research community—its passage was inevitable with the bipartisan public support it enjoyed. He gave me a little hug and said he admired my courage. (A few years later, I was devastated to learn that he had been killed in a plane crash.) After the hearing, I returned home, relieved beyond measure, my spirit elevated by what Leland had said, and feeling as if I had been part of making history.

Representative Leland was, indeed, correct. Although I rashly told the press that the law could not pass until 2010, it passed in 1985. In fact, two laws passed. One was an amendment to the Animal Welfare Act, and the other was the National Institutes of Health (NIH) Reauthorization Bill, which required that the NIH, as the major source of funding for biomedical research, enforce the guidelines and principles that it historically had ignored. For example, the *NIH Guide to the Care and Use of Laboratory Animals,* first written in the 1960s, explicitly forbade using multiple survival surgery to save money. Yet, as discussed, this practice was rife in human and veterinary medical schools. When I documented this in the late 1970s, I told the NIH. The reply: "What do you want us to do? We're not in the enforcement business."

While working on the legislation, I came to know many major figures in the animal research community and even came to think of them as friends. One was Dale Schwindeman, head of the Federal Animal and Plant Health Inspection Service, the group charged with enforcing the Animal Welfare Act. Another was Thomas Wolfle, the head of the Research Resources Division of the NIH, of whom I speak more later. Both are highly intelligent men who came genuinely to understand the ethical issues in animal research. When the laws passed, I received separate calls from both of them. They said essentially the same thing: "Congratulations. You've established the first rights for animals in these laws."

8

The Deeper Meaning of the Laws

The history of the regulation of animal research is, in essence, the history of the emergence of a meaningful social ethic for animals in society. For virtually all of Western intellectual history, essentially no discussions existed of ethical obligations toward non-human beings, with the exception of the writings of some isolated thinkers such as Plutarch, Schopenhauer, and Bentham. Even more important, virtually no legislative history existed of constraining actions toward animals, with the exception of the prohibitions against overt cruelty, which are clearly expressed in the Old Testament, were defended by Thomas Aquinas during the Middle Ages, and were encoded in the laws of Western societies beginning in roughly 1800.

These anti-cruelty ethics and the laws mirroring them, particularly in their medieval and modern incarnations, moreover, did not portray animals as direct objects of moral concern. Instead, they focused on the indirect effects of cruelty on humans. Aquinas and Kant were quite explicit in forbidding animal cruelty on the grounds that, if such behavior were condoned in society, the perpetrators would be likely to advance to the abuse of humans, a psychological insight buttressed by three recent decades of research. On such a view, if a person demonstrably would not graduate to hurting people, presumably animal cruelty would not be morally problematic. Indeed, if people were known to be expunged of their sadistic urges toward people by engaging in animal cruelty, presumably such actions could be construed as obligatory.

In the nineteenth century, it became apparent that society interpreted the anti-cruelty laws in the same Thomistic way. In one revealing case in nineteenth-century Missouri (*State v. Bogardus* 1877), a man was charged with cruelty after throwing pigeons into the air and shooting them to demonstrate his skill. After killing the birds, he ate them. The court ruled that the pigeons were not "needlessly or unnecessarily killed" but that the killing was done "in the indulgence of a healthful recreating during an exercise tending to promote strength, bodily agility and courage." In discussing a similar nineteenth-century case of a tame-pigeon shoot in Colorado (*Waters v. the People* 1896), the court affirmed that "every act that causes pain and suffering to animals is not prohibited. Where the end or object in view is reasonable and adequate, the act resulting in pain is . . . necessary and justifiable, as . . . where the act is done to protect life or property, or to minister to the necessities of man." To the credit of the Colorado court, it did not find that such tame-pigeon shoots met the test of "worthy motive" or "reasonable object." Even today, however, there are jurisdictions where tame-pigeon shoots and "canned hunts" do not violate the cruelty laws. ("Canned hunts" involve shooting drugged or tame animals in small areas.)

Part of the historical reason for the poverty of animal ethics, be it theoretical or social, lies in the nature of traditional animal use. As mentioned in Chapter 4, the overwhelming uses of animals were agricultural, and the key to agricultural success was good husbandry—putting the animals into the optimal conditions they needed to thrive, then augmenting their natural survival skills with food during famine, water during drought, protection from predation and extremes of weather, and so on. This generated a happy symbiosis, wherein both human and animal partners to this ancient contract did well if and only if the other did well. A sanction far stronger than social ethics—self-interest—underwrote the husbandry relationship. The anti-cruelty laws were there to cover the sadists and those who were heedless of self-interest.

It is only in the mid-twentieth century that the stage was set for social demand for animal ethics, and even then in a halting and ambiguous fashion. Two factors created this demand. First, husbandry-based animal agriculture was superseded by industrial agriculture, the application of industrial methods to the production of animals. Antibiotics, vaccines, air-handling systems, and other tools allowed us to keep animals alive and profitable while miserable, confined in small spaces, deprived of social interaction, and fed restricted diets.

Second, the mid-twentieth century witnessed the rise of massive amounts of animal-research funding with the founding of the National Institutes of Health (NIH), as well as the development of large amounts of toxicity or safety testing of cosmetic, drugs, and food additives. Here again was a new and significant use of animals in which animal welfare was no longer ensured by the nature of that use. Animals were harmed for human (and animal) benefit, with no compensatory benefit to the animal subjects. Yet no social ethic or government regulation existed to ensure that such suffering was minimized, even when its presence was unnecessary or counterproductive to science.

As a movement, antivivisectionism—moral objection to invasive animal research—in fact, goes back to the beginnings of modern animal research. It is arguable that Descartes' successful depiction of animals as organic machines lacking sentience laid the groundwork for significant experimentation on animals in terms of anatomy and physiology, with Descartes' disciples at the Port Royal Abbey in France pioneering in literal vivisection—"cutting while alive." This sort of work in turn sparked significant opposition, particularly in Britain, with the forces opposed to animal research generating sufficient political clout to cause an antivivisection bill to be presented to the House of Lords in 1875. After much testimony and controversy, Parliament passed the Act of 1876 (Cruelty to Animals Act), which restricted some uses of animals in research and teaching and set up a system of licensure and certification governing the use of animals in British science.

No such movement of similar political clout developed in the United States. The closest relevant concern was over the seizure of animals from pounds via a series of state laws enacted paralleling the rise of significant amounts of animal research after World War II; these laws (known as "pound seizure laws") allowed research laboratories to obtain dogs and cats from pounds to use for experimentation. Though such laws elicited much opposition from animal advocates, some are still extant, while some states, such as Massachusetts, have disallowed even the use of dead pound animals in research.

In general, the biomedical research community successfully countered any legislative intrusion into the research process from World War II until the 1960s, cannily portraying animal research as a scientific necessity, not as an ethical issue, and further portraying those who raised moral questions about animal research as misanthropes unconcerned about human health—that is, "animal lovers and people-haters." This view was not merely a cynical political posture but, in fact, an ideology widely accepted in the biomedical community. In the mid-1960s, however, two events took place that made it politically necessary for Congress to address animal research, at least on a superficial level.

Here is the first incident as described in the *Legislative History of the Animal Welfare Act* (2007):

> In July 1965, a Dalmatian named Pepper disappeared from her backyard and was later spotted by a family member in a photograph of dogs and goats being unloaded from a Pennsylvania animal dealer's truck. The family discovered that Pepper had been sold to a dog dealer in New York State. When the family confronted the dealer, they were refused entry onto the property. . . . Events led to a telephone call to Congressman [Joseph] Resnick's office in the [d]istrict where the dog dealer was located. However, even Mr. Resnick's intercession failed. Angered by the dealer's refusal to admit the family, Congressman Resnick decided to introduce a bill to prevent such wrongs. Pressure from the Pennsylvania State Police led to an admission that Pepper had actually been sold to a hospital in New York City. In the end, Pepper had been used in an experiment and was euthanized. Pepper's disappearance, however, had galvanized several members of the House and Senate to introduce legislation to prevent future incidents. (Laboratory Animal Act of 1966, 89 P.L. 544, 80 Stat. 350)

During the course of the hearing, passage of the bill was virtually ensured by a story in *Life* magazine accompanied by dramatic photographs of emaciated, terrified dogs taken by Stan Wayman during a raid by the Maryland State Police on a dog dealer who provided animals for research. The photographs documented serious dog abuse. The resulting public outcry led to quick passage of the law.

It is absolutely essential to note that there was no attempt to deal with rational animal ethics per se in this legislation. The unabashed reasons for these laws are protection of human sensibilities (i.e., concern that their beloved possessions, their pets, not be dognapped or catnapped and end up in experiments) and calming public hysteria. Furthermore, Wayman's photographs struck at the heart of American's love for dogs. In particular, his stark nighttime photo of an emaciated greyhound, little more than a bag of bones, held by a dealer was bound to galvanize a major emotional response.

From the point of view of rational ethical content, this legislation is appalling. First, the act defines "animals" in research as "live and dead dogs, cats, monkeys (non-human primate animals), guinea pigs, hamsters, and rabbits." The regulations specifically exclude mice, birds, farm animals, and horses used for food and fiber research. Given that rats and mice were estimated to make up more than 90 percent of the animals used in research, this was hardly a comprehensive research-animal welfare act. In addition, the regulations state that "animal" shall mean, in addition to the animals listed above, any "other such warm-blooded animal as the Secretary [of Agriculture] determines is being used, or is intended for use, for research, testing, experimentation." Absurdly, the law authorizes the secretary to determine (i.e., find out) which animals are used for research and cover them, yet also to decide, as in the regulations, not to cover certain animals that are, in fact, so used. Not surprisingly, the animals covered were ones that aesthetically appeal to members of the public. As one USDA inspector told me in the 1970s, he could bring charges against a researcher or dealer who "abuse[d]" a dead dog yet would be powerless against a scientist who was biting the heads off mice and spitting them into garbage cans.

In tandem with this most ethically unsound definition of "animals" came a very restricted notion of the scope of the act:

> The Secretary [of Agriculture] shall establish and promulgate standards to govern the humane handling, care, treatment and transportation of animals by dealers and research facilities. Such standards shall include minimum requirements with respect to the housing, feeding, watering, sanitation, ventilation, shelter from extremes of weather and temperature, separation by species, and adequate veterinary care. The foregoing shall not be construed as authorizing the Secretary to prescribe standards for the handling, care, or treatment of animals during actual research or experimentation by research facility as determined by such research facility. (U.S. Code, Title 7, chap. 54, sec. 2131)

In other words, the act is designed to ensure the welfare of research animals without prescribing standards for "handling, care, or treatment during actual research or experimentation." This is relevantly analogous to a sex manual that covers cohabitation and foreplay but disavows concern with anything having to do with sexual intercourse. In 1970, the act was amended to include ensuring proper use of anesthesia, analgesia, and tranquilization by the research facility during an experiment. However, the absurdity therein was that the regulatory requirement could be met by the research facility's affirming in its annual report that it saw no need for anesthesia, analgesia, or tranquilization, even if it was, in fact, performing painful research.

Armed with the philosophical framework I assembled earlier, our legislation-writing group saw its task as creating moral checks on animal use in research, the most important of which was the legally mandated control of pain and distress if animals were to be used in ways that caused pain.

Further, the approach to legislation seemed to follow logically and in accord with common sense: If animals were not getting the best treatment possible consistent with their use in research—indeed, if poor treatment was sometimes even compromising research by introducing uncontrolled stress and pain variables—we had a societal opening to find a middle way between those in the research community who insisted on no constraints on the use of animals in research and those animal advocates who would forbid research altogether. Society as a whole, we surmised, was in the middle on those matters.

We learned much in the ensuing five years until the bill passed. In the first place, and contrary to our expectations, we learned that the research community absolutely and completely opposed any legislative ensurance of proper animal treatment. A long tradition had already existed in the medical research community of seeing anyone who raised questions about the ethics of animal use as an "anti-science, anti-human, anti-progress, anti-vivisectionist." Thus, for outlining the legislation in *Animal Rights and Human Morality,* I was called a "Nazi and a lab-trasher" in a review in the *New England Journal of Medicine* in 1982. It was as if, to the scientific community, we were hell-bent on stopping medical progress. I only gradually learned that scientific thought was guided by a powerful and immovable ideology that declared science to be "value-free" in general and "ethics-free" in particular, an offshoot of rampant logical positivism (a philosophical school that held that there was a complete difference between empirical assertions and assertions of value, declaring only the former to be meaningful). Furthermore, this ideology required agnosticism about animals' thought, feeling, consciousness, or pain as empirically unknowable. Furthermore, one day after I was attacked in the *New England Journal,* I received a copy of *Agenda,* an animal activist magazine that reviewed the same book and pronounced me a "sell-out" for "accepting the reality of science." That criticism stems from a radical viewpoint according to which animal abuse cannot be remedied incrementally but requires revolutionary change. The famed activist Henry Spira, though an abolitionist vis-à-vis animal use, nonetheless has pointed out that all social revolution in the history of the United States has been incremental.

We were secure in our belief that we had seized ground that society in general would support—namely, ensuring more humane treatment for laboratory animals. Nonetheless, we were told explicitly that we had an uphill battle, if only because the medical community had such a powerful lobby to oppose us. We needed to justify, persuasively and painstakingly, every provision we proposed to make mandatory.

At the root of our laws was control of pain and of distress, the latter encompassing such negative emotional states as fear, loneliness, and boredom. We also mandated that, if a procedure would hurt humans, it could be presumed to hurt animals. The research community outrageously claimed to control pain already. We proved this false by doing a literature search on animal analgesia in 1982 when I went before Congress. The result? There were only two papers on the subject. One of them said, "There ought to be papers"; the other said that not much was known. Such evidence of neglect of pain control could not be ignored. If pain control were truly used, there would be scientific papers on its use.

In addition to mandating pain control, the legislation we proposed was intended to break the hold of agnosticism about ethics and mental states among scientists. We did this by requiring Institutional Animal Care and Use Committees (IACUCs), which would include scientists and non-scientists, to review prospectively all protocols and discuss them in terms of proper numbers of animals, control of pain and suffering, statistical design, species, and so on. Such mandated discussion, we felt, would help ideology crumble—and it did. Committees also reviewed all teaching and inspected facilities and checked to make sure protocols were performed as approved.

Finally, we proposed in our bill that all laboratory animals (including rats and mice, which had been excluded from the Animal Welfare Act) be housed and kept in ways that met their biological and psychological needs and natures. Unfortunately, Congress was unwilling to grant this, instead mandating only exercise for dogs and environments for non-human primates that "enhanced their psychological well-being." Other provisions included prohibiting the use of paralytic drugs without anesthetic, prohibiting multiple surgery unless justified to test a single hypothesis, establishing an animal welfare information service at the National Agricultural Library, and requiring research facilities to institute and oversee training for researchers and staff on humane practice and experimentation. In addition, the USDA, which enforced the Animal Welfare Act and these amendments, was to share efforts with the NIH, which, beginning in the 1960s, already had good guidelines for proper care and use of laboratory animals but failed to enforce them. (The NIH guidelines were, in fact, turned into law at the same time our amendments passed in 1985.) Both of these laws went into effect in 1986.

Virtually all vertebrate animals used in research were covered by one or another of these laws. However, in a very reactionary move in 2002, when the USDA was planning to include rats and mice under the Animal Welfare Act, the chief biomedical research lobby group, the National Association for Biomedical Research, convinced Senator Jesse Helms to sponsor legislation that declared rats and mice not to be animals for the purposes of the act. By then, such a move was not very popular with the scientific community, as many scientists felt it made them look ridiculous in the eyes of the public. Nevertheless, it prevailed, and rats and mice are still exempted from many of the protections of the law.

The laws, and particularly the regulations interpreting them, established by the Animal and Plant Health Inspection Service (APHIS), and to a lesser degree by the NIH, are far more complicated than this thumbnail sketch might suggest. For example, there are detailed rules concerning surgery, veterinary care, psychological well-being, and so forth. But conceptually, at least, we now know enough to understand why these laws are, indeed, revolutionary breakthroughs in animal ethics. In the first place, some of the absurdities manifest in the laws of 1966 have been largely corrected. Although the claim disavowing any legal control over the actual conduct of research remains, the procedures mandated clearly belie that claim. Similarly, although the Animal Welfare Act amendment and the Helms law deny legal protection to rats and mice, the NIH law covering all federally funded institutions does cover them in most settings, though there are still some exempted contexts. Farm animals used in biomedicine are clearly covered, and many IACUCs demand that the same biomedical level of control of pain be used for farm animals as that used for animals in biomedical research, even in agricultural research. Many committees have also applied pain-control rules to invertebrates such as cephalopods, where there is excellent scientific reason to believe pain (and even distress) are present.

In addition, the laws have significantly eroded the ideology that creates a radical cleavage between ethics and science. Protocol review (i.e., prospective review of animal research projects by the IACUC) is inherently replete with substantial ethical discussion, which inevitably becomes more sophisticated with time. When my own institutional committee began in 1980 (voluntarily to show Congress that such a system could work), we might have covered twenty protocols in a ninety-minute meeting, including time to eat lunch and schmooze. Now judging the same number of protocols consumes three to four hours, and a single controversial protocol can consume an entire meeting.

Moreover, scientists serving on these committees understand that the current system is their last chance at self-regulation and that loss of federal funds for a whole institution can be a penalty for not obeying the law. The result is more and more scientists taking the issues of animal care and use very seriously and growing hostility among committees to the handful of researchers who try to get around the system. Friends at the NIH even told me that, within five years of the laws' going into effect in 1987, some committees were discussing cost–benefit issues in terms of animals' suffering, even though the law does not mandate such discussions. Though most protocols are not rejected, many are modified to the benefit of animals. The biggest problem that remains with the laws is that primacy is still given to the science being done, not to animal welfare.

It is also obvious that, from their inception, the laws have eroded and displaced the ideological denial of animal mentation, particularly pain. Given that knowledge of and concern for animal pain was almost nonexistent when the laws passed, the USDA wisely concentrated on enforcing control of pain. It is only in the past few years—now that pain control is solidly established, and the vast majority of young scientists and graduate students acknowledge pain in animals as axiomatic, and the literature on animals' pain has become vast and increases exponentially—that USDA has mentioned, as a word to the wise, that it will start monitoring "distress," even though, as was the case initially regarding pain, people are stumbling in the dark regarding this difficult-to-define concept.

When we drafted this legislation, our group was adamant that the role of the law should be analogous to what Wittgenstein said of his philosophy: an educational ladder that allows or, rather, compels scientists to transcend their previous agnostic position regarding the ethics of research and the pain and distress of animals and negotiate routinely in what historically was terra incognita. Given that the law has been in effect for only twenty-four years, our goal seems well on the way to being achieved. Ultimately, we hoped to produce a generation of scientists to whom what are now legal stipulations are second nature and who have re-appropriated common sense and common decency.

The social furor that reflected public distrust of scientists' treatment of animals in the 1970s and early 1980s has diminished. There is no question that revelations by People for the Ethical Treatment of Animals and other activists about the mistreatment of macaque monkeys in a neuroscience lab run by Dr. Edward Taub in Maryland in 1981; atrocities at the University of Pennsylvania Head Injury Laboratory in 1984, in which baboons were egregiously mistreated; and the misconduct revealed at the City of Hope cancer-research facility in 1985 all fueled the passage of our laws. And correlatively, it is clear that the passage of the laws blunted constant media coverage of atrocities and the misuse of animals in research, though occasional flares still emerge, particularly in the area of primate use.

To use the famous language of W.M.S. Russell and R. L. Burch regarding alternatives to animal use, published in *The Principles of Humane Experimental Technique* (1959), we may recognize three alternative approaches known as "the three Rs": replacement of animals by non-animals, reduction in numbers of animals, and refinement in animal use. In the short run, the laws have greatly affected reduction by focusing researchers' attention on previously neglected statistical precision. (To be fair, though, sometimes committees may see the animal sample as statistically inadequate and demand more animals.) It is amazing that researchers seeking answers to the same sort of question will ask to use thousands of mice but only a few horses. Their requests are not governed by the logic of the experiment but by nonscientific, economic considerations.

Even more than reduction, perhaps, the laws have focused attention on refinement of procedures—notably, by demanding early end points (i.e., points for euthanasia) and precise end points decided in advance. Whereas researchers used to use death as an endpoint in disease studies, a point that can involve significant suffering, today the researcher must specify the earliest possible moment of termination. Similarly, while in the 1970s I saw tumors grown in animals larger than the animal itself, today the size of such tumors is strictly limited and small.

Animal activists, however, favor *replacement* of animals (e.g., by computers) as the most desirable alternative. Unfortunately, replacement is difficult, as it requires both significant money for research and equally significant amounts for validation. Science tends to be conservative and demands what it considers full proof of the viability of an alternative before replacing animals as the historical "gold standard," whether they are or not. That is not to say the laws have not encouraged replacement. Particularly in teaching, invasive animal use, especially use involving suffering, is a thing of the past. Whereas once science classes included multiple survival surgery and poisoning of animals, today even terminal surgery for teaching is declining, and IACUCs are increasingly asking, "Why can't you film it?" A famous example is hemorrhagic shock labs in which medical and veterinary students were forced to bleed animals out and watch the stages leading to death. Today such labs, once ubiquitous, have been replaced by films or computer simulations in most medical and veterinary schools.

In short, the laws have provided an ongoing mechanism for the scientific community to reflect both on what it does and on what society thinks about it in ethical terms. Having said all this, it is necessary to sound a cautionary note and address the fact that the laws are far from perfect. At best, they represent the first real steps of ethical evolution in thinking about animal research, which, in the light of previous history, is not a trivial point.

Despite the real progress in these laws, they are only steps on the way to a full-blown social ethic for laboratory animals. Some implicit assumptions that underlie these laws are at least morally questionable in today's society, if not downright unacceptable. One such assumption is that the importance of the scientific question being researched on animals takes precedence over the welfare of the animals. This assumption is built into the prohibition against committees' rejecting certain research as being too invasive to perform (though, as mentioned, some committees do on occasion exceed their statutory authority and reject certain research). In a showdown between good science and animal welfare, good science will usually take precedence. Hence, the provision from the original Animal Welfare Act affirming that these laws are not intended to infringe on the design or conduct of research except in the specific ways enumerated is still extant. It is by no means clear that society as a whole would say this, and there is no doubt that very many citizens would be prepared to dispense with certain scientific advances if they can be achieved only with the expense of great suffering. There is, in fact, some research that I am sure most citizens would reject because far too much suffering is caused to balance the benefits. In fact, a survey commissioned by the Humane Society of the United States shows that public support for animal research declines in direct proportion to how much the suffering the animal endures in pursuit of that knowledge.

Thus, I have no doubt that many, if not most, citizens would approve of painless killing of many mice to cure cancer, or even of the painful death of a thousand rats if we were pretty certain the result would be a cancer cure. But when a researcher blinds a thousand hamsters to study circadian rhythms, I seriously doubt most people would approve, given the lack of any demonstrable benefit to human health.

At the moment, the scientific community justifies invasive animal use by citing the benefits to humans or animals that result from such use. In the current system, the scientific community ultimately judges both cost and benefit; IACUCs exist to ensure that everything that can be done to mitigate suffering is, in fact, being done. Much research on animals is done with public money. That which is done with private money is still allowed to go forward in the public arena because people implicitly trust the scientific community's cost–benefit assessments. In the face of these points, it would be reasonable to allow committees to judge whether a given piece of research should be done at all, not just how it should be done. The degree of suffering allowed to be inflicted on other creatures should be judged by society in general, since the question at issue is inherently a matter of social ethical judgment, not merely the judgment of those who have a vested career interest in the outcome. If what results from an experiment on animals is worth the animals' suffering, ordinary people should be able to see that balance clearly and unequivocally.

Thus, because the justification of animal research depends on social moral decisions, it seems appropriate that those adjudicating that decision should be representatives of society in general—in whose alleged interest the invasive manipulation is to be done—rather than representatives of those whose personal careers and futures depend on doing those manipulations, regardless of their actual social value. This is a fortiori true when the research is funded by tax money.

In other words, the next reasonable step in creating morally sound laws governing the use and treatment of laboratory animals would be to allow the decisions for which invasive animal research is to be done or not done to fall on those who *allegedly* will benefit from it rather than on those who clearly stand to gain from doing more research. To the claim that ordinary people could not make such a judgment, I would reply that, even if they find it difficult, scientists are capable of explaining what and why they need to do what they want to do. Furthermore, it is far more respectful of citizens' autonomy in a democracy to allow them to decide for themselves which activities are to be conducted in their names. People should at least be allowed to directly affirm, "I will not accept this amount of animal suffering as a cost of this amount of human health improvement or increase in knowledge."

Such a system would be a major moral step forward. But a doubt remains that public sentiment would necessarily give priority to animals' interests. In addition, other difficulties exist in the current system that could render it even less effectual than it currently is. A key feature of the current laws is prospective review by committees of suggested animal studies—an examination of the hypothesis proposed, what is to be done to test the hypotheses, and the degree and nature of resulting suffering, as well as modalities for its control. But more and more, as biology is increasingly based in molecular genetics, this old model is being superseded. Much of today's research doesn't allow plausible prediction of what the experiment will affect. For example, ever increasing amounts of molecular biology involve gene or sequence ablation or gene or sequence addition or insertion. No one has the foggiest notion of what results such insertions or ablations will engender—the phenotypic results—in the animals themselves. So committees really cannot predict what effects on welfare such manipulations may engender.

As one of my friends at a major medical school put it, very few schools can keep up with the nature of the new "try it and see" approaches to molecular biology—namely, those schools with large numbers of postgraduate residents already trained in laboratory animal medicine who can tour laboratories to catch unexpected results engendering pain or suffering for the animals. In other words, if we lack the ability to anticipate phenotypic effects of genetic manipulation, controlling pain and suffering in a timely way becomes very labor-intensive and correlatively cost-prohibitive.

It is also plain that society has grown increasingly sensitive to animals' suffering, and protocols that were acceptable—or, at least, unquestioned—twenty years ago can become today's scandals and capable of damaging an institution considerably. A case in point occurred at the Tufts University Veterinary School in 2004. An IACUC carefully examined a protocol that involved fracturing young dogs' legs and repairing the fractures with two different sorts of external fixation apparatuses. The committee and the veterinary staff worked tirelessly to minimize the animals' pain and distress and succeeded quite well. Yet the general public, the student body, and the mass media were horrified that the limbs of young dogs were being fractured, regardless of the benefit. In other words, certain manipulations on certain animals are socially unacceptable, period. This is likely to be a moving target, both in terms of kinds of animals and in terms of kinds of manipulations.

The issue of research that oversteps the bounds of decency is certainly a social ethical issue concerning which current laws are silent. Phil Kosh, dean of veterinary medicine at Tufts, agonized over this issue for a long time and finally instituted a potential additional level of oversight not embodied in the federal laws. On his proposed model, senior administrators can flag certain protocols as not morally acceptable in their context, regardless of how they are done or what benefit they produce, except under conditions of national emergency for humans (such as AIDS) or animals (such as parvovirus). How such additional oversight will work, whether researchers will accept it, and how it will stand up to legal challenges all remain to be seen. But it does demonstrate the probable next step in law and ethics that society will demand, wisely foreseen by a thoughtful and prescient administration.

A second example of going beyond current law helps to solidify the point. When Patricia Olson became senior administrator at the Morris Animal Foundation, a very influential research foundation devoted largely to pet animal health, one of her first concerns was that the foundation funded significantly invasive research. She found this morally, politically, and pragmatically disturbing: How could a group specializing in the well-being of dogs, cats, and other animals do invasive research on them? When she asked me to talk to the foundation's board and to Dr. Mark Morris, its leader, I did, arguing that there was much possible non-invasive research that could benefit animals—for example, certain types of behavioral research. After all, the largest single cause of death for pet animals is euthanasia for behavioral problems. I also explained that groups such as the American Kennel Club already refused to fund invasive research. The board and Dr. Morris concurred, and the foundation's policy now allows for invasive research only in emergencies. Thanks to that policy, it received a million-dollar gift from a pet-food company. I currently serve as chairman of Morris's ethics committee.

Finally, a more adequate ethic for research animals would address the physical, social, behavioral, and psychological needs of research animals—what I have elsewhere called providing living conditions that accommodate their *telos,* or nature, as we proposed in our original draft bill. Only about 10 percent of research animals are used in invasive, painful protocols involving unrelieved pain, but 100 percent of such animals are kept in conditions that violate some aspects of their nature. To cite some glaring examples, nocturnal animals are kept in twenty-four-hour daylight; social animals are kept isolated; burrowing animals are kept in polycarbonate cages. I strongly believe that, just as uncontrolled pain affects the quality of research, so does violating animals' nature. In the end, the justification for not only preventing miserable lives for research animals but actually striving to create happy lives for them is a moral one, calling us back to the hard moral fact that research on captive animals is irreducibly morally problematic.

9

A Philosopher Looks at Scientific Ideology

Being criticized by the *New England Journal of Medicine* and by the animal-activist journal *Agenda* genuinely surprised me. I thought that animal activists would welcome anything that improved the condition of laboratory animals, but *Agenda* took the position that short-run improvements for animals' well-being would calm protestors and slow down societal rejection of animal research. They espoused revolution. Fat chance.

I was more astounded by the extreme language in the *New England Journal* review. I believed that we had written laws that balanced the needs of science with the demands of ethics. I did not understand how very bright scientists could fail to understand the ethical issues involved in research, not only on animals but on humans as well, as the well-publicized Tuskegee experiment revealed when black prisoners were left untreated for syphilis. Even when scientists would speak to me, they could not seem to hear the ethical questions, however bright they were, and I often felt like a college sophomore debating religion with classmates.

My thesis, then, is that an ideologically ubiquitous denial of the relevance of values in general, and of ethics in particular, to science created blinders among scientists to issues of major concern to society.

I was further perplexed by the apparent blindness displayed in science toward animals' pain and suffering: no literature on the use of analgesia; paralytic drugs used in surgery instead of anesthetics; teaching via multiple survival surgery and atrocious laboratories; unwillingness to accommodate students who did not want to hurt animals and dismissal of their moral concerns as "squeamishness," rendering them unsuitable for careers in science and medicine. I could not understand how biomedical scientists could profess to be evolutionarily based but deny the phylogenic continuity of consciousness, ignore what was patently pain in animals, and dismiss it as merely reflex. Eventually I stopped trying to convince scientists rationally of the relevance of ethics and the reality of animals' pain and consciousness and came to the conclusion that all of that needed to be legislated. It took until the late 1980s for me to begin to understand what was going on, as articulated in *The Unheeded Cry: Animal Consciousness, Animal Pain, and Science* (Rollin 1989), and until well into the twenty-first century to fully understand it, as expressed in *Science and Ethics* (Rollin 2006c).

Nor could I fathom the low status of animal care and the little regard for it in biomedical sciences, not only in human medical schools but even in veterinary schools. Yet I learned that the situation was worse than Dave Neil had portrayed it as I traveled to research institutions to lecture. The official line of the research community was that animals were essential to biomedical progress, yet they were not treated anywhere near as well as pieces of equipment (being cheaper). A researcher who would never dream of dragging a microtome to work behind a pickup truck would leave the care of his animals in the hands of students or technicians paid the minimum wage, who often didn't bother to check the animals for days at a time or even to replenish food and water on weekends.

Yet animals are infinitely more sensitive to stress than machinery. I made it my business to learn as much as possible about the relationship between animal care and treatment and scientific results both to get legislation passed and to try to educate researchers. Indeed, following the passage of the laws in 1985, I was almost immediately approached by a science publisher, CRC Press, to do a book on the proper care and use of laboratory animals to ensure adherence to the law and good science. Enlisting my staunch veterinary ally, Lynne Kesel, and many colleagues around the world, we produced *The Experimental Animal in Biomedical Research* (1989–1995), a two-volume, fifty-two-chapter work on everything from ethics to analgesia and a species-by-species survey of optimal care for laboratory animals. The book is a classic (if I do say so myself) that is still recommended by the National Institutes of Health (NIH) as a reference.

How we keep animals may well cause them more distress than what we do to them. Only a small percentage of research protocols are painful, yet all laboratory animals are kept under conditions that violate their *telos,* their psychological and biological needs and natures, dramatically affecting not only the animals' welfare but also the research results. In fact, as the thrust for enriched environments for laboratory animals has gained momentum, much traditional "baseline data" have had to be thrown out because the animals' physiology and metabolism mirrored the highly unnatural conditions under which they were kept.

To exemplify these points: mice and rats are nocturnal burrowing animals yet were, and are, kept in polycarbonate cages under twenty-four hours of daylight. One researcher, an expert on the rat retina as a model for that of humans, did not know that long-term exposure to light leads to retinal degeneration. Another who had done thirty years of work with guinea pigs thought his colony had a wasting disease when they lost weight; he had not trimmed their teeth, which were so maloccluded that the animals could not eat. Every laboratory-animal veterinarian can tell of being scolded by indignant researchers because they supplied "sick dogs" with body temperatures higher than 98.6 degrees Fahrenheit. (The normal temperature for a dog is 101 degrees.) Most egregious was the treatment of non-human primates. In one primate center, I saw baboons (social animals of high intelligence) caged singly in three-by-three-by-three-foot cages. I was horrified and asked the director why. "Because they're vicious and hard to handle," he replied. I had visited an Australian baboon colony that roamed freely in a huge enclosure in which the animals had been trained using food rewards to present an arm for blood sampling. I asked this director to consider that how his baboons were being kept was what was making them vicious. Indeed, smart researchers have been able to train animals to do all sorts of things by using food and play rewards. Lynne Kesel did it with dogs and injections and blood samples.

Lynne tells the story of a research project she did on a vaccine for parvovirus. Once a day, she took blood samples from the dogs and played with them. One day as she was leaving the dog runs, one of the dogs began to howl and yelp, as if in pain. Thinking he was injured, she ran to check him. He had no physical problem. After a moment, Lynne realized he was telling her she had forgotten to take the blood sample, and he missed his play with her and treats. Shortly thereafter, I adopted the dog, a shepherd mix about a year old, and dubbed him "Parvo." He lived with us until his death fifteen years later.

My experience alone with the profound stupidity and ignorance displayed by many researchers about the animals they use could fill a good-size book. Indeed, one activist publishing a book invited me to contribute a chapter on the biggest atrocity I knew of in animal research. After a good deal of thought, I wrote an essay saying that the greatest atrocity was the fact that one could earn a master's or doctorate or M.D./Ph.D. in some animal-using area of research, set up a lab to do such research, and never learn anything about the animals (or their needs) except that they model some human disease or syndrome. He rejected the contribution, making it clear that he wanted *National Enquirer*–type material. Yet my point stands. More suffering grew out of such ignorance than ever came from hideous experiments such as burning pigs.

An example: One university I visited maintained a beagle colony for research on mammary tumors. When I toured the colony, I was told I had to wear shooting earmuffs because the noise levels were constant and damaging. Noise is well known to be a stressor to animals. I asked whether the dogs wore earmuffs. "No," they replied. "Why?" "Because," I said, "there was a paper in *Science* some months ago showing that beagles exposed to stressors (including noise) developed more mammary tumors."

All sorts of things are stressors to animals. A tiny change in ambient temperature can radically alter responses to drugs and toxins. R. M. Nerein and co-workers showed in 1980 in *Science* that if two groups of rabbits are put on a 2 percent cholesterol diet and one group is petted and fondled while the other is simply fed and watered, the rabbits treated with tender loving care will develop 60 percent fewer atherosclerotic lesions. Even more dramatic, K. Gärtner and colleagues (1981) studied the effects on twenty-five blood characteristics of simply moving rats in their cages or exposing them to one minute of ether. The effect of these apparently minor interventions was very dramatic; in fact, they create a microcirculatory shock profile.

If something as apparently trivial as moving a cage can cause such profound effects, then it goes without saying that the innumerable other intrusions on animals' natures can have similar consequences. Indeed, this information served me well in one very dramatic incident well worth recounting in detail. In the early 1980s, I was invited to Jackson Lake Lodge in the Grand Tetons of Wyoming to be the dinner speaker at the annual general meeting of the Shock Society, a large group of researchers who study circulatory shock or circulatory collapse, the ultimate cause of death for all living things. To study shock, a phenomenon that can come from multiple causes—such as trauma when people lose blood internally after an accident until circulation collapses or from bacterial poisons (endotoxins) that block circulation (endotoxic or septic shock)—animals are used. Creating these states in animals is brutal, requiring traumatizing or infusing toxins into the animals. Knowing I was going to deal with a tough audience, I did a good deal of study before the meeting.

I expected to be treated like an Orthodox Jew at a Nazi rally, and that was partially true but also partially false. The first evening, I sat with a group of young researchers who were very concerned about the ethics of what they did. They implored me to raise the issue that when trauma was inflicted on animals, they were forbidden to use anesthesia because the human trauma victim being "modeled" was not anesthetized. One way to create trauma was by using the infamous Noble-Collip drum, a device like a clothes dryer that contained protuberances in which the animals were tumbled to produce random trauma.

Jackson Lodge employed retirees and college students as staff, these researchers told me. Earlier that day, a presentation had been given accompanied by a film of dogs placed in the drum. The film projector was run by a student. At the end of the lecture, he sought out the president of the society and angrily said, "I speak for all of us here. We can't wait for you sons of bitches to get out of here." Horrified, I began to modify my lecture to include discussing the use of anesthesia.

I was not scheduled to talk until dinner the next day and decided to attend some sessions. I was drawn to what was advertised as a debate on "vivisection." Intrigued, I went and watched in growing rage as one society member lampooned an idiotic emotional antivivisectionist while another refuted such claims as "Research doesn't even help humans." At the end, I stood up and said, "How dare you mock an issue you have no understanding of! How dare you make light of serious moral questions!" Their response: "We didn't know you would be here."

Evening came. It was time for my talk. I got up and began to speak about ethics and animals. Then I launched into the issue I had been asked by the young researchers to raise. I sarcastically praised the members of the society for their attempt to produce high-fidelity models. If they were so scrupulous as to avoid anesthesia in the name of good science, surely they knew about Gärtner's results. I wrote the name on the board. No one had heard of it. I expressed amazement. Gärtner showed that simply moving a cage or uncorking a bottle of ether creates a microcirculatory shock profile. How can you not control for that? How can you not control for the myriad stressors you don't even recognize? And if you don't, I trumpeted, how dare you withhold anesthesia in the name of science! I pulled a hundred dollars out of my wallet and said that I would bet them the money against a Coke that I could use anesthesia and predictably map the anesthetized animal onto the unanesthetized animal—in other words, adjust for the effect of anesthesia. They agreed. "Then how dare you [a phrase I was using a lot that trip] withhold anesthesia, a moral requirement!" I said. The room grew very quiet. The grand old man of the field, and editor of the Shock Society's journal, raised his hand. "I'm glad you raised the issue," he said. "I was going to announce that henceforth we will only accept papers describing work on anesthetized animals." Boom—just like that. Gone were all the pieties about the accuracy of models. The young researchers thanked me effusively.

But my time on the hot seat was not over. As soon as I was finished, I asked for questions. Before anyone could ask anything, up jumped an eminent researcher. In a comic-opera German accent, his face flushed with rage, he said, "Vell, you speak vit some vit und you are superficially entertaining. But you don't know vat you are talking about, and your science is all wronk." He then turned on his heel and strode out. I shouted after him, "Cheap shot! Come back and tell me why and where my science is wrong." He did not. This was, in fact, a tipping point, as his rudeness turned the audience sympathetically toward me. Playing the injured martyr—"It's all right. I've heard worse," I said—I then entertained serious questions for more than two hours.

The last example of scientists' cutting their own throats epistemologically comes from pigs. Because pigs are omnivores whose digestive systems and cardiovascular systems are quite similar to those of humans, they were deemed ideal for certain experiments. But the pigs used historically were big, smart, and not disposed to suffer injury in silence. Researchers were scared to death of them. When the time came to take blood samples, they dispatched a big group of rednecks to snare the pig, wrestle it to the ground, and draw blood. (I actually saw a film of this at a conference.) Given what the reader now knows from Gärtner, I ask you to imagine how valid the results obtained from that blood sample were.

Let us also recall that uncontrolled pain is a stressor that has profound physiological results, ranging from neuroendocrine disruption to retarding healing and disposing toward infection. That will give you a good idea of why our laws actually helped improve research.

But our original question remains: How can researchers engage in behavior that so violates common sense and common decency? How can intelligent people believe that science, a human activity embedded in a societal context, can be value-free in general and ethics-free in particular? How can anyone who possesses ordinary common sense not realize that an animal is in pain if you step on its foot or do surgery on it? How can anyone who possesses common decency not feel an imperative to control pain inflicted on an animal in the course of research? And even more incredible, how can people who treat lab dogs that way go home and dote on the family poodle? How could Descartes, who raised spaniels and gave them as gifts to friends, see animals simply as machines?

It took me until the mid-1980s to understand how scientists could deny the relevance of ethics to science and deny the reality of consciousness. A realization dawned on me as I worked on the puzzle of how science could be Darwinian, positing the phylogenetic evolutionary continuity of morphological and physiological traits, yet deny similar continuity of consciousness regarding mind, despite Darwin's firm belief in animal mentation.

As I worked on this, I became aware that, while I was an undergraduate, I had been taught precisely the patterns of thinking I was now criticizing. In psychology, I had learned that one could not study consciousness, even in humans; in science classes, I had learned—and believed—the mantra "Science is value-free in general and ethics-free in particular." I realized that scientists were learning a set of beliefs along with the data of the science even as people learn logically questionable precepts in their religious education, precepts that are presented as axiomatic, indubitable, not subject to questioning or criticism, and presuppositional to science. I saw that these beliefs were very much like religious belief and that no amount of rational argument could dislodge them—in other words, that an *ideology of science* was taught to nascent scientists from the beginning of their education and solidified as they proceeded through doctoral training.

Those beliefs, which I discuss at length in *Science and Ethics,* are never questioned. They constitute a hardened and unshakeable ideology that I have called "scientific common sense" or "scientific ideology," which stands in the same relationship to scientists' thinking that ordinary common sense does to the thinking of non-scientists. It is to this ideology we now turn.

What is an ideology? In simple terms, an ideology is a set of fundamental beliefs, commitments, value judgments, and principles that determine the way someone embracing those beliefs looks at the world, understands the world, and is directed to behave toward others in the world. When we refer to a set of beliefs as an "ideology," we usually mean that, for the person or group entertaining those beliefs, nothing counts as a good reason to revise those beliefs and, correlatively, raising questions critical of those beliefs is excluded dogmatically by the belief system. As David Braybrooke has stated, "Ideologies distort as much by omitting to question as by affirming answers" (Braybrooke 1967, 126).

The term "ideology" is perhaps most famously associated with Karl Marx, who described capitalist ideology (or free-market ideology) as involving the unshakeable beliefs that the laws of the competitive market are natural, universal, and impersonal; that private proprietary ownership of the means of production is natural, permanent, and necessary; that workers are paid all they can be paid; and that surplus value should accrue to those who own the means of production.

We all encounter ideologies on a regular basis. Most commonly, perhaps, we meet people infused with religious ideologies, such a biblical fundamentalism, who profess to believe literally in the Bible as the Word of God. I have often countered such people by asking them whether they have read the Bible in Hebrew and Greek, for surely God did not speak in antiquity in English. Further, I point out, if they have not read the original language, they are relying on interpretations rather than the literal meaning, since all translation is interpretation, and interpretation may be wrong. To illustrate this point, I ask them to name some of the Ten Commandments. Invariably, they say, "Thou shalt not kill." I point out that the Hebrew, in fact, does not say, "Though shalt not kill"; it says, "Thou shalt not *murder.*" This, then, should be enough to convince them that they do not believe the Bible literally, if only because they cannot read it literally. Does it do so? Of course not. They have endless ploys to avoid admitting that they can't possibly believe it literally, such as "The translators were divinely inspired."

We, of course, are steeped in political ideology in grade school and high school—for example, on issues of "human equality." Ask the average college student (as I have done many times) the basis for professing equality when people are clearly unequal in brains, talent, wealth, athletic ability, and so on. Few will deny this, but most will continue to insist on "equality" without any notion that "equality" refers to a way we believe we ought to treat people, not a factual claim. If they do see equality as an "ought" claim, almost none can then provide a defense of why we believe we ought to treat people equally if, in fact, they are not equal. And so on. But almost never will such a student renounce the belief in equality.

Of late, students have been steeped in the ideology of diversity and multiculturalism, affirming that no culture is superior to any other and an admixture of cultures is always best. Few can respond to the query I tender: "Are you telling me that a culture where clitorectomies are performed without consent and without anesthesia on helpless female children is as good as a culture that disavows such mutilations?" Similarly, no one but the Taliban would argue that the Taliban culture, wherein women are not allowed to be educated and are beaten for laughing in public and men are beaten for flying kites or listening to music, is a culture as good as ours. In the same vein, I point out that the price of diversity is often friction and tension. No sane New Yorker leaves his or her apartment unlocked; in rural Wyoming, unlocked doors are de rigeur. People share grazing land, and someone may be rounding up cattle when a storm strikes, so everyone leaves ranch houses unlocked in case someone needs refuge. A person in trouble is expected to enter the empty house, use the bed, make a meal, tidy up, and leave. In return, one does the same thing for others. Similarly, if one has an accident or car trouble in Wyoming, every passing car stops to help. In my view, this is possible because the culture is monolithic rather than diverse, and everyone shares the same values, beliefs, and expectations.

Thus, despite one's ability to provide cases in which ethnic multiplicity or diversity has downsides and other cases in which common sense shows that some cultures are worse than others, students who have been ideologically brainwashed simply filter out such arguments, even as Marxists filter out and ignore counterexamples to their basic ideology and religious fundamentalists do the same.

Ideologies are attractive to people; they give pat answers to difficult questions. It is far easier to give an ingrained response than to think through each new situation. Militant Muslim ideology, for example, sees Western culture as inherently evil and corruptive of Islam and the United States as "the Great Satan," the fountainhead of Western culture that in turn aims to destroy Islamic purity. The United States is thus automatically wrong in any dispute, and any measures are justified against that country in the ultimate battle against defilement.

What is wrong with ideology, of course, is precisely that it truncates thought by providing simple answers and, as Braybrooke indicates, cutting off certain key questions. Intellectual subtlety and the powerful tool of reason, making distinctions, are totally lost to gross oversimplifications. Counterexamples are ignored.

But the problem is not only that ideology constricts thought. The problem is also that it can create monsters out of ordinary people by overriding common sense and common decency. We have seen this manifested plainly throughout the history of the twentieth century. The recent experiences of Eastern Europe and Africa make manifest that ideologically based hatreds, whose origins have been obscured by the passage of time, may like anthrax spores re-emerge as virulent and as lethal as ever, unweakened by years of dormancy. Most strikingly, perhaps, the historian David Goldhagen has demonstrated the enormous power of ideology to overwhelm and obscure both common sense and common decency even among the most civilized people. In his monumental *Hitler's Willing Executioners* (1996), Goldhagen shows that under the Nazis, ordinary Germans willingly volunteered to engage in genocidal activities, even when it was patently open to them to refuse to do so without fear of recrimination. The killers Goldhagen studied were neither sadists and psychopaths of the sort attracted to the Schutzstaffel (SS) nor the sort of street brawlers and bullies that composed the ranks of Ernst Röhm's Sturmabteilung (SA). Rather, they were normal, largely nonviolent family men who operated neither out of fear of punishment for disobedience nor out of blind respect for authority, as suggested by Stanley Milgram (1975) and often invoked to explain the Nazis' killing. According to Goldhagen, neighbors became killers because of their immersion in two centuries of ideological dogma depicting Jews and others as pathogens in the body politic, rendering that body ill and infirm and demanding radical excision of the disease-causing organisms. As absurd as this seems to those of us not steeped in similar ideology, it was common sense to Goldhagen's Germans and straightforward justification for actions they would recoil from in non-ideological contexts.

As we have seen, ideologies operate in many different areas: religious, political, sociological, economic, ethnic. Thus, it is not surprising that an ideology would emerge with regard to science, which, after all, has been the dominant way to know about the world in Western societies since the Renaissance. Indeed, knowing has had a special place in the world since antiquity. Among the pre-Socratics—or *physikoi,* as Aristotle called them—one sometimes needed to subordinate one's life unquestioningly to the precepts of a society of knowers, as was the case with the Pythagoreans. The very first line of Aristotle's *Metaphysics*—or *First Philosophy*—is "All men by nature desire to know." Thus, the very *telos* of humanity, the "humanness" of humans, consists in exercising the cognitive functions that separate humans from all creation. Inevitably, the great knowers, such as Aristotle, Francis Bacon, Isaac Newton, and Albert Einstein, felt it necessary to articulate what separated legitimate empirical knowledge from spurious knowledge and jealously to guard and defend that methodology from encroachment by pretenders to knowledge.

Thus, the ideology underlying modern (i.e., post-medieval) science has grown and evolved along with science itself. A major—perhaps the major—component of that ideology is a strong positivistic tendency, still regnant today, of believing that real science must be based in experience, since the tribunal of experience is the objective, universal judge of what is really happening in the world.

If one asked most working scientists what separates science from religion, speculative metaphysics, or shamanistic worldviews, they would unhesitatingly reply that it is an emphasis on validating all claims through sense experience, observation, or experimental manipulation. This component of scientific ideology can be traced directly back to Newton, who proclaimed that he did not "feign hypothesis (*hypotheses non fingo*)" but operated directly from experience. (The fact that Newton, in fact, *did* operate with non-observable notions such as gravity or, more generally, action at a distance did not stop him from making ideological proclamations affirming that one should not do so.)

It is instructive to review some dramatic examples of this ideology evoked in response to my work, both on legislation and on ethics and animal consciousness. I have, in fact, argued that this ideology not only has allowed major abuse in science of objects of moral concern but also distances ordinary people from science and the scientific community.

Astute people in the scientific community are well aware of the many threats to science. They include appalling scientific illiteracy among the public and the unfortunate resurgence of "magic thinking," reflected in the reappearance of a creationism that is hostile to evolution and billions of dollars spent on evidentially baseless "alternative medicine," the fact that cryptozoology books sell more copies than all bio-science books, and ubiquitous iconic Frankensteinean imagery informing public reaction to scientific advances in biotechnology (as I describe in my book on the ethics of biotechnology, *The Frankenstein Syndrome* [1995b]). One threat I describe here, however, has escaped mainstream serious attention. I begin by relating a series of fairly shocking anecdotes whose unifying thread is that they are rooted in the Common Sense of Science (some of the subsequent discussion is drawn from Rollin 2007b):

1. In about 1990, the director of the NIH, and therefore, arguably the chief representative of biomedicine in the United States, was visiting his alma mater. He was talking to a group of students informally and apparently was unguarded in his remarks, not realizing that a student reporter for the school newspaper was present. The students asked him about the ethical issues associated with genetic engineering. His astonishing reply: Although "scientific advances like genetic engineering are always controversial, science should never be hampered by ethical considerations" (quoted in Rollin 2007b).
2. Around 1980, when I was developing and pressing for the federal legislation for laboratory animals passed in 1985, I was invited by the American Association for Laboratory Animal Science (AALAS) to discuss my reasons for supporting legislative constraints on science on a panel with a half-dozen eminent laboratory-animal veterinarians. To make my point, I asked them to tell me which analgesic would be best for a rat used in a limb-crush experiment, assuming that analgesia did not disrupt the results that were being studied. The consensus response was, in essence, "How should we know? We don't even know for sure if animals feel pain." Interestingly, five years later, after the laws passed, I phoned one of those veterinarians and pointed out that he was now *required* to know the answer to my question. He rattled off five different analgesic regimens. I asked him where he had gotten his information. "From the drug companies." he said. Puzzled, I asked whether they now worked on rat analgesia. "No," he said, "but all human analgesics are tested on rats." The point is that he had known this five years earlier but did not see it then as relevant to rats' pain.

3. At another AALAS meeting in the early 1980s, I ran a full-day session on ethics and animal research. At the end, reporters present converged on the association's president, asking him to respond to my points. "Oh, there are no issues in animal research," he said. "God said we can do whatever we want with animals." When the reporters asked me to respond, I facetiously said that what he said could not possibly be true. The association's president, I pointed out, "is at the —— Vet School, and if God chose to reveal himself at a vet school, it would surely be Colorado, which is, after all, God's Country."
4. At the American Veterinary Medical Association (AVMA) pain panel convened in 1986 by Hiram Kitchen at the request of Congress, I was asked to write the prologue to the report. I presented it to the group. I approvingly pointed out that according to the great skeptical philosopher David Hume, few things are as obvious as the fact that animals have thoughts and feelings and that this point does not escape "even the most stupid." A representative from the National Institute of Mental Health (NIMH) stood up, indignant, and declared, "If we're going to talk mysticism, I'm leaving." He did, never to return. I have seen many scientists walk out on ethics talks, particularly mine.
5. As late as the mid-1980s, and even into the current century, many veterinary and human medical schools *required* that students participate in bleeding out a dog until it died of hemorrhagic shock. Although the veterinary school at Colorado State University (CSU) had abolished that laboratory in the early 1980s for ethical reasons, the department head who took that action was *defending* the practice ten years later at another university. He explained to me that if he didn't, his faculty would force him out. As late as the mid-1990s, the associate dean at a medical school told the dean of CSU's veterinary school that his faculty was "firmly convinced" that one could not "be a good physician unless one first killed a dog." In his 1981 autobiographical *Gentle Vengeance,* which deals with an older student going through Harvard Medical School, Charles LeBaron remarks in passing that the only purpose he and his peers could see to the dog labs was to ensure that the students were divested of any shred of compassion that might have survived their pre-medical studies. At one veterinary school, a senior elective class provided each student with a dog, and the student was required to do a whole semester of surgery on the animal. One student anesthe-

tized the animal, beat on it randomly with a sledgehammer, and spent the semester repairing the damage. He received an "A."

6. In 2001, I was part of the World Health Organization group that was charged with setting guidelines for the use of antibiotics in animal feed because their indiscriminate use was driving the evolution of microbial resistance to anti-microbials and thus endangering human health. I was asked to give the keynote speech defining the ethical dimensions of the issue. When I finished, I asked for questions. One veterinarian, who was, in fact, the U.S. Food and Drug Administration (FDA) employee in charge of managing the issue, said that she was offended. "By what?" I asked. "By the presence of an ethics talk at a scientific conference. Ethics has nothing to do with this issue. It is strictly a scientific question." Stifling an urge to strangle her, I calmly said, "Let me show you that you are wrong. Suppose I give you an unlimited research budget to determine when to stop or curtail the use of antibiotics in feeds. We do the research and find out that current use levels kill (or sicken) one person in five hundred, or five thousand, or fifty thousand, or five hundred thousand, or five million. Even when we know these data, they do not tell us where the risk of morbidity or mortality tells us to discontinue such antibiotic use. That is an ethical decision." She kept quiet for the rest of the conference.
7. In the early 1980s, when my colleagues and I had pretty well drafted the key concepts of our proposed federal laboratory-animal legislation and Representative Pat Schroeder of Colorado had committed to carrying it forward, we were told by congressional aides that we must provide clear evidence of the need for such law, both because the medical-research community was a major financial contributor to war chests for congressional campaigns and because the same community claimed already to be controlling pain in research animals. In essence, I was charged with proving they were not. I did so by performing a literature search on analgesia for laboratory animals—or, indeed, any animals. What did I find? The two references mentioned earlier, one of which said there ought to be papers on this issue, and the other saying we don't know much, but here is the little we do know—aspirin, morphine, and that was about it. If analgesia were, indeed, widely used, I told Congress, I would have been able to find a significant literature on its theory and practice.
8. In 1979, I attended a conference on animals' pain at which I debated a prominent scientist. I defended the view that animals

could feel pain, while he denied the claim. I thought we had enjoyed an amicable discussion until I returned to CSU, whereupon I discovered that, after the debate, he had called the dean of veterinary medicine and told him that I was "a viper in the bosom of biomedicine" who should not be allowed to teach in a veterinary program.

9. The first textbooks of veterinary anesthesia published in the United States, by W. V. Lumb (1963) and W. V. Lumb and E. W. Jones (1973), do not as much as mention *felt* pain (the fact that pain *hurts*), even as a reason for anesthesia; instead, they list positioning the limbs, avoiding getting hurt by the animal, and so forth. And *Animal Pain: Perception and Alleviation* (Kitchell and Erickson 1983), in part designed to assure the public of science's concern with animals' pain, oddly does not talk about either perception or alleviation but focuses on the "plumbing"—electrochemistry and physiology—of pain, with only one small reference to its alleged purpose in the paper "Species Differences in Drug Disposition as Factors in Alleviation of Pain," by Lloyd Davis.
10. As the Talmud says, "The last is the most beloved," so I end this list with one of my most loved anecdotes. A few years before Dolly the cloned sheep was announced, I received a call from a research official at the Roslin Institute asking me to chat about the ethics of the "hypothetical" production of a cloned animal. "It's your nickel," I said (finally deploying that wonderful locution stolen from hard-boiled detective novels and noir films of the 1940s). "Keep talking." I told the official that there were two major concerns: Does cloning harm the animal, and does it create any social or ecological danger or danger of disease? More important than these legitimate concerns, I continued, was what I called a "Gresham's Law for Ethics." Gresham's law in economics asserts that "bad money drives good money out of circulation"; in the same way, "bad ethics drives good ethics out of circulation." So, for example, after World War I, German currency (the deutsche mark) was so inflated that it took a wheelbarrow full of bills to buy a loaf of bread. In such an economy, rational people pay their outstanding debts with deutsche marks, not with gold, which they hoard. The same happens in ethics, I said. Any new technology, be it the computer or biotechnology, creates a vacuum in social ethical thought and fear. "What effect will this have on our lives? Is it good or bad? What do we need

> to control?" If the scientists do not inaugurate rational discussion, that lacuna will be filled by doomsayers with vested interests. "So," I concluded, "that is your biggest worry. You must create an educated populace on cloning and help them define the issues, or the public will be told that it 'violates God's will,' and how can you respond to that?" As I suspected, it was as if our conversation had never taken place. Some years later, the creation Dolly was announced to a completely uninformed public. Time Warner conducted a survey one week after the announcement. Fully 75 percent of the U.S. public affirmed that cloning "violated God's will."

There are many other, similar stories. For example, there was a period where open-heart surgery was done on neonatal humans without anesthesia using curariform paralytic drugs, or when Robert Rissler, chief of the APHIS, approached the primatology branch of the American Psychological Association after the laboratory-animal laws passed in 1985 to help define "psychological well-being of primates." When he was told, "Don't worry—there is no such thing," he classically replied, "There will be after January 1, 1986, whether you people help me or not." Or I could cite the debate I had with a famous pain physiologist in London who had argued for an hour that, since the electrochemical activity in the cerebral cortex of a dog was different from that in a human, and since the cortex controls consciousness, the dog didn't "really feel pain as humans did." My refutation was uniquely brief. "Dr. X," I said. "You're a famous pain researcher. Am I correct that you do your work on dogs? . . . And you extrapolate those results to people?" "Yes." he replied. "Then either your talk is false, or your life's work is." But I have said enough, I hope, to establish our universe of discourse.

The ideological insistence on experience as the bedrock for science continues from Newton to the twentieth century, where it reaches its most philosophical articulation in the reductionistic movement known as logical positivism, a movement that was designed to excise the unverifiable from science and, in some of its forms, to systematize science in a formal way so that its derivation from observations is transparent. A classic and profound example of the purpose of the excisive dimension of positivism is in Einstein's rejection of Newton's concepts of absolute space and time on the grounds that such talk cannot be tested. Other examples of positivist targets were Henri Bergson's (and other biologists') talk of life force (*élan vital*) as separating the living from the non-living and the embryologist Hans Driesch's postulation of "entelechies" to explain regeneration in starfish.

Although logical positivism took many subtly different and variegated forms, the message, as received by working scientists and passed on to students (including me), was that proper science ought not allow unverifiable statements. This was no doubt potentiated by the fact that one British philosopher, a logical positivist named Alfred J. Ayer, wrote *Language, Truth, and Logic,* an aggressively polemical book that defended logical positivism. It first appeared in 1936 and has remained in print ever since. Easy to read and highly critical of wool-gathering, speculative metaphysics, and other soft and ungrounded ways of knowing, the book was long used in introductory philosophy courses and, in many cases, represented the only contact with philosophy that aspiring young scientists—or even senior scientists—enjoyed.

Be that as it may, the positivist demand for empirical verification of all meaningful claims became a mainstay of scientific ideology from the time of Einstein to the present. Insofar as scientists thought at all in philosophical terms about what they were doing, they embraced the simple but, to them, satisfying positivism I have described. Through it, one could clearly, in good conscience, dismiss religious claims, metaphysical claims, or other speculative assertions not merely as false and irrelevant to science, but as meaningless. Only what could be verified (or falsified) empirically was meaningful. "In principle" meant "someday," given technological progress. Thus, although the statement "There are intelligent inhabitants on Mars" could not, in fact, be verified or falsified in 1940, it was still meaningful, since we could see how it could be verified: by building rocket ships and going to Mars to look. Such a statement stands in sharp contradistinction to the statement "There are intelligent beings in heaven" because, however our technology is perfected, we don't know what it would be like to visit heaven because it is not a physical place.

What does all this have to do with ethics? Quite a bit, it turns out. The philosopher Ludwig Wittgenstein, who greatly influenced the logical positivists, remarked in "Lecture on Ethics" (1965) that if you take an inventory of all the *facts* in the universe, you will not find it a *fact* that killing is wrong. In other words, ethics is not part of the furniture of the scientific universe. You cannot, in principle, test the proposition that "killing is wrong." It can neither be verified nor falsified. So in Wittgenstein's view, ethical judgments are empirically and scientifically meaningless. From this, it was concluded that ethics is outside of the scope of science, as are all judgments regarding values rather than facts. Thus, the slogan I learned in my science courses in the 1960s and that is still being taught in too many places—that science is value-free in general and ethics-free in particular.

The particular denial of the relevance of ethics to science was taught both explicitly and implicitly. One could find it explicitly stated in science textbooks. For example, while I was researching a book on animals' pain in the late 1980s, I looked at basic biology texts, two of which a colleague and I actually used, ironically enough, in an honors biology course we team taught for twenty-five years in the attempt to combine biology and the philosophical and ethical issues it presupposed and to which it gave rise. James Gould and William Keeton's widely used textbook *Biological Science* (1986), for example, in what one of my colleagues calls the "throat-clearing introduction," wherein the authors pay lip service to scientific method, a bit of history, and other "soft" issues before getting down to the parts of a cell and the Krebs cycle, loudly declares that "science cannot make value judgments . . . cannot make moral judgments." In the same vein, in the popular text *Biology: Evolution, Diversity, and the Environment,* Sylvia S. Mader asserts that "science does not make ethical or moral decisions" (Mader 1987). The standard line affirms that science at most provides society with *facts* relevant to making moral decisions but never itself makes such decisions.

The logical positivism that informed scientific ideology's rejection of the legitimacy of ethics dismissed moral discussion as empirically meaningless. That is not, however, the whole story. Positivist thinkers felt compelled to explain why intelligent people continued to make moral judgments and continued to argue about them. They explained the former by saying that when people make assertions such as "killing is wrong," which seem to be statements about reality, they are, in fact, describing nothing. They are "emoting," or expressing their own revulsion at killing. Rather than describe some state of affairs, "killing is wrong" really *expresses* "killing, yuk." And when people seem to debate about killing, we are not really arguing ethics (which can't be done any more than you and I can debate whether we like or don't like pepperoni); rather, we are disputing each other's facts. So a debate over the alleged morality of capital punishment is my expression of revulsion at capital punishment while you express approval, and any debate we can engender is over such factual questions as whether capital punishment serves as a deterrent in society against murder.

It is therefore not surprising that when scientists were drawn into social discussions of ethical issues, they were every bit as emotional as their untutored opponents. Because their ideology dictates that these issues *are nothing but emotional,* the notion of rational ethics is seen as an oxymoron, and he who generates the most effective emotional response "wins." So, for example, in the debate on the morality of animal research of the 1970s and 1980s, scientists either totally ignored the issue or countered criticism with emotional appeals to the health of children. For example, in the film *Will I Be All Right, Doctor?* (the question is asked by a frightened child to a pediatrician), made by defenders of unrestricted research, the answer given was "Yes, if *they* leave us alone to do what we want with animals." So appallingly and unabashedly emotional and mawkish was the film that, when it was premiered for a subsection of laboratory-animal veterinarians at the AALAS meetings—a putatively sympathetic audience—the only comment from the audience came from a veterinarian who affirmed that he was "ashamed to be associated with a film that is pitched lower than the worst antivivisectionist clap-trap."

Other advertisements placed by the research community have affirmed that 90 percent of the animals used in research are mice and rats, animals "people kill in their kitchens anyway." Sometimes questions raised about animal use, as once occurred in an editorial in a science journal, elicited the reply that "animal use is not an ethical question—it is a scientific necessity," as if it cannot be, and is not, both. My thesis, then, is that an ideologically ubiquitous denial of the relevance of values in general and ethics in particular to science created blinders among scientists to issues of major concern to society.

10

Ideology and Consciousness

A second component of scientific ideology that harmonizes perfectly with the value-free dictum is the positivistic/behavioristic thesis that science could not legitimately talk about consciousness and subjective experiences, which led to a question about their existence. (John Watson, the founder of behaviorism, came close to saying that we don't have thoughts, that we only think we do.)

It is quite perplexing that such a view should emerge at all in twentieth-century science, which considers itself Darwinian, or that it should come from positivistic empiricism. After all, the historical ancestor of positivism, the eighteenth-century philosophy David Hume, most unequivocally affirmed the existence of animal thought and mentation. Arguably the greatest skeptic in the history of philosophy, who denied the ultimate knowability of mind, body, God, causation, the past, and the future, Hume nonetheless extended no doubt to the animal mind. In Section 16 of *A Treatise of Human Nature,* titled "Of the Reason of Animals," he affirms, "Next to the ridicule of denying an evident truth, is that of taking much pains to defend it; and no truth appears to me more evident, than that beasts are endowed with thought and reason as well as men. The arguments are in this case so obvious, that they never escape the most stupid and ignorant" (Hume [1739] 1896, 176). (The last sentence is presumably directed at Descartes, who denied animals' consciousness.)

Pet owners can tell innumerable stories about their animals' demonstrating a full range of mental life. In my own long experience with a welter of companion animals, two stories stand out as the most extraordinary incidents I ever witnessed. One took place in 1976. We had just moved into a house on a lake half a mile from the nearest neighbor. The house had been unoccupied for a long time and had become a hangout for groups of young people and some gangs. I was starting to travel to lecture and was concerned about leaving my wife alone. I answered an ad in the paper offering a guard dog to anyone willing to pay the kennel fee where he had been boarded when not rented to construction sites. He was a huge, 140 pound German Shepherd cross who had never bonded with a human but had been given to an outlaw biker in exchange for labor. With some reservations, I took him and devoted a great deal of time to bonding with him. In time, he developed a normal relationship with my wife and me but was fierce with any other human being or vehicle that set foot on our property. (He once bit the rearview mirror off a truck that drove up.) If anyone came, we had to restrain him.

One day, a turkey belonging to my neighbor walked up the driveway. We quickly restrained the dog and called the neighbor, who came for the bird. The next day, the turkey came back and established himself on a patch of grass adjacent to the dog's house. Amazingly, the dog did not attack. We phoned the neighbor, who said, "Keep him." We watched with trepidation, but soon the turkey was sharing the dog's dinner and, on warm days, sleeping on the dog. They became inseparable, with the dog following me, and the turkey following the dog, and the turkey gobbling at intruders when the dog barked.

The relationship grew over the next two years. Then the dog developed degenerative spinal disease that paralyzed his hind legs. I went home four or five times a day to move and clean him, because he could not walk. The turkey stayed with him. One evening when my wife and I came home from late-evening grocery shopping, we opened the car door, and a giant Malamute jumped in. Our amusement became horror when we saw that his muzzle was bloody. We followed a trail of blood and feathers into the backyard, where our dog lay. There, between his forepaws, was the turkey, torn open but still alive. He had come to his friend for protection after being attacked, and the German Shepherd had kept the Malamute away by snarling and growling, as he did while we watched. Though the turkey eventually died of his injuries, I will never forget that paralyzed dog bravely protecting his companion, crossing species boundaries and training boundaries to protect what must be called his friend.

The second story is about horses. Earlier, I mentioned my beloved horse Raszam. Some years after I acquired him, I began to board two horses for my friend Lynne Kesel. Both were well-bred Morgans—an older, very large gelding named Festus and a smaller, younger gelding named Jubilee. I kept them for almost twenty years, and they got along well. That notwithstanding, they established the usual pecking order, or "dominance hierarchy," that horses do. Festus was at the top, Raszam was next, and Jubilee was at the bottom. The more dominant horse would chase the less dominant away from food, and much nipping and (largely) fake kicking would routinely take place. Once established, these hierarchies usually endure.

One day, Raszam developed a condition of temporary blindness, colloquially known as "moon blindness." He could not see and could not locate his food or water. My wife and I watched in amazement as Jubilee, the lowest-ranking horse, began to nudge and guide Raszam to food and water, and, *mirabile dictu,* to protect him from Festus. What was most extraordinary was how Jubilee would keep Festus away from Raszam, breaking the hierarchy, and would not eat his own food until Raszam had finished and no longer needed protection. This behavior occurred at every feeding for two weeks; Jubilee would even guide Raszam to the shelter that protected them from wind and rain and provided shade. Linda and I were deeply and profoundly touch by this deviant and selfless behavior, and she vowed that Jubilee would never want for a home. When Raszam's sight returned, things reverted to normal. Ordinary people can no more understand people who deny animal thought, feeling, and emotion than they can empathize with the Taliban.

The certainty of animal thought is affirmed throughout post–Humean empiricist British philosophy, with Jeremy Bentham and John Stuart Mill drawing moral consequences from animals' ability to feel pain and thus, of necessity, being included in the scope of utilitarian moral concern. (Mill, in fact, was such a thoroughgoing empiricist that he thought mathematics to be inductively based.) Bentham's famous remark in *An Introduction to the Principles of Morals and Legislation* was this:

> Other animals, which, on account of their interests having been neglected by the insensibility of the ancient jurists, stand degraded into the class of things. . . . The day has been, I grieve it to say in many places it is not yet past, in which the greater part of the species, under the denomination of slaves, have been treated . . . upon the same footing as . . . animals are still. The day may come, when the rest of the animal creation may acquire those rights which never could have been withholden from them but by the hand of tyranny.

> The French have already discovered that the blackness of skin is no reason why a human being should be abandoned without redress to the caprice of a tormentor. It may come one day to be recognized that the number of legs, the villosity of the skin, or the termination of the os sacrum, are reasons equally insufficient for abandoning a sensitive being to the same fate. What else is it that should trace the insuperable line? Is it the faculty of reason, or perhaps, the faculty for discourse? . . . The question is not, Can they reason? nor, Can they talk? but, Can they suffer? Why should the law refuse its protection to any sensitive being? . . . The time will come when humanity will extend its mantle over everything which breathes. (1789, 311)

Mill, in turn, affirmed in *Principles of Political Economy* that "the reasons for legal intervention in favor of children apply not less strongly to the case of those unfortunate slaves—the animals" (Mill 1852, 546).

We can see that from Locke through the utilitarians, the assumption exists in empiricism of animal mentation, from Hume's claim of animal reason to Bentham's and Mill's affirmation of animals' ability to feel pain. The scientific culmination of this stance on animal consciousness, however, is reached in the works of Charles Darwin. Darwinian science gave new vitality to ordinary common-sense notions that attributed mental states to animals but that had been assaulted by Catholics and Cartesians. For Darwin, the guiding assumption in psychology was one of continuity, so the study of mind became comparative, as epitomized by Darwin's marvelously blunt title *The Expression of the Emotions in Man and Animals* (1872), which brazenly hoists a middle finger to the Cartesian tradition, since Darwin saw emotion as inextricably bound up with subjective feelings. Furthermore, in *The Descent of Man* (Darwin [1871] 1971, 448), Darwin had specifically affirmed that "there is no fundamental difference between man and the higher animals in their mental facilities" and that "the lower animals, like man, manifestly feel pleasure and pain, happiness, and misery." In the same work, Darwin attributed the entire range of subjective experiences to animals, taking it for granted that one can gather data relevant to our knowledge of such experiences. Evolutionary theory demands that psychology, like anatomy, be comparative, for life is incremental, and mind did not arise de novo in man, fully formed like Athena from the head of Zeus.

Darwin was not, of course, content to speculate about animal consciousness. He explicitly turned over much of his material on animal mentation to a trusted spokesman, George John Romanes, who in turn published two major volumes, *Animal Intelligence* (1882) and *Mental Evolution in Animals*

(1884), both of which richly demonstrate phylogenetic continuity of mentation. In his preface to *Animal Intelligence,* Romanes acknowledges his debt to Darwin:

> [He] not only assisted me in the most generous manner with his immense stores of information, as well as with his valuable judgment on sundry points of difficulty, but has also been kind enough to place at my disposal all the notes and clippings on animal intelligence which he has been collecting for the last forty years, together with the original manuscript of his wonderful chapter on "'Instinct." This chapter, on being recast for the "Origin of Species", underwent so merciless an amount of compression that the original draft constitutes a rich store of hitherto unpublished material. (1883, xi)

While Romanes's work focuses mainly on cognitive ability throughout the phylogenetic scale, he also addresses emotions and other aspects of mental life, all of which, for a Darwinian, ought to demonstrate some continuity across animal species.

In addition to the careful observations he made, Darwin also pursued a variety of experiments on animal mentation. He placed great emphasis on verifying any data subject to the slightest question. Toward this end, for example, he contrived some ingenious experiments to test the intelligence of earthworms, a notion that he clearly felt was far beyond the purview of anecdotal information and that was sufficiently implausible as to require controlled experimentation. These experiments, now virtually forgotten, occupy some thirty-five pages of *The Formation of Vegetable Mould through the Action of Worms with Observations on Their Habits* (1886). The question Darwin asked was whether the behavior of worms in plugging up their burrows could be explained by instinct alone or by "inherited impulse" or chance, or whether something like intelligence was required. In a series of tests, Darwin supplied his worms with a variety of leaves, some indigenous to the country where the worms were found and others from plants that grew thousands of miles away, as well as parts of leaves and triangles of paper and observed how they proceeded to plug their burrows and whether they used the narrow or the wide end of the object first. After quantitative evaluation of the results of these tests, Darwin concluded that worms possess rudimentary intelligence in that they show plasticity in their behavior, some rudimentary "notion" of shape, and the ability to learn from experience. Darwin is no romantic anthropomorphist; he clearly distinguishes the intelligence of the worms from the "senseless or purposeless" manner in which even higher animals often behave, as when a beaver cuts up logs and drags them about when there is no water to dam, or a squirrel puts nuts on a wooden floor as if he had buried them in the ground.

As Darwin's work quickly became the regnant paradigm in biology and psychology, one would expect that the science of animal mentation would have steadily evolved during the subsequent century and a half as a subset of evolutionary biology. Strangely enough, this is not the case. Despite Darwin's influence, animal mentation disappeared as a legitimate object of study not only in a Europe influenced by Cartesianism but in the Anglo-American world, as well.

Before we turn to the remarkable story of how this occurred, a story that shakes the foundation of how science believes itself to change, it is worth mentioning that Darwin's work inspired a spurt of concern about the moral status of animals. While Darwin himself did not follow out in the moral realm the logic of attribution of the evolutionary continuity of consciousness to animals, save for occasional comments such as "The love for all living creatures is the most noble attribute of man," a number of his contemporaries did—most notably, Edward P. Evans in *Evolutional Ethics and Animal Psychology* (1898) and Henry Salt in *Animal Rights Considered in Relation to Social Progress* (1892). The obvious extension of moral concern to animals as continuous with humans phylogenetically *and* mentally seems to have been forestalled by a self-serving interpretation of Darwin affirming that, since humans were "at the top of the evolutionary pyramid," they were "superior" to lesser beings, and thus we didn't need to worry about them morally.

Scientific common sense—the uncritical ideology associated with science for well over a hundred years and believed by most scientists—decrees that there are only two ways that established scientific theories or hypotheses can be overturned. The first and most obvious way is through empirical disconfirmation: We gather data or do experiments to show that what was believed is factually falsified. Thus, we may believe that "all swans are white" until we find a black swan or that stress causes ulcers until we find that the primary cause is helicobacter pylori. (For simplicity, we are leaving aside the Quinean critique of straightforward verification or falsification.) The secondary way to reject a theory or hypothesis is by showing that it is conceptually or logically flawed. Thus, Einstein demonstrated that Newton's account of absolute space and time was incoherent, for its postulation required of us the ability to measure absolute simultaneity, yet the events that we call "simultaneous" depend on the observer's measuring of them. In a similar way, Bertrand Russell showed Gottlob Frege's definition of number to generate logical absurdity. This form of disconfirmation is, of course, much rarer.

From even before the time of Darwin, the existence and knowability of animal mentation was taken as axiomatic through the early years of the twentieth century. But after 1920, and to some extent even today, few British or American psychologists or classical European ethologists would accept that view. (The classic volume *Instinctive Behavior* [Schiller 1957] chronicles the first interactions of Anglo-American behaviorists with European ethologists of the school of Konrad Lorenz and Nikolaas Tinbergen. Although the two schools agreed about little else, they were of one mind in denying consciousness or its knowability in animals.) The obvious question that arises, of course, is whether the assumption of animal mind was empirically disconfirmed or found to be conceptually flawed. The surprising answer is: neither. There was no empirical disconfirmation of animal consciousness, nor was any conceptual or logical flaw found in its postulation. In fact, far from being disproved, the knowability of animal consciousness was *disapproved,* disvalued, banished by a valuational revolution cloaked in rhetoric about how to make psychology a "real" science and all of science allegedly wholly empirical.

In fact, there is quite a significant history of science's changing in virtue of valuational considerations rather than by these accepted methods. It is perhaps surprising that the Scientific Revolution can be so viewed.

To begin with, we must recall that all human cognitive enterprises, of which science is, of course, a paradigm case, rest on certain foundational presuppositions—what Aristotle called *archai.* As in the transparent case of geometry, all such activities must make certain assumptions to function. Again, as in geometry, one cannot prove the assumptions, for it is on these assumptions that the possibility of proof itself rests. If one could prove the assumptions, it would of necessity be on the basis of other assumptions, which must themselves either be taken for granted or based in other assumptions, and so on ad infinitum. That is not, of course, to suggest that one cannot criticize the assumptions: We have already pointed to examples of logically flawed assumptions in Newton and Frege. But we have also seen that in the case of the assumption that animals possess and demonstrate mentation and feeling, no such incoherence was discovered.

Are assumptions in science discarded for reasons other than demonstrable logical fallaciousness? Are they adopted for reasons other than to replace fallacious ones or to better account for recalcitrant data? One is compelled to assert that this is, indeed, the case. They may change for valuational reasons, as well. One need look no further than the Scientific Revolution to buttress this claim.

It is well known that the Scientific Revolution inaugurated by Galileo, Descartes, Newton, and others marked a major discontinuity with medieval/Aristotelian science. Aristotelian science was concerned with explaining the world that we find through our senses, which were assumed to be a mainly reliable source of information about that world. As the senses tell us, the world is a world of qualitative differences—of things alive and not alive, hot and cold, wet and dry, solid and liquid, good and bad, beautiful and ugly. To be adequate, science must do justice to that world. Aristotle specifically affirms that there thus can be no one master science of everything; each thing must be explained according to its own kind, and each domain of scientific inquiry rests on assumptions uniquely appropriate to it. A science of inert matter can never serve to explain the behavior of living things. This is a conceptual and methodological necessity based in the patent empirical differences we find in the world. Thus, Aristotle definitively rejects the Platonic notion of an underlying reality that required only one language—that of mathematics. The only reason mathematics fits everything, says Aristotle, is that it is so vague and general as to be vacuous, like the "interesting paper" comment that professors who are at a loss to say anything else scrawl on students' essays. For Aristotle, science should tell us what is unique to a domain, not what is common to all domains.

The science of Galileo and others thoroughly rejects the Aristotelian story. It is not that the revolutionaries discovered empirical facts that *falsify* or *disconfirm* the core of Aristotle's account. *Any* empirical facts (data gathered by the senses) are grist for Aristotle's mill, or are compatible with Aristotle's worldview, because they, by definition and of necessity, bespeak a world of qualitative differences. What the proponents of revolution must do instead is disvalue certain facts and ways of looking at the facts that Aristotle holds dear. Aristotle disvalues the quantitative dimensions of the world; the revolutionaries stand him on his head and glorify the quantitative while trivializing the qualitative. This is not disconfirmation; it is, rather, a difference in seeing brought about by a difference in valuing, in much the same way that a son and his parents might look very differently at his potential spouse—he stressing sex appeal and excitement, they stressing reliability and good sense. Looking at the same woman, they thus find very different characteristics in their respective lists of her strengths and faults.

The Scientific Revolutionaries value mathematical unity over sensory diversity, universal intelligibility over fragmented intelligibility, reason over experience, Plato over Aristotle, geometry over natural history, physics over biology. As Paul Feyerabend (1975) and others have pointed out, they defend their approach at least as much by appeal to value as by appeal to fact.

Consider, for example, the classic case of Descartes' defense of the quantitative approach in *Meditations on First Philosophy*. His tack, as every freshman philosophy student knows, is to disvalue the senses as a reliable source of information about reality, striking directly at Aristotle's notion of "what you see is what you get." Descartes' argument essentially proceeds as follows: There are numerous examples where the senses deceive us. Nothing in sense experience is absolutely certain—we are all familiar with the sorts of mistakes the senses make. Since we can be wrong about any sensory experience, we could conceivably be wrong about every such experience, and if we could be wrong about every such experience, we should categorically reject the senses as a source of information. From this basis, Descartes proceeds to deduce what one could not be wrong about: his own existence and, eventually, a priori, geometrical knowledge of the world of the sort favored by the New Science.

As soon as one scrutinizes this argument, it is patent that it does not logically compel the abandonment of Aristotelianism any more than new data could empirically compel the rejection of Aristotelianism. Descartes' argument is flawed in many ways. For one thing, by parity of reasoning, one can construct the following argument: As Arthur Danto points out, since one *could* be right (as well as wrong) about any type of empirical knowledge, one *could* be right (as well as wrong) about every item of empirical knowledge; therefore, one should accept all such knowledge—clearly a fallacious argument isomorphic to Descartes'. Second, as Hume pointed out, we might be wrong in any of our mathematical calculations and proofs (e.g., by misreading a symbol or simply by erring, as we do when learning geometry). Thus, even if Descartes is correct about the infallibility of his self-knowledge, that same infallibility does not extend to mathematical physics, both because we can make mathematical errors and, even more important, because we need to apply our mathematical physics to real-world situations, and for this we need to rely on sense experience. Descartes' reply is that a benevolent deity would not deceive us, at least regularly, a response that is equally appropriate for the Aristotelian against whom Descartes marshaled his arguments in the first place.

Thus, Descartes, Galileo, and other figures in the Scientific Revolution neither falsify the Aristotelian approach empirically nor show it to be conceptually flawed at root in ways that could not be turned back on their own positions. Once we realize this, we are in a position to understand that the orthodox notion of how scientific ideas are abandoned will not always stand up. It appears that scientific ideas can change not only because of disconfirming data or because of the discovery of basic logical flaws but also because of the *rise of new values that usher in new philosophical commitments or new basic assumptions.* Thus, in the case we have been discussing, a variety of new values, ranging from preference for Plato over Aristotle by a group of prominent intellectuals to greater concern about precision in the prediction of projectile movement because of the advent of artillery, to a penchant for reductionism over pluralism, led to a change in basic assumptions about what science should be doing and how it should be doing it. (In the same vein, it has been pointed out that new technology or tools can determine even basic theoretical approaches and assumptions in science, notably in medicine, which situation accords with neither of the classical accounts of scientific change but does fit better with our valuational account. New technology is valued sufficiently to subordinate medical approaches and assumptions to their use.)

It is within this new category that we attempt to place the abandonment of the common-sense or Darwinian approach to animal mentation. It appears that the view that animals have subjective experiences and that these could be studied was given up not because it did not generate fruitful research programs. It surely did in the hands of people such as Darwin and George Romanes. Nor was it given up because it did not explain or allow us to predict animals' behavior. It surely did. Nor was it shown to be logically inconsistent or incoherent. Rather, it was abandoned because of some major valuational upheavals and concerns.

What values come into play that worked against the knowability of animal consciousness in the early twentieth century? Most important, perhaps, was the marvelous salesmanship of the twentieth-century psychologist J. B. Watson in selling behaviorism. (Let us recall that Watson was a major force in developing modern advertising techniques.) Watson sold to scientists but also sold to the general public. He was one of the rare scientists who loved to talk to reporters about the social utility of the science he advocated. Watson promised nothing less to his peers than the creation of a new psychology as credible as physics and chemistry.

One has only to examine Watson's own work to see that he was attempting to sell a new philosophical-valuational package. In the manifesto "Psychology as the Behaviorist Views It" (1913), Watson urges psychology to "throw off the yoke of consciousness." Only by so doing can psychology become a "real science." By concerning itself with consciousness, "it failed signally . . . to make its place in the world as an undisputed natural science" such as physics and chemistry. To be a "real science," it must behave like a real science and study what is "observable." Thus, he writes, "Can image type be experimentally tested and verified? Are recondite thought processes dependent mechanically upon imagery at all? Are psychologists agreed upon what feeling is?" Watson assumes, but does not demonstrate, that the answer to all of these questions is negative. What is observable is behavior. What we find in the world are "stimulus and response, habit formations, habit integrations and the like." (In fact, of course, these are not directly observable; they are theoretical notions.) "I believe we can write a psychology, define it as Pillsbury [i.e., as the science of behavior], and never go back upon our definition: never use the terms consciousness, mental states, mind, content, introspectively verifiable, imagery, and the like" (Watson 1913, 463).

Note that Watson does not prove that we *should* do this; he merely affirms that psychology will be more like physics and chemistry if we do and thus advocates it. (The physics Watson admired, of course, is nineteenth-century physics. Twentieth-century physics soon soared beyond mechanism.) To the objection that the abandonment of consciousness is a very heavy price to pay, a violation of what we all know to be part of the furniture of the universe (some would say the best-known part of all the furniture), Watson said little except that he didn't "care" about consciousness.

In most of his written work, Watson did not go so far as to say explicitly that there are no such things as consciousness, mental images, and the like, but it is clear that this is his bottom line. Throughout his life, he contended that thoughts, images, and the rest were "implicit behavior," small muscular movements in the larynx or other organs that we would be able to detect if we had a more advanced technology. Watson, in essence, paradoxically held that "we don't have thoughts, we only think we do." Subjective mental states are at best dispensable psychic trash and at worst, nonexistent. Watson's own deepest mental states are inaccessible to us, of course, not least because he is dead. But he was certainly interpreted as I have outlined by his contemporaries and co-workers such as the psychologist Karl Lashley.

If behaviorism was to be significantly different from other approaches that preceded it, including the Darwin–Romanes approach, it had to deny the reality of consciousness in humans and animals—or, at least, its knowability. In this regard, Watson is his own version of a consistent Darwinian. In fact, in a bizarre dialectical turn in "Psychology as the Behaviorist Views It," he accuses those who argue for a phylogenetic continuum of consciousness of anthropocentrism because "it makes consciousness as the human being knows it, the center of reference for all behavior" (Watson 1913, 459–460), just as Darwinian biology was anthropocentric in attempting first and foremost to describe the evolution of Homo sapiens.

Behaviorism played well to the general public, especially the American public, because it promised a science that would birth a technology—the ability to control and shape behavior. With it, we could rehabilitate criminals, educate children properly, produce a better society. With its contempt for genetic bases of behavior, it fit perfectly into American optimism about social engineering and the ability to shape humans, just as we conquered the frontier and shaped nature. This side of behaviorism reached its culmination in the work of Watson's student B. F. Skinner.

Behaviorism also fit well with other early-twentieth-century cultural tendencies, in particular with the reductive tendency manifest in that era to eliminate frills, excesses, and superfluities. This value may be found in diverse quarters: the composer Arnold Schönberg's reaction against Richard Wagner and Gustav Mahler and others, the reaction of the Bauhaus against excessive ornamentation in art and design, the rise of formalism in criticism—all express the same spirit that invaded science in the form of positivism. Thinkers such as Ernst Mach, Albert Einstein, and, later, the logical positivists all sought to excise metaphysical and speculative baggage from science, to clearly delineate the realm of science as the realm of the empirical and observable, a tendency that had been part of science since Newton. (The positivists also had political reasons and values that justified their hard empiricism: the elimination of meaningless but inflammatory rhetoric from political discourse.) Since animal consciousness could not become a direct empirical datum for us, it was automatically suspect on positivist grounds. Ironically, then, the phenomenalistic empiricism of Locke and Hume, which took animal consciousness as axiomatic, was stood on its head by their twentieth-century successors.

While scholars debate the influence that logical positivism had directly on behaviorism, there is no doubt that it at least created an environment highly congenial to the elimination of consciousness. Indeed, as I argued in the previous chapter and argue more fully in *Science and Ethics* (2006c), positivism was a powerful force for removing consciousness *and* ethics from legitimate scientific discourse, thereby accelerating what I have called "scientific ideology." In *Science and Ethics,* I trace the pernicious ethical consequences of this ideology for issues that range from the treatment of research subjects to pain management in medicine and science's image in the public mind.

To add insult to injury, behaviorist historians throughout the twentieth century wrote as if Watson were the logical and inevitable culmination of a variety of thinkers who succeeded Darwin. In *A History of Experimental Psychology* (1950), for example, Edwin Boring cites Lloyd Morgan, Jacques Loeb, H. S. Jennings, E. B. Titchener, and Edward Thorndike as leading inevitability to behaviorism. We all know that history is written by the victors. That notwithstanding, the tracing of psychology from Romanes to Watson is as egregious a distortion of the history of ideas as I have ever encountered. In *The Unheeded Cry* (Rollin 1989), I did something quite heretical and actually *read* the psychologists cited as leading to Watson. Amazingly enough, none of them ever even suggested the need to eliminate consciousness; indeed, all presupposed it in their own writings.

Consider, for example, the self-assured, unequivocal historical claim advanced by Melvin Marx and William Hillix in *Systems and Theories in*

Psychology about the pivotal role of Conway Lloyd Morgan in paving the way for behaviorism:

> Romanes was demonstrating continuity by finding mind everywhere; Morgan also wished to demonstrate continuity, but suggested that it might be done as well if we could find mind nowhere. Morgan's appeal to simplicity and rejection of anthropomorphism would seem, from a modern perspective, to have made the development of a scientific behaviourism inevitable. (1963, 168)

They are here referring to the dogma (for behaviorists) that Morgan's Canon, as articulated in *An Introduction to Comparative Psychology,* eliminated consciousness. Sometimes erroneously seen as a special case of Occam's razor, the Canon says with regard to an animal's behavior, "In no case may we interpret an action as the outcome of the exercise of a higher psychical faculty, if it can be interpreted as the outcome of the exercise of one which stands lower in the psychological scale" (Morgan [1904] 2000, 53). Anyone who reads Morgan as a proto-behaviorist has not read Morgan. The Canon is not intended to eliminate consciousness; it instead *presupposes* consciousness. Morgan believes unequivocally that if consciousness exists anywhere on the phylogenetic scale, it must exist everywhere, at least in simple form, even in bare nature. He is, in fact, a raving speculative metaphysician, a monist, a pan-psychist, a Spinozian, a believer that everything in nature has both a physical and a psychological dimension. The Canon is simply meant to warn against confusing higher consciousness with lower, not to *eliminate* consciousness. Morgan's own words end any debate:

> We have . . . taken for granted the existence of consciousness, and the fact that there are subjective phenomena which we, as comparative psychologists, may study. We have also proceeded throughout on the assumption that subjective phenomena admit of a natural interpretation, as the result of a process or processes of development or evolution, in just the same sense as objective phenomena admit of such interpretation. ([1904] 2000, 323)

The truth notwithstanding, for much of the twentieth century, psychologists believed in the inexorable, logical, empirical victory of behaviorism. The two mutually reinforcing components of scientific ideology taken together have caused incalculable damage to science, society, and objects of moral concern in science's failure to engage ethical issues. I showed earlier some of the ways that animals suffered.

This second component of scientific ideology, affirming that scientists need to be agnostic about subjective states in people and animals, led to all of the following consequences: the denial of the scientific reality of pain that in turn resulted in open-heart surgery performed on neonatal humans until the late 1980s using paralytic drugs, not anesthetics; the failure to provide adequate analgesia to all human patients, as recounted in Richard Marks and Edward Sachar's famous paper "Undertreatment of Medical Inpatients with Narcotic Analgesics" (1973), about pain in cancer patients; and the failure to control any animal pain in research at the expense of both animals and science. A healthy dose of philosophy of mind (as well as legislation) was needed even to begin to correct this. This hurt not only innocent creatures but science itself through a nearly total failure to control pain and stress variables. All of this ramified in major neglect of pain control in the practice of both human and veterinary medicine.

In the area of human research, the abuses of humans have been legion, from the Tuskegee Institute's studies (1932–1972) on black prisoners with syphilis who were told that they were being treated for the disease but, in fact, were not and were allowed to get sicker and sicker for forty years; to the recent death of sixteen-year-old Jesse Gelsinger in a gene-therapy trial, where the boy was killed by a researcher violating his own protocol under pressure from investors; to the radiation studies performed on humans by the U.S. Department of Energy; to the release of pathogenic microbes in subway systems; to the administration of LSD to soldiers and mental patients without informed consent; to the exposure of mentally retarded children to hepatitis at the Willowbrook State School in the 1960s. (For detailed discussion of these and other egregious research abuses, see Rollin 2006c, chap. 4). The results for science have been equally pernicious: the federal imposition of draconian rules for researchers, the changing of rules according to political correctness (allowing pregnant woman to serve as research subjects after banning them earlier, the flurry over what to call Indians when they were the subjects of research [the government insisted on "Native Americans" until it actually *asked* the Indians], asking that alcoholics serve on committees evaluating studies of alcoholics). The net effect is that researchers see these rules as bureaucratic hoops to jump through with absolutely no grasp of the ethical issues, further creating hostility to doing human research properly.

It is my contention that a good part of the reason that society has moved from the optimistic, naïve, Buck Rogers and Jetsonion adoration of a science-shaped future of the 1950s to today's wholesale skepticism about science—seen in the alternative-medicine movement, neo-fundamentalist anti-Darwinism, the rejection of stem-cell technology and (especially in

Europe) the large-scale rejection of biotechnology, the representation of scientists in popular culture as mad megalomaniacs—is what I call Gresham's law for ethics. In the absence of scientists' responsibly articulating the dangers and moral issues raised by science, opportunists such as theologians, Rifkins, Luddites will leap into the breach and fill the gap with lurid, uninformed but highly marketable pseudo-ethical issues, as we see in the case of Dolly the cloned sheep. Unless science begins to engage ethics in serious ways, the forces of darkness and unreason and anti-intellectualism will prevail, which in any case are lurking not terribly far from the surface in society as Richard Hofstadter documented in his Pulitzer Prize–winning book *Anti-intellectualism in American Life* (1964). George Gaskell and his colleagues (1997) have revealingly shown that Europeans reject biotechnological modalities for reasons of moral concern, not out of fear, as is widely believed.

As I see it, there is only one way to resolve this malignancy: through education of a new generation of scientists trained to think of ethics and science together. Only education can displace, uproot, and supplant ideology. When I worked to draft the federal laws for laboratory animals, it was not to create a regulatory bureaucracy—or, as I put it then, to put "a cop in every lab." I personally tend toward resistance to laws; I will not ride my Harley-Davidson in states that have mandatory helmet laws. But I was enough of a product of the 1960s to understand the lesson I learned from Martin Luther King Jr. and Lyndon Johnson: Just because we may have too many laws in some areas does not mean we have enough in others. We drafted the animal-research laws in the way Wittgenstein saw his philosophy: as a ladder to reach a higher plane, which ladder can later can be thrown away. Just as Martin Luther King envisioned a generation that possessed racial tolerance and did not need marshals or paratroopers to escort children to school, I saw the laws as forcing animal researchers to reflect in ethical terms so the laws eventually would not be needed. And it worked. From the two meager papers on animals' pain I found in 1982, the literature has grown to over eleven thousand papers in twenty-five years. And, of course, Institutional Animal Care and Use Committees routinely discuss ethical issues. This ideology is nowhere near as ubiquitous as it was twenty-five years ago.

But recall, and note well, that a different bill was being pressed by activists: the "Research Modernization Act," which would have cut the federal research budget by up to 60 percent and put the money into "alternatives." What did "alternatives" mean? As the chief proponent once said, "Oh, you know: plastic dogs that howl when cut and bleed ketchup so they can do their experiments." This is the potential price of ignoring ethics.

The National Institutes of Health seemed to have somewhat grasped the need for ethics training when they mandated courses in science and ethics for institutions where students received training grants. As I understand it, the institutes were prompted to do this by increasing numbers of reports of data falsification, plagiarism—what is generically called "misconduct in science." As I pointed out to some NIH officials in the early 1980s, "You can't teach students that science is value-free in general and ethics-free in particular and then fault them for not behaving ethically."

I have been teaching science and ethics in some form steadily since 1976. For more than twenty years, I taught a year-long honors biology course with a biologist in which ethical and conceptual issues arising in science were included as integrally related to the science we taught—as cake, not icing. The course was wildly successful and influenced generations of students who are researchers, physicians, or faculty members.

The only way to escape the quicksand into which support for science is sinking is to create educational requirements for every graduate student and undergraduate majoring in any area of science. Too many undergraduates are still taught the mantra "Science is value-free." We can rest only when the examination of ethical issues presuppositional to and generated by science are as much second nature to scientists as are the double helix or the Krebs cycle and when we fully expunge the pernicious ideology described here. Increasingly draconian regulation of the sort we have seen imposed by the government in the human research area can only alienate researchers. Especially for thinking people, ethics is far more valuable than regulation.

What, specifically, should be taught? In the first place, one must provide students with a historical perspective on science's neglect of ethics. Very few students are aware of the atrocities perpetrated on humans throughout the twentieth century. Even fewer know about the denial and ignoring of animals' pain and distress. Once students face these shocking facts, one can go beyond the sensationalistic stories to the underlying ideology. This approach works well. Students, initially shocked and horrified, eventually come to the realization that, in their own careers, they must do everything possible to restore moral concern to scientific activity. Given the natural idealism in most college-age people, our approach has an indelible impact.

11

Ethical Issues in Animal Research and the Research-Animal Laws

Successes and Inadequacies

Before I discuss the effects of the laws on research and on the scientific ideology just examined, I should identify the ethical issues occasioned by animal research. I believe that one can find three layers or levels of ethical issue in the activity of animal research. Unfortunately, our laws address only the last, and the least profound, level, but we can hope that the unraveling of scientific ideology will make the research community more receptive to the other two. In any case, it is likely that, as animal ethics evolves in society, these other issues will be addressed.

The most fundamental moral question is this: What entitles us to use animals for human benefit in invasive research that causes them pain, fear, distress, loneliness, injury, boredom, and so on? This issue was raised by Peter Singer in *Animal Liberation* (1975), by me in *Animal Rights and Human Morality* (1981), by Tom Regan in *The Case for Animal Rights* (1983), by Steve Sapontzis in *Morals, Reason, and Animals* (1987), and by numerous other philosophers in the ensuing years. Most of the arguments follow the logic I outlined in an earlier chapter about providing for serious moral status for animals in our moral deliberations. The same arguments regarding an inability to define morally relevant differences between people and animals also cast doubt on our moral entitlement to use animals invasively in

Portions of this chapter are drawn from Bernard E. Rollin, "Animal Research: A Moral Science," *EMBO Reports* 8, no. 6 (2007): 521–525.

research for our benefit (or even for the benefit of other animals). If animals are legitimately in the moral arena, and what we do matters to them, neither human superiority, alleged lack of a soul, absence of reason in animals, nor any other argument entitles us to use them in ways that hurt them any more than we could so use humans. Certainly, if we do not allow the use of so-called marginal humans—children, the insane, the senile, the mentally retarded, the comatose—for invasive experimentation, we similarly should disallow the invasive use of animals. (I address killing animals painlessly in my later discussion of killing animals for food.)

To be sure, scientists did use disenfranchised humans in all sorts of research for all of the twentieth century: soldiers, prisoners, mentally retarded people, insane people, poor people, foreigners in Third World countries, prisoners of the Nazis, Russians, Japanese, Chinese concentration camp victims, students—indeed, any sort of person in a position of weakness. But society has roundly condemned and decried such invasive use, even when it was beneficial. (The syphilis experiments at Tuskegee are a paradigm case of such use and such public outrage.) To the claim that humans can provide informed consent to allow them to participate morally in invasive experiments that benefit other humans while animals cannot, the philosopher Steve Sapontzis has offered a very clever response: Open the cages and we will know if they wish to participate.

To the basic moral question of whether we are morally justified in using animals invasively against their will, little morally sound discussion has been forthcoming from the research community. By the same token, animals continue to be used invasively. If one presses researchers for a response, it usually takes one of two forms. They say that we are "superior" to animals and can do as we wish. We have already questioned the adequacy of this logic. What does superior mean? More powerful? If we follow out that position, the mugger or rapist is justified in victimizing the weak, which is, in fact, what much of ethics is designed to prevent. Does it mean intellectually superior? Why is that morally relevant? Does it mean morally superior? If so, victimizing something sentient because we can is hardly evidence of moral superiority. But most commonly, the reply is tendered in terms of costs and benefits: invasive animal research is justified because it produces more benefit to humans or animals than harm to the animals. Aside from the fact that our consensus social ethic does not accept hurting the minority for the benefit of the majority, this argument is open to a much more practical, nondebatable point.

Let us assume that invasive animal research is justified only by the benefit produced. It would then seem to follow that the only morally justifiable research would be research that benefits humans (or animals). But there is, in fact, a vast amount of research that does not demonstrably benefit humans or animals. Much behavioral research, weapons research, and toxicity testing as a legal requirement are obvious examples, as is much of basic research that is invasive but has no clear benefit. Obviously, a certain amount of research meets that test. (Peter Singer recently announced that some invasive neuroscience work on primates, in his view, does provide benefits that outweigh the cost.) But a great deal does not. Someone might respond that "we never know what benefits might emerge in the future" and appeal to serendipity or unknowns. But if that were a legitimate point, we could not discriminate in funding between research that is likely to produce benefit and research that is unlikely to do so. Yet we do. If we appeal to unknown but possible benefits, we are forced to fund everything, which we do not. We do, in fact, weigh cost versus benefit in human research and in animal research. Why not weigh cost to the animal subject as a relevant parameter?

Thus, we find a second moral issue in animal research. To recapitulate: The first issue arises from the suggestion that any invasive research on an object of moral concern is morally problematic. In response, researchers invoke the benefits of research. Even assuming that this is a good argument, it gives rise to another moral issue: *Why do we not do only animal research that clearly produces more benefit than cost to the animals?* Even if we disregard the general point about the morality of invasive animal research, we are still left with the fact that much of animal research does not fit researchers' own moral justification for it. In other writings, I have referred to this moral claim about justifying invasive research by appealing to benefits as the "utilitarian principle": If one accepts the benefit argument, we are left with the conclusion that the only justifiable animal research is that which produces results yielding more benefit than harm (however this is measured).

Thus, even if we retreat to the utilitarian argument in moral defense of invasive animal research, we find that a good deal of such research fails to meet that "more benefit than harm" criterion. But this is not all. Yet another ethical issue arises. Suppose we ignore the cost–benefit criteria discussion, as well as the first argument questioning the morality of all invasive animal research. This is, of course, what we do in actual practice. Would it not, then, at least be morally required that we treat the animals in the best possible manner commensurate with their use in research? To put the question another way: Are research animals given the best possible treatment they could get while being used in research? Regrettably, the answer is no, as one can easily demonstrate both historically and in the present.

The demand that, if we do use animals in invasive research, we at least do our best to meet their interest and needs, minimize their suffering as much as possible, and respect their *telos* (nature) seems to be a requirement of common decency, particularly if we are using them in a way that ignores the moral problems recounted thus far. Sadly, this is not the case. Historically—in the United States, at least—basic animal care has been a very low priority in animal research, ironically harming the science by failing to control pain, stress, and other variables and very much failing to meet the ideal set forth in the third set of moral issues just enumerated. In helping to draft and defend the 1985 laws for laboratory animals before the U.S. Congress, it was my business to know about the deficiencies in animal care if I was to be able to prove to Congress the need for legislation strongly opposed by much of the research community, who claimed that it would be obstructive of research and prohibitively expensive. What I found could easily be chronicled in a whole book, but I restrict myself to two paradigmatic examples: pain control and housing.

Ordinary common sense would dictate that one of the worst things one can do to a research animal is to cause it unrelieved pain. Since animals do not understand sources of pain, particularly the sort of pain inflicted in experiments, they cannot rationalize that "this will end soon." Rather, because they cannot anticipate its cessation, their whole life becomes the pain. This insight, as mentioned earlier, has led the veterinary pain specialist Ralph Kitchell to surmise that animals' pain may be worse than humans' pain; as I put it, humans have *hope.* Further, pain is a stressor and can skew the results of experiments in numerous ways. Thus, for both moral and scientific reasons, one would expect pain control to be a major emphasis when scientists undertake painful experiments. If someone were conducting fracture research, for example, one would think that he or she would use pre-emptive and postsurgical or post-traumatic analgesia liberally, since the pain is not the point of the experiment and unmitigated pain actually retards healing.

A central component of the federal legislation of 1985 was to mandate control of pain in research animals after we showed Congress the lack of pain control. In the same vein, many veterinarians to this day—typically veterinarians trained before the mid-1980s—still equate anesthesia with "chemical restraint" or "sedation" and use these words synonymously. The first U.S. textbooks on veterinary anesthesia do not even mention pain control as a reason for anesthesia (they do, however, mention using it to keeping the animal still to prevent injury), and they do not mention analgesia.

Some of the neglect of felt pain in animals goes back to veterinary medicine's historical roots as ancillary to agriculture and, thus, its concern only with the animal's economic and productive role. In a textbook on veterinary surgery from 1906, Louis Merillat thus bemoans the failure of veterinarians even to use *anesthesia* for surgery, with the episodic exception of the practitioners who treated canines and whose clients presumably valued their animals enough in non-economic terms to demand anesthesia.

As we saw, the two components of scientific ideology—denial of ethics in science and denial of the knowability of consciousness—worked synergistically to the detriment of laboratory animals, creating a formidable barrier against awareness of the ethical issues inherent in animal research and against recognition of the pain and distress sometimes created in the research process. As important as the infliction of pain and suffering, which only sometimes arises in research, is the fact that 100 percent of the animals used in research have their basic biological and psychological needs thwarted by how they are kept. This is why, in the initial drafts of the legislation, we worked out mandated housing and husbandry for all research animals that met their natures. Unfortunately, this did not pass. Nonetheless, it did ramify in an awareness of "environmental enrichment" that can benefit the animals only as their accommodations better meet their *telos.*

In my view, new laws and, more important, the growing societal concern for animals that drove their passage have had salubrious consequences for the moral status of animals in research. For one thing, they vividly underscore the fact that society sees invasive animal research as a significant moral issue. For another, they explode the scientific ideology that precludes ethical engagement by animal-research scientists with the issues their activities engender. Finally, they have led to what I call the "reappropriation of common sense" with regard to the reality and knowability of animals' suffering and the need for its control. One can be guardedly optimistic that animal research will evolve into what it should have been all along: a moral science.

We can now turn to the question of how well these laws have succeeded in introducing ethical vectors into animal research and consider another major criticism of their potential to bring about change. This was expressed best in *The Animal Rights Movement in America* (1994), in which the philosophers Lawrence and Susan Finsen, thoughtful and rational animal advocates, derided the value of Institutional Animal Care and Use Committees (IACUCs), the conceptual and operational foundation of federal legislation protecting research animals, as "a new set of clothes for the emperor"—or, in other words, as a sham. According to the Finsens' view, a perspective also shared then and now by many others in the animal-rights and animal-welfare movements, such committees generally act as a rubber stamp for researchers' use of animals, since "the membership of these committees are [*sic*] typically selected because they are favorably disposed toward research. Yet that these review committees exist allows researchers to claim that protocols are all carefully reviewed to assure that no 'unnecessary' suffering occurs in laboratories" (Finsen and Finsen 1994, 260). Many others have echoed this concern, claiming that current oversight mechanisms amount to little more than the fox watching the henhouse. Because both major 1985 laws protecting laboratory animals—the National Institutes of Health (NIH) Reauthorization Act and the amendments to the Animal Welfare Act—do amount to what one Australian sociologist has aptly described as "enforced self-regulation," the Finsens' criticism is a serious one. In this critique's most interesting and strongest version, it suggests that current laws cannot move the treatment of animals beyond the status quo and certainly cannot bring about major protective changes. If they are correct, our hopes for advancing the proper treatment of animal research and the general public's deep concern for research animals, which led to the passage of these laws even in the face of significant opposition from the research community, come to nothing.

I argue on both conceptual and empirical grounds that the "fox watching the henhouse" view is misguided and that IACUCs must inevitably move beyond the status quo—and, indeed, have done so already. The Finsens' concern probably best applies to the rate at which change occurs, not the fact of such change.

Implicit in the Finsens' charge is an "us" versus "them" gestalt. Ordinary people who put their faith in the laws for laboratory animals presumably possess one moral view of animals, and researchers possess a radically different and incommensurable one. Thus, the Finsens claim, self-regulation must inevitably fail. In one sense, the Finsens are historically correct. Where they go astray, I think, is in misunderstanding the role of the laws. In my view, these laws must inevitably serve to bridge the gulf, not to perpetuate it. They exist not to divide scientists from the public on the moral status of animals but, rather, to ensure that "from a moral point of view," as Pogo says, "they is us."

Certainly, the Finsens are historically correct when they say that science denied any concern with ethics. Scientific ideology denied the relevance of morality to science in general and, a fortiori, to the issue of animal use in research. Perhaps the most extreme example of this position can be found in a letter from the researcher Robert White, professor of surgery at Case Western Reserve, to the *Hastings Center Report* in 1990 condemning the journal for even treating the use of animals in research as a moral issue:

> I write in reference to the Special Supplement entitled "Animals, Science, and Ethics," which appeared in the May/June (1990) issues of the *Hastings Center Report.*

> I am extremely disappointed in the particular series of articles, which, quite frankly, has no right to be published as part of the *Report.*
>
> Animal usage is not a moral or ethical issue and elevating the problem of animal rights to such a plane is a disservice to medical research and the farm and dairy industry.

The result of this component of scientific ideology was, of course, blindness to moral issues raised by animal research. Typical of this reaction was the response I received at a formal dinner in the early 1980s from a prominent medical researcher who asked me to outline my concerns about animal research. I indicated that my chief concern was that many scientists do not even admit that there are any moral issues in this area. He then accused me and "all others like [me]" of attempting to "lay [our] trip on everyone else." "Morality," he told me, was "a matter of taste in a free country." To attempt to pass legislation restricting research using animals was "fantastic" and "totalitarian." I was entitled to my opinion, he admitted, but ought not to try to impose it on him. He continued in that vein at length and wound down only when I pointed out that absence of constraints on the use of animals in research meant that he was "imposing his trip on me," which was equally reprehensible by his argument.

The second component of scientific ideology that insulates researchers from what ordinary common sense views as morally problematic in animal research has been the denial of scientific reality to animal consciousness, thought, and feeling. This component merged synergistically with the denial of ethics. Both components cleared the decks so that scientists could do whatever they felt needed to be done and protected them from the guilt and anguish that ordinary beliefs that animals were conscious would raise in any ordinary person who inflicted harm on animals.

The two components of scientific ideology taken together represented a formidable barrier to the development of scientific thinking about the moral issues associated with animal research. In the role of scientist, scientists would don scientific common sense along with their lab coats and doff them when they went home to their role as ordinary people. Scientific common sense and ordinary common sense were, as psychologists put it, very well compartmentalized. Score one for the Finsens.

In general, then, science and common sense coexisted like multiple personalities in the same body. These are the barriers the laws were intended to breach. Somehow, one had to break down the separation between ordinary common sense (and its ordinary consensus morality) and scientific ideology's denial of morality in science and consciousness in animals. In essence, the task was to force scientists to reappropriate ordinary common sense and ordinary morality.

Our idea therefore was to remind scientists of what they as ordinary citizens must adhere to in the treatment of animals—very likely an idea that they accepted when they were not wearing their lab coats. (More than 85 percent of the general public and 90 percent of the eight thousand or so western ranchers I have addressed believe that animals have rights in the sense I have described.) Laws, to paraphrase Plato, are social ethics "writ large," so if the law states that animals suffer and that such suffering must count and be dealt with in scientific deliberations, and that animal-care committees must work on the playing field of these assumptions and deliberate about what are clearly ethical issues, scientific ideology or scientific common sense is suppressed in favor of ordinary common sense and consensus social morality. If federal law states that animals feel pain and suffer, scientific ideology cannot respond with agnosticism about animals' consciousness. If federal law states that it is morally wrong to ignore animals' suffering, scientific ideology cannot say that the science is morally neutral and value-free. Indeed, although the laws say that committees may not look at cost–benefit issues in animal research the way human Institutional Review Boards (IRBs) do, such deliberations are impossible to avoid in practice, particularly when research is very invasive.

Thus, the laws force the scientific community, through the vehicles of the IACUCs, to engage animal research in terms of common morality—to "recollect"—and to reappropriate common sense about animals' consciousness and pain. For members of IACUCs and, indirectly, for the scientists they represent, notice is served that scientific ideology is no longer adequate to determine the rules for animal research. I have seen this work well in human-subjects committees. In the thirty-four years I have served on CSU's IRB, I have seen sensitivity move from a low point of "What is wrong with using your students for nutrition experiments?" to a point of such sensitivity that the board prohibits researchers from bothering people who don't return questionnaires.

This, then, is the conceptual part of the response to the Finsens' objection. Insofar as the 1985 laws force the thought of scientists into ethical channels and channels that recognize the reality of animals' pain, suffering, and distress, they must change the way scientists think and act. For this reason alone, the Finsens' prediction that the use of animals in science would be essentially untouched by these laws must be false. Members of IACUCs start to think differently and, through their decisions and dialogue, spread this thinking to their colleagues.

Perhaps what the Finsens meant is that change has not yet taken place to any significant degree in animal care and use. That is an empirical question and would itself represent a strong objection to the current regime. If it is going to take a hundred years to get scientists to think differently and act differently, the current laws are inadequate for now, whatever their eventual outcome may be.

I do not think that this version of the Finsens' claim is correct either. Having served on an IACUC since the late 1970s and on a human-subjects IRB since the mid-1970s; having persuaded my institution to review animal-research protocols meaningfully since 1980; having successfully defended the concept of IACUCs to the U.S. Congress and to the Dutch, Australian, and South African governments; and having consulted for many IACUCs across the United States, I know that these laws do, in fact, work to improve the situation of animals. It is true that they follow no predictable timetable, because different institutions, like different individuals, vary in their cultures, personalities, receptivity, and so on. With the advent of the Internet, however, insights are quickly shared, and more homogeneity in ethical response has inevitably emerged.

The following list cites some examples of where animals are immeasurably better off by virtue of IACUCs' activities in accordance with the laws:

1. The recognition and control of animals' pain has grown rapidly in theory and in practice. Most dramatically, control of animals' pain has become a growth industry. Thousands of papers on the subject have now been published. The passage of the laws led lab-animal veterinarians to a new perspective on old data generated from the practice of testing analgesics on animals. Social concern with pet animals has also given a boost to the study of pain and distress control, and Rimadyl and other forms of analgesia for arthritic pain in older dogs have become billion-dollar products.
2. Control of care has moved more and more into the hands of experts (laboratory-animal veterinarians and, in many institutions, a centralized animal-care facility with specially trained staff). In the past, everyone believed he or she was an expert. As one prominent physiologist remarked to me, "M.D./Ph.D.s used to say, 'Hell, if we can take care of people, we can take care of animals,'" even though it was possible to earn an M.D. or a Ph.D. in an animal-using area of science, begin a major animal-research program, and never learn anything about the animals except that they modeled a particular disease or syndrome, and even though the researcher was accountable to no one regarding animal care. Furthermore, care and husbandry were often provided by stu-

dent employees paid the minimum wage, which meant, in practice, erratic feeding and watering, failure to detect disease, and failure to control other variables that led to bad animal care and bad scientific results. Committees increasingly demand central care by trained personnel and researchers' demonstration of some mastery of basic principles of research—for example, surgery. Furthermore, courses are being mandated for nascent researchers in various aspects of animal care and use.

3. Many committees have extended the law beyond its letter—for example, to concern about pain in invertebrates, which are not covered by the laws, or about surgery and pain control in farm animals used for agricultural research, who are also exempt from legal protections.
4. Committees have undertaken or forced the undertaking of research to the benefit of animals. For example, at CSU, the IACUC mandated that a toxicology researcher who never used anesthesia in his painful studies because he feared skewing his results look at a variety of anesthetic regimens to see whether such skewing actually occurred. (He ended up finding a regimen that did not affect his data.) CSU also funds small research projects that aim to benefit the animals.
5. Euthanasia protocols are tightly controlled. In the past, researchers used (or tried to use) such methods as succinylcholine or magnesium sulfate paralytics that suffocated animals. Now committees even worry about animals being euthanized in the presence of other animals, and there is an emerging distrust of killing using carbon dioxide.
6. Many researchers are undertaking work on enriched environments for species that are not legally mandated to have such environments, such as mice and rats.
7. Committees are forcing teachers to think through anew the invasive uses of animals in teaching. Correlatively, many committees have mandated providing alternatives for students who don't wish to hurt or kill an animal in the name of education.

These are just a few clear examples of changes that belie the notion that the laws don't effect change. Nonetheless, it does seem at times that committees move very slowly. In my experience, a peculiar phenomenon, which I call a breakthrough experience, is required to help move things forward until a certain momentum is reached. I don't believe that breakthrough experiences can be orchestrated, but they do inevitably occur as people became increasingly sensitized. For example, one researcher on CSU's IACUC tended to view the protocol-review activity as a "waste of time" because researchers "know what they're doing." However, when we reviewed a research proposal to drown pigs to study refloat time for human drowning victims, he was shocked out of his sanguine stance. Under his leadership, the committee rejected the proposal, and he pointed out that a simple alternative was available: to study gas formation in slaughterhouse gut taken after animals are killed. Since that event, he has taken protocol review very seriously.

As another example, and as mentioned earlier, the CSU committee initially reviewed protocols very quickly—thirty in an hour, with time for lunch—and I despaired of members' seriously engaging the issues. One day, we were discussing a protocol that had been carried over from a previous meeting that involved trapping coyotes in a steel-jawed trap. The research protocol had made numerous concessions, including padding the jaws of the trap and using bait laced with tranquilizers. The committee was about to pass it when one very strong member—an equine surgeon—walked in. After being apprised of where we were, he slammed his fist down and shouted, "If we're supposed to be an animal care committee, there is no way on God's green earth that I will approve a steel-jawed trap protocol. That is barbaric." Some members pointed out that he induced lesions in horses to study lameness and questioned why that was morally justifiable. We were off to the races, and our pace of protocol review slowed significantly.

This was quite typical. Our first committee chairman was Jim Voss. He made it clear that he thought the whole process was nonsense and that all researchers were competent. What turned him around was a protocol by one of his own department members—a full professor—who proposed euthanizing a cow with magnesium sulfate (Epsom salts), which killed by paralyzing the diaphragm muscles and creating suffocation. That, for him, was a breakthrough experience.

We found in general that if we encountered researchers hostile to the process, we should put them on the committee. Inevitably, they, too, would have breakthrough experiences and change their views (and stop being problems for us).

Having, I hope, cleared the laws of the charges raised, I conclude by pointing out some limitations and inadequacies in the laws. Despite the salubrious developments I have sketched here, the "new" laws are by no means ideal or even totally adequate. First, they do not cover all animals used in research. Neither of the laws applies to all rats and mice, farm animals, or birds used in industrial research because the current interpretation of the Animal Welfare Act by the U.S. Department of Agriculture (USDA) still does not consider these creatures animals, and the NIH law applies only to recipients of federal grants and to those in the NIH's own labs. Clearly, the Animal Welfare Act must be extended to cover all animals; a federal judge ruled that the exclusion by the USDA of rats, mice, birds, and farm animals used in biomedicine actually seems to go against the intent of the law.

In addition, these laws are currently restricted in their application to warm-blooded animals (the Animal Welfare Act excludes rats, mice, and birds) and to vertebrates (NIH law). These exclusions are clearly arbitrary, and many committees, to their credit, have extended the application of the principles in the laws to such higher invertebrates as squids, where there are good scientific reasons to suspect the presence of thought and feeling. The scope of these laws should be statutorily expanded to include all animals where there are solid reasons to infer the presence of pain or consciousness. Unfortunately, the right-wing biomedical lobby convinced Senator Jesse Helms (R-N.C.) to pass an amendment to the farm bill in 2002 that permanently excluded rats, mice, and birds from the Animal Welfare Act. (Many thoughtful scientists are appalled by this.)

Another marked inadequacy in these laws pertains to animals used in agricultural research. The Animal Welfare Act specifically excluded from its purview farm animals used in agricultural research. Yet millions of farm animals are used in research in ways that may be as invasive and bring about as much pain and suffering as biomedical research. Such agricultural projects may include surgery, deficient diets, food and water deprivation, total confinement, and induced disease, yet these animals enjoy no legal protection. Thus, suppose one has twin male lambs, one of which goes to an NIH-funded biomedical research project and the other to an agricultural research project. Both are to be castrated. The NIH lamb will get anesthesia and postsurgical analgesia and will be castrated under aseptic conditions. The agricultural lamb may have the testicles removed under field conditions in standard ways, which even include having them bitten off.

To their credit, many committees now apply NIH standards to all surgical procedures done on their campuses—even for agricultural research. Nonetheless, agricultural animals clearly need to be included under standards as rigorous as those governing the treatment of biomedical animals. Although the agricultural-research community has adopted voluntary guidelines for their research animals, they are, not surprisingly, far too weak and have no enforcement structure to back them. Yet another criticism stems from the fact that researchers are on the honor system to do what they say they will do in their protocols. For this reason, a movement is starting for post-approval monitoring, or monitoring of laboratory procedures after the protocols have been approved.

The major criticism of these new laws, however, is that they don't go far enough. Powerful arguments are being made that, ultimately, there is no moral justification for using animals invasively in research at all. When researchers attempt to answer this sort of argument, they respond in cost–benefit terms: that the good to humans and animals coming out of research outweighs the cost in pain and suffering to the research animals. Leaving aside the cogency of this response, one can, indeed, acknowledge that the statement seems to capture the current state of social moral thought on the question. But if this is, indeed, the case, it naturally follows that the only invasive research that ought to be pursued is research in which the benefit to humans or animals likely to emerge outweighs the cost in suffering to the animals.

This maxim suggests that much invasive research, which is aimed at "pure knowledge," should not be allowed. One standard response to this principle by researchers is to invoke the serendipity argument: They argue that, although it may not appear that a particular piece of research will produce foreseeable benefit, one never knows what will arise adventitiously. The response to that is simple. By definition, one cannot plan for serendipity. Society does not fund a great deal of research for a wide variety of reasons. Much research is turned down by the granting agencies because it is perceived as poorly designed, less important than other research, and so on. If the serendipity argument were valid, one could not make such discriminations, and one would be logically compelled to fund everything.

Admittedly, such cost–benefit calculation is fraught with difficulties: How does one weight one parameter against a disparate one? But the crucial point to remember is that we do currently make such cost–benefit decisions in a variety of areas about research on humans. All that needs to be done is to export such calculations to the area of animal use. Certainly, there will be hard cases, but at least extreme cases will be clear. Invasive research aimed at developing a new weapon or a new nail polish or at discovering knowledge of no clear benefit to humans or animals—for example, territorial animal aggression studies—obviously would not be permitted.

Clearly, then, some mechanism needs to be developed that will exclude invasive research that produces no benefit but simply advances trivial knowledge or researchers' careers. Some types of psychological research, for example, are highly vulnerable to this criticism. The current mechanism of peer review, whereby experts in the field judge the value and fundability of research, plainly does not address these concerns. Researchers who throughout their careers have taken a particular sort of invasive animal use for granted in their field are not the best source for eliminating such a use from the field. A better alternative, perhaps, would be to allow local committees with greater representation from the citizenry at large to rule on the value of a piece of animal research; researchers ought to be able to defend to a set of citizens their need to spend public money to hurt animals. This approach works for our justice system. Perhaps researchers need to persuade a jury of their need to hurt animals for the sake of research. Thus, I argue that local committees should also be charged with deciding whether a given piece of invasive research ought to be done and that the majority on such committees be made up of non-scientists representing the public in general.

The final major area of deficiency stems from the fact that the laws focus on pain and suffering growing out of inadequate husbandry and housing only in the cases of dogs and primates. I argue that moral concern, when applied to research animals, demands another principle, which I have called the "rights principle" (Rollin [1981] 2006, 180). That principle asserts that all research should be conducted in such a way as to maximize the animal's potential to live its life according to its nature, or *telos,* and that certain fundamental interests should be preserved regardless of considerations of cost. In other words, if we are embarking on a piece of research that meets the utilitarian principle, we by no means have carte blanche; we must attend to the interests that follow from the animal's nature—the interest in being free from pain, being housed and fed in accordance with its nature, in exercise and companionship if it is a social animal, and so on. The animal used in research should thus be treated, in Kant's terminology, as an end in itself, not merely as a means or tool.

I therefore argue that the laws should mandate the creation of husbandry and housing systems that allow animals to live lives approximating those dictated by their *telos* to ensure their happiness, as well as the mitigation of their pain and suffering. Precedents for this already exist in the work done on enriched environment for zoo animals. It has been argued, in fact, that animals suffer more from how we keep them than from what we do to them. I believe that the social ethic eventually will move in the direction I have sketched.

12

Pain and Ideology

Pain, as one recent book on the history of anesthesia called it, is "the worst of evils." This is made plain in many ways: People commit suicide to avoid torture; people seek assisted suicide to avoid unalleviable pain and the attendant degradation and loss of self that follow in its wake. One of my friends, a highly successful food-animal veterinarian and department head, has told me that, when he is stricken by lower back pain, he is no longer a veterinarian or academic or administrator. He *is* the pain.

The impact of the second component of scientific ideology—agnosticism or total denial of the scientific reality of subjective awareness, including pain—on human and animal welfare must therefore be recounted to help the reader grasp the full horror of the pernicious effects of scientific ideology.

Obviously, concern about how a person or animal feels—in pain, fearful, threatened, stressed—looms large in the tissue of ethical deliberation. If such feelings and experiences are treated as scientifically unreal—or, at least, as scientifically unknowable—that will serve to eliminate what we may term a major call to ethical deliberation and ethical thought. Insofar as modern science tends to bracket subjectivity as outside its purview, the tendency to ignore ethics is potentiated. For example, in the discussion of

Portions of this chapter are drawn from Bernard E. Rollin, *Science and Ethics* (Cambridge: Cambridge University Press, 2006).

animal research, I have alluded to the absence of pain control until it was mandated by federal legislation.

While this is certainly a function of science's failure to recognize ethical questions in science, society in general (except for issues of overt cruelty) also historically neglected ethical questions about animals. Ordinary people, however, were comfortable in attributing felt pain to animals (a matter of ordinary common sense) and adjusted their behavior accordingly, even though an explicit ethic for animals was not prevalent in society. In fact, no one before Descartes even thought to deny pain in animals. Scientists, however, having been trained out of ordinary common sense regarding animals' subjective experience, were not moved by what non-scientists saw as plainly a matter of pain. Hence, one of my veterinarian colleagues responded to my concern about howling and whining in his experimental surgery dogs by saying, "Oh, that's not pain. It's after-effects of anesthesia." In other words, the denial of the reality (or the scientific knowability) of pain in animals provided yet another vector for ignoring ethics, since ethical concern is so closely linked to recognizing mental states. We shall, surprisingly, shortly document a similar problem in human medicine.

Historically, medicine was, and aspired to be, a combination of science and art. The science component came, of course, from its attempt to develop generalizable, lawlike knowledge that would remain invariant across space and time. Such knowledge was sought regarding the working of the body, the nature of disease, and valid therapeutic regimens, although medicine often fell short of the mark in all of these areas. The element of art was patent in medicine. Art deals with the individual, the unique; with the domain of proper names; with the person, not merely the body; with that which does not lend itself to generalization; with the subjective psychological aspects of a person as well as with the observable. A physician was thus expected to be both lawlike and intuitive, the latter not in any mystical way but, rather, in a manner that is focused on this particular individual and his or her subjectivity and felt experience. In understanding the individual—by definition, unique—all information, whether it consisted of first-person reports or objective measurements, was relevant. In the twentieth century, however, medicine became increasingly viewed in biochemical terms. Biology became reducible to chemistry. This in turn fueled positivistic ideology and the ignoring of the subjective.

In some ways, the physicalization of medicine was a boon to sick people: A science and evidence-based way to develop and test drugs and other therapies for safety and efficacy now existed. But in other ways, it was a detriment. In the first place, how patients felt became significantly subordinated to how they objectively "were." Medical success came to be measured in terms of how long patients lived—alive, not dead—and for how long was an objective parameter that could be quantified.

Cancer medicine provides an excellent example of this view. Oncology was directed at eliminating the tumor and buying a measurable increment in life span, or time before death. Quality of life, suffering attendant on chemotherapy or radiation, loss of dignity in the course of treatment, psychological and economic toll on family were not measures that scientific medicine was wont to adopt. "Buying extra time" was the goal. Yet, as numerous authorities have told us, a patient's concern is primarily about suffering, not about death per se.

In general, people who seek voluntary euthanasia do so because they fear pain, loss of dignity (e.g., of the sort that comes from incontinence), helplessness, dependence, stress on the family. Obviously, they fear such experiences more than they fear death. Yet scientific medicine does not worry about such "hindrances" to prolonging life. In particular, and crucial to the argument in this chapter, felt pain becomes not fully medically real, since it is not observable or objective, or mechanistically definable. In that regard, I vividly recall what one nursing dean told me: "The difference between nurses and doctors is that we worry about *care*; they worry about *cure*." In turn, recall that the institution that has most concerned itself with and done the most for the terminally ill is hospice, and hospice was founded and is dominated by nurses, not by physicians.

In 1973, Richard Marks and Edward Sachar published the seminal "Undertreatment of Medical Inpatients with Narcotic Analgesics" in *Annals of Internal Medicine,* in which they demonstrated that almost three out of four cancer patients studied in two major New York hospitals suffered (unnecessary) moderate to severe pain because of under-medication with readily available narcotic analgesics. Marks and Sachar were psychiatrists brought in to consult on patients who putatively were having a marked emotional reaction to their disease. On examination, they determined that the problem was under-treatment of pain leading to emotional responses rather than psychiatric problems. Although the article received a great deal of attention, this disgraceful state of affairs was confirmed by other studies and by an extraordinary editorial in *Pain* fourteen years later, in 1987, by John Liebeskind and Ron Melzack, two of the world's most eminent pain researchers:

> We are appalled by the needless pain that plagues the people of the world—in rich and poor nations alike. By any reasonable code, freedom from pain should be a basic human right, limited only by our knowledge to achieve it.

> Cancer pain can be virtually abolished in 80–90% of patients by the intelligent use of drugs, yet millions of people suffer daily from cancer pain without receiving adequate treatment. We have the techniques to alleviate many acute and chronic pain conditions, including severe burn pain, labor pain, and postsurgical pain, as well as pains of myofascial and neuropathic origin; but worldwide, these pains are often mismanaged or ignored.
>
> We are appalled, too, by the fact that pain is most poorly managed in those most defenseless against it—the young and the elderly. Children often receive little or no treatment, even for extremely severe pain, because of the myth that they are less sensitive to pain than adults and more easily addicted to pain medication. Pain in the elderly is often dismissed as something to be expected and hence tolerated.
>
> All this needless pain and suffering impoverishes the quality of life of those afflicted and their families; it may even shorten life by impairing recovery from surgery or disease. People suffering severe or unrelenting pain become depressed. They may lose the will to live and fail to take normal health-preserving measures; some commit suicide.
>
> Part of the problem lies with health professionals who fail to administer sufficient doses of opiate drugs for pain of acute or cancerous origin. They may also be unaware of, or unskilled in using, many useful therapies and unable to select the most effective ones for specific pain conditions. Failure to understand the inevitable interplay between psychological and somatic aspects of pain sometimes causes needed treatment to be withheld because the pain is viewed as *merely "psychological."* (1987, 1–2; emphasis added)

The final line of this editorial eloquently buttresses the account I have given of the capture of medicine by a mechanistic and physicalistic ideology that denies reality to subjective experience. Also highly relevant to the subsequent discussion is Liebeskind and Melzack's strong claim that pain is most egregiously ignored in the young and the elderly (i.e., those who are most vulnerable and defenseless).

The fact of ignoring pain is further buttressed in "High Tech Comfort: Ethical Issues in Cancer Pain Management for the 1990s" (Ferrell and Rhiner 1991). According to Ferrell and Rhiner, although pain can be controlled effectively in 90 percent of cancer patients, it is, in fact, not controlled in 80 percent of such patients. An article in *Nursing Standard* by Elizabeth Gray shows that the problem brought to light by Marks and Sachar continued into the new century. Gray affirms that "more recent studies have shown that there has been little improvement over the years" (Gray 1999, 32). Supporting the points made earlier, the author is a nurse, not a doctor.

As pain was seen as medically unreal and subjective, control of pain was historically determined by strange ideological dicta, even after the discovery of anesthesia in the nineteenth century. In *A Calculus of Suffering* (1985), the historian Martin Pernick has shown this point eloquently by comparing hospital records of that time on anesthetic use with ideological pronouncements and finding very high correlations. For example, although affluent white women were generally the class receiving the most anesthesia for most medical procedures, this was not true for childbirth, because it was believed that childbirth pain was divine punishment for Eve's transgression and that women would not bond with the children unless they felt pain. Farmers, sailors, and other members of "macho" professions received very little anesthesia, as did foreigners. Black women, even when being used for painful experiments, received no anesthesia at all. Limb amputation was classified as "minor surgery." Children received more pain control because of their "innocence" (which, as we shall see, has been reversed under current ideology). Worries were expressed that anesthesia gives the doctor too much (sexual) control over the patient. The key point is that pain control even then was more a valuational and ideological decision than a strictly scientific medical one.

Thus, even with regard to anesthesia, precedent existed for odd and arbitrary, ideologically dictated use. Inevitably, given the tendency to see felt pain as scientifically less than real—and, in any case, unverifiable—and further given the ethics-free ideology we have discussed, a morally based dispensation of pain control was unlikely to be regnant.

There is ample evidence for this claim. Gary Walco and colleagues (1994) demonstrated that infants and children (who are, of course, powerless or defenseless in this sense) received less analgesia for the same procedures than did adults undergoing the same procedures in the 1990s. But there is a far more egregious example of the same point in the surgical treatment of neonates—an example that never fails to elicit gasps of horror from audiences when I recount it. This was the practice of doing open-heart surgery on neonates (newborns) without anesthesia, instead using "muscle relaxants" or paralytic drugs such as succinylcholine and pancuronium bromide, until the late 1980s. After surgery, no analgesia was given to control pain.

Let us pause for a moment to explain some key concepts. Anesthesia literally means "without feeling." We are all familiar with general anesthetics, which put a patient to sleep for surgery. With general anesthesia, a person should feel no pain during a procedure. Similarly, local anesthetics, such as Novocain for a dental procedure, remove the feeling of pain from a particular area while procedures such as filling a tooth or sewing up a cut are performed, so the patient is conscious but does not feel pain. Though there are many qualifications to this rough-and-ready definition, they do not interfere with the point here.

Muscle relaxants or paralytics block transmission of nerve impulses across synapses and thus produce flaccid paralysis but not anesthesia. In other words, one can feel pain fully but cannot move, which may, indeed, make pain worse, since pain is augmented by fear. First-person reports by knowledgeable physicians and researchers of paralytic drugs, which paralyze the respiratory muscles so the patient is incapable of breathing on his or her own, recount the terrifying nature of the use of paralytics in conscious humans who are aware of what is happening. Analgesics are drugs that attenuate pain or raise patients' ability to tolerate pain. Examples are aspirin and Tylenol for headaches, morphine, Demerol, and Vicodin. Thus, babies were receiving major open-heart surgery using only paralytic drugs, and they were experiencing countless procedures that ranged from circumcision and venipuncture to frequent heel sticks with no drugs to alleviate pain at all—neither anesthetics nor analgesics.

The public became informed about the open-heart surgery in 1985, when a parent whose child died undergoing this sort of surgery, complained to the medical community, was essentially ignored, and went public supported by some operating-room nurses who felt strongly that babies experienced pain. The resulting public outcry caused the medical community to reexamine the practice and eventually to abolish it.

The reasons anesthesia was ignored in neonates were multiple and familiarly ideological. First, the medical community believed that pain is "subjective" and thus not medically real. Second, since babies do not remember pain, they claimed, pain doesn't matter. Third, it was argued and widely accepted that the neonatal cortex or other parts of the nervous system were insufficiently developed to experience pain. For example, it was said that babies' nerves were insufficiently myelinated for babies to feel pain. Fourth, since all anesthesia is considered "selective poisoning," it was argued that anesthesia was dangerous. Many of the claims on which the objections to anesthesia were based were deftly handled in the classic "Pain and Its Effects in the Human Neonate and Fetus" (Anand and Hickey 1987).

To the first claim that pain is (merely) subjective, the reply is simple: It is equally true for adults, and what is subjective is very real for the one who experiences it. The essence of pain is that it *hurts.* To the claim that forgotten pain doesn't matter, the simple response is that, once experienced, pain is biologically active and retards healing and is immunosuppressive even if it is forgotten. To this day, painful procedures such as bronchoscopy and colonoscopy are often performed under amnesic drugs in adults, who may feel much pain during the procedure but do not remember because the drug is deliberately causing amnesia of the event. Failure to remember does not justify the infliction of pain. Furthermore, babies give evidence of memory when they are brought back to rooms in which they underwent surgery.

Third, Anand and Hickey convincingly debunk the claim that neonates—and even pre-term babies—do not feel pain. There are convincing physiological arguments that both myelination and cortical development in neonates suffice to attribute pain to infants. Behavioral changes also buttress this point.

Fourth, *all* anesthesia is dangerous, particularly when administered to sick people. The key point is that adequate anesthesia regimens exist to tilt the cost–benefit ratio in favor of using anesthesia. In a later paper, Anand and Hickey (1992) showed that neonates given high doses of anesthesia and analgesia for surgery fared better in terms of morbidity (sickness) and mortality than children treated with light anesthesia. They demonstrated that when infants undergoing open-heart surgery were deeply anesthetized and given high doses of opiates for twenty-four hours after the operation, they had a significantly better recovery and significantly fewer postoperative deaths than a group that had received a lighter anesthetic regimen (halothane and morphine) followed postoperatively by intermittent morphine and diazepam for analgesia. The group that received deep anesthesia and profound analgesia "had a decreased incidence of sepsis, metabolic acidosis, and disseminated intravascular coagulation and fewer postoperative deaths (none of the 30 given sufentanil versus 4 of 15 given halothane plus morphine)" (Anand and Hickey 1992, 9).

Anand and Hickey concluded:

> Numerous lines of evidence suggest that even in the human fetus, pain pathways as well as cortical and subcortical centers necessary for pain perception are well developed late in gestation, and the neurochemical systems now known to be associated with pain transmission and modulation are intact and functional. Physiologic responses to painful stimuli have been well documented in neonates of various gestational ages and are reflected in hormonal, metabolic, and cardiorespiratory changes *similar to but greater than* those observed in adult subjects. Other responses in newborn infants are suggestive of integrated emotional and behavioral responses to pain and are retained in memory long enough to modify subsequent behavior patterns. In decisions about the use of these techniques, current knowl-

> edge suggests that humane considerations should apply as forcefully to the care of neonates and young, nonverbal infants as they do to children and adults in similar painful and stressful situations. (1987, 1329; emphasis added)

It is interesting to note that, as in the case of pain in animals, the scientific "reappropriation of common sense" about infants' pain occurred only at the instigation of, and subsequent to, public moral outrage about standard practice.

The powerful and sensitive article "Pain, Hurt and Harm: The Ethics of Pain Control in Infants and Children" (Walco, Cassidy, and Schechter 2004) reviews and criticizes some of the major arguments leading to withholding pain control from children and infants, echoing points made by Anand and Hickey (1987, 1992). These include the subjectivity of pain, the belief that children are not reliable reporters of pain, the failure to recognize individual differences in children (despite solid scientific evidence to the contrary), misinformation about the neurologic capacity to feel pain, and the "no memory" argument. Recent evidence indicates that the last point is particularly egregious: that not only does unrelieved pain disturb eating, sleeping, and arousal in the neonate but also "infants retain a memory of previous experience, and their response to a subsequent painful experience is altered" (Lee 2002, 233–237) and failure to control pain in infants leads to aberrant nerve growth, causing additional pain later in life (Beggs 2003).

Walco and his colleagues also raise and refute the claim that opioid analgesics cause respiratory depression or arrest. They point out that "the risk of narcotic induced respiratory depression in adults is about 0.09 percent, whereas in children it ranges between 0 percent and 1.3 percent" (Walco, Cassidy, and Schechter 2004). In most cases, the problem is solved by reducing the dosage, and opiate overdoses can be reversed. They also indicate that fully 39 percent of physicians worry about creating addicts by using opioids, yet this concern is baseless, with "virtually no risk of addiction associated with the administration of narcotics" (Walco, Cassidy, and Schechter 2004). Another set of arguments affirms that masking pain masks symptoms (a very common reason given for not using analgesia in children and in animals in veterinary medicine), an absurd claim regarding major postoperative surgical pain. An additional argument affirms that "pain builds character," again an absurd argument in an infant or a suffering child. As Walco and his colleagues declared, "If there is a therapeutic benefit from a child's pain, one must be exquisitely economical with it" (Walco, Cassidy, and Schechter 2004).

The conclusion of "Pain, Hurt, and Harm" is as morally sensitive and powerful as the rest of the article:

> There are now published guidelines for the management of pain in children, which are based on recent data. However, guidelines and continuing medical education do not necessarily alter physicians' behavior. Specific administrative interventions are required. For example, hospitals may include standards for the assessment and management of pain as part of their quality-assurance programs. The Joint Commission on Accreditation of Healthcare Organizations has established standards for pain management. To meet such standards, multidisciplinary teams must develop specific treatment protocols with the goal of reducing children's pain and distress. In addition, pressure from parents and the legal community is likely to affect clinical practice.
>
> All health professionals should provide care that reflects the technological growth of the field. The assessment and treatment of pain in children are important parts of pediatric practice, and failure to provide adequate control of pain amounts to substandard and unethical medical practice. (Walco, Cassidy, and Schechter 2004, 544)

Many of the points made in "Pain, Hurt, and Harm" have direct implications for other areas where pain is neglected. For example, large portions of the medical community have steadfastly opposed the use of narcotics in terminally ill patients on the dubious grounds that such patients may become addicted. The first response for people who have a short time to live, is, of course, "So what if they become addicted? These drugs are cheap." In any case, the medical community's ignorance in this area is appalling, as Walco, Cassidy, and Schechter (2004, 543) reveal:

> It is essential to distinguish between physical dependence (a physiologically determined state in which symptoms of withdrawal would occur if the medication were not administered) and addiction (a psychological obsession with the drug). Addiction to narcotics is rare among adults treated for disease-related pain and appears to depend more on psychosocial factors than on the disease or medically prescribed administration of narcotics. Studies of children treated for pain associated with sickle cell disease or postoperative recovery have found virtually no risk of addiction associated with the administration of narcotics. There are no known physiologic or psychological characteristics of children that make them more vulnerable to addiction than adults.

Large numbers of physicians also are vehemently opposed to the medical use of marijuana. It appears that such physicians have gullibly bought into simplistic government "One shot and you're hooked" propaganda about drugs and addiction. In fact, many soldiers in Vietnam were regular users of heroin; when they no longer found themselves in stressful situations after returning home, they gave up the drug use and were not addicted. Again, we see ideology trump both science and reason—in this case, the ideology that underlies U.S. drug policy.

Another glaring example of medicine's ignoring of subjective states can be found in the history of the drug ketamine. This illustration is particularly valuable in that it demonstrates the cavalier attitude that has obtained (and, indeed, still obtains) with regard to negative subjective experiences in humans and animals. Ketamine is a cousin of phencyclidine (also known as PCP), which was developed in the 1950s but was found to be very dangerous because it caused hallucinations, violent behavior, confusion, and delusions and because it could easily be abused. Various derivatives of PCP were tried until 1965, when ketamine was found to be most promising. In 1970, it was released for clinical use in humans in the United States.

Ketamine was heralded as the "ideal" anesthetic because overdose was virtually impossible and the drug did not cause respiratory depression. Furthermore, it could be administered via intravenous, intramuscular, oral, rectal, or nasal routes. Ketamine is profoundly analgesic (pain relieving) for somatic, or body, pain, though it is of no use for visceral (gut) pain. It has been particularly useful in human medicine for treating burn patients and changing dressings.

In the 1980s, while researching a paper on animals' pain, I looked at ketamine in some detail. In the first place, I found that it was used very frequently in research as a sole surgical anesthetic in small rodents and other animals and in veterinary practice as a standard "anesthetic" for spays. Since it is emphatically not viscerally analgesic, this meant that in such procedures it was being used as a restraint drug. (We encountered this in the story about the atrocious lab in which cats were fed cream and visceral surgery was done using ketamine.) Under ketamine, animals are "disassociated"—they experience a strong feeling of disassociation from the environment—and are immobilized in terms of voluntary movement. When I watched a visceral surgery on a cat done with ketamine, I could see obvious signs of pain—jerking, vocalizing—when the viscera were cut or manipulated. In essence, this means that when ketamine alone was used for visceral procedures, the animals felt pain but were immobilized.

In human medicine, ketamine was used for a wide variety of somatic procedures, such as the changing of burn dressings and plastic surgery. But by 1973, the medical community had become aware that ketamine was capable of engendering significantly "bad trips" in a certain percentage of patients, though many experienced pleasant hallucinations. A watershed contributing to this awareness was a letter published in *Anesthesiology* in 1973 in which Robert Johnstone, an anesthesiologist, graphically described his own experiences as a research subject under ketamine. It is important to stress that Johnstone had taken several different narcotics and sedatives before the ketamine experience and had had no problems. His experience with ketamine, however, was quite different:

> I have given ketamine anesthesia and observed untoward psychic reactions, but was not concerned about this possibility when the study began. After my experience, I dropped out of the study, which called for two more exposures of ketamine. In the several weeks since my ketamine trip, I have experienced no flashbacks or bad dreams. Still I am afraid of ketamine. I doubt I will ever take it again because I fear permanent psychologic damage. Nor will I give ketamine to a patient as his sole anesthetic agent. (Johnstone 1973, 460–461)

Here is Johnstone's description of what occurred:

> My first memory is of colors. I saw red everywhere, then a yellow square on the left grew and crowded out the red. My vision faded, to be replaced by a black and white checkerboard which zoomed to and from me. More patterns appeared and faded, always in focus, with distinct edges and bright colors.
>
> Gradually I realized my mind existed and could think. I wondered, "What am I?" and "Where am I?" I had no consciousness of existing in a body; I was a mind suspended in space. At times I was at the center of the earth in Ohio (my former home), on a spaceship or in a small brightly-colored room without doors or window. I had no control over where my mind floated. Periods of thinking alternated with pure color hallucinations.
>
> Then I remembered the drug study and reasoned something had gone wrong. I remembered a story about a man who was awake during a resuscitation and lived to describe his experience. "Am I dying or already dead?" I was not afraid, I was more curious. "This is death. I am a soul, and I am going to wherever souls go." During this period I was observed to sit up, stare and then lie down.
>
> "Don't leak around the mouthpiece!" were the first real sounds I heard. I couldn't respond because I didn't have a body. Thus began my cycling into and out of awareness—a frightening experience. I perceived the laboratory as the intensive care unit; this meant some-

> thing had gone wrong. I wanted to know how bad things were. I now realized I wasn't thinking properly. I recognized voices, then I recognized people. I saw some people who weren't really there. I heard people talking, but could not understand them. The only sentence I remember is "Are you all right?" Observers reported a panicked look and defensive thrashing of my arms. I screamed "They're after me!" and "They're going to get me!" I don't recall this or remember the reassurances given me.
>
> I then became aware of my body. My right arm seemed withered and my left very long. I could not focus my eyes. Observers reported marked nystagmus (jerky eye movements). I recognized the ceiling, but thought it was covered with worms (apparently cued by the irregular depressions in the soundproof blocks). I desperately wanted to know what was reality and to be part of it. I seemed to be thinking at a normal rate, but couldn't determine my circumstances. I couldn't speak or communicate, but once, recognizing a friend next to me, I hugged him until I faded back to abstractness.
>
> The investigators gave me diazepam, 20 mg, and thiopental, 150 mg, intravenously because I was obviously anxious, and I fell asleep. When I awoke it was five hours since I had received ketamine. I promptly vomited bilious liquid. Although I could focus accurately, I walked unsteadily to the bathroom. I assured everyone "I'm OK now." Suddenly I cried with tears for no reason. I knew I was crying but could not control myself. I fell asleep again for several hours. When I awoke I talked rationally, was emotionally stable and felt hungry. The next day I had a headache and felt weak, similar to the hangover from alcohol, but functioned normally. (1973, 460–461)

Today, of course, ketamine (known by the street name "Special K") is classified as a Schedule III highly controlled drug, not only because it is widely abused but also because it has become a rape drug in virtue of the immobility and "paralysis of will" it produces. And there are countless examples in literature of vivid depictions of bad ketamine trips going back to 1973. (Animals, too, may have bad experiences. As one of my friends who is a veterinary anesthesiologist puts it, "Most cats see little pink mice, but some see giant menacing pink rats.") An additional troubling dimension of ketamine use became known at that time: the tendency of the drug to produce unpredictable "flashbacks," much in the manner of LSD.

When researching this in 1985, my main interest was ketamine's use in animals. I therefore approached some world-renowned colleagues in veterinary anesthesia, who confirmed, first of all, its misuse for visceral surgery. I then asked about "bad trips." There was no literature on this, I was told, but such occurrences were obvious to observers. Nevertheless, I have never seen any discussion in the veterinary literature of bad trips. Similarly, there is no literature on deviant behavior indicating possible flashbacks in animals, but I have been told about owners who have reported complete personality changes in animals after ketamine dosing, one woman claiming that the hospital had given her back the wrong animal. The failure of veterinary medicine even to discuss such potential problems eloquently attests to the perceived irrelevance of animals' bad subjective experiences to scientific veterinary medicine.

Continuing my research on ketamine in 1985–1986, I was curious about how its use had changed since the revelations in 1973 of bad trips and flashbacks. Much to my amazement, I found that ketamine was largely being used by the medical profession "on the very young (children) and the very old (the elderly)." For the next few months, I searched the anesthesia literature—journals and textbooks—to find out what unique physiological traits were common to the very young and the very old that made ketamine a viable drug at these extremes but not for people in the middle. I got nowhere. Finally, by sheer coincidence, I happened to attend a party with an anesthesiologist who treats humans and asked him about the differing physiologies. He burst out laughing. "Physiology?" he intoned. "The use has nothing to do with physiology. It's just that the old and the young can't sue and have no power." In other words, their bad subjective experiences don't matter. This was confirmed by one of my students, who had had a rare disease since birth that was treated at a major research center. He told me that procedures were performed under ketamine, which he had loathed because of the "bad trips." When he turned sixteen, he was told, "Ketamine won't work anymore."

If there ever was a beautiful illustration of ideological, amoral, cynical denial of medical relevance of subjective experience in human and veterinary medicine, it is this account of ketamine. Unfortunately, there is more to relate on this issue. I now turn to the definition of pain given by the International Association for the Study of Pain (IASP), which was widely disseminated until it was finally revised in 2001 to mitigate some of the absurdity I discuss here.

The IASP is the world's largest and most influential organization devoted to the study of pain. Yet its official definition of pain claimed that infants, animals, and non-linguistic humans did not feel pain. In 1998, I was asked to criticize the official definition of pain, which I felt was morally outrageous in its exclusion of these groups and in reinforcing the ideological denial of subjective experience to a large number of beings to whom we have moral obligations. Leaving such a definition to affirm the scientific community's stance on felt pain was a matter that caused moral mischief and, ultimately, a loss of scientific credibility. The discussion that follows is drawn from my remarks at the IASP convention in 1998 and a subsequent essay published in *Pain Forum* (Rollin 1999).

It is a major irony that although the definition of pain adopted by the IASP was cast into its current form for laudable moral reasons, it has given succor to neo-Cartesian tendencies in science and medicine, and, in fact, has the potential for supporting morally problematic behavior. Harold Merskey, a principal architect of the definition, explained at the American Pain Society meeting in San Diego in 1998 that the initial definition of pain as "an unpleasant sensory and emotional experience associated with actual or potential tissue damage, or described in terms of such damage" was later modified in a note to allow for the reality of pain in adult humans where there was no organic cause for the pain and no evident tissue damage. The IASP's Web site affirms:

> Pain is always subjective. Each individual learns the application of the word through experiences related to injury in early life.
>
> Many people report pain in the absence of tissue damage or any likely pathophysiological cause: Usually this happens for psychological reasons. There is usually no way to distinguish their experience from that due to tissue damage if we take the subjective report. If they regard their experience as pain and if they report it in the same ways as pain caused by tissue damage, it should be accepted as pain.

In other words, linguistic self-reports of pain should be accepted as proof of the existence of genuine pain in linguistically competent beings, a move designed to encourage medical attention to pain even in the absence of a proximate stimulus involving tissue damage. This was clearly a praiseworthy, morally motivated move, which also spurred research into areas such as chronic pain that might have been ignored in the absence of a definition stressing the subjective side of pain and its linguistic articulation.

Unfortunately, however, the definition's emphasis on the connection between pain and full linguistic competence has led to a neo-Cartesian tendency to make such linguistic competence a necessary and sufficient condition for attributing pain to a being. (Descartes had famously argued that only creatures with language could be said to possess mind.) "Mere" behavior that is nonlinguistic, such as a moan or withdrawal of limb, does not license the confident or certain attribution of pain to an organism, because only words evidence the subjective. As Merskey said, "The behavior mentioned in the definition is behavior that describes the subjective state and that is how matters should remain." Merskey has also stated:

> The very words "pain behavior" are often employed as a means to distinguish between external responses and the subjective condition. I am in sympathy with Anand and Craig in their wish to recognize that such types of behaviour are likely to indicate the presence of a subjective experience, but the behavior cannot be incorporated sensibly in the definition of a subjective event. (1996, 209)

Despite Merskey's professed belief that "there is an almost overwhelming probability that some speechless organisms suffer pain, including neonates, infants and adults with dementia" (he does not mention animals), he nonetheless classifies such pain as "probable" or "inferred," in contradistinction to the certainty that accompanies claims by linguistic beings (1996, 209). This ultimately creates a large ontological and epistemological gulf between linguistic and nonlinguistic beings in relation to the presence and certainty of experienced pain. This, in turn, helps to justify the well-documented tendency of researchers and clinicians to under-treat or fail to treat altogether pain in neonates, infants, young children, and animals, all of whom lack full linguistic ability.

It is thus disturbing to find a neo-Cartesian element infiltrating these discussions of pain, suggesting that only linguistic beings are capable of experiencing pain as something of which they are aware and that only verbal reports allow us to "really" know that a being is in pain. Aside from the ethical damage that such a view can create by implying that animals, neonates, and prelinguistic infants do not "really feel pain," promulgation of this view is dangerous to the methodological assumptions underlying science, as well as to scientific credibility in society in general.

The thesis that only linguistic beings can *feel pain* or be aware of pain or give us evidence that they have pain is precisely such a metaphysical thesis, to which no amount of data is ultimately relevant. To illustrate the methodological pitfalls inherent in such a view, consider the thesis once raised by Bertrand Russell: How do we know that the world was not, in fact, created 10 seconds ago, complete with fossils, etc. and us with all of our memories? Or better yet, consider the following critique of the very possibility of science: Look here. Science claims to give us explanations of phenomena that take place in the physical world we all share. Yet, in point of fact, our only access to the real physical world is through our experiences, our perceptions, which are totally *subjective,* unique to each perceiver. After all, it is notorious that I can't know what you perceive. You may not see red as I do or hear sounds as I do. How, then, do we ever get to an "objective" world by summing a whole bunch of inherently subjective perceptions and experiences?

This, of course, is an argument for solipsism that few if any scientists worry about when they attempt to explain the nature and causes of disease, earthquakes, atomic and subatomic phenomena, mind, and so forth. Why don't they worry about it? Because both of the concerns described above, like the existence of God or of an immaterial soul, are ultimately *metaphysical* hypotheses that can never be refuted or confirmed by gathering data or doing experiments, and scientific activity is archetypically tethered, however indirectly, to what can be confirmed by observation and experiment.

We all recognize that when we judge that another person feels pain, we are making a fallible claim. The person (i.e., the linguistic being) may be malingering, faking, or acting. So we seek other evidence: signs of injury, knowledge that the injury or condition in question produces pain generally. We check our ability to lessen the pain with anesthetics or analgesics; we look for involuntary moans and groans that the person may emit when fully or partially asleep. Like all empirical claims, judgments that someone is in pain are in principle falsifiable. The presence of language is certainly not definitive, as language can be used to mislead and befuddle, as well as to inform. In practicing science or medicine, we go with the weight of evidence: the presence of inflammation, guarding of a limb, change in pallor, reluctance to eat, and so forth. No scientist of any credibility would affirm that he or she is withholding judgment that another person feels pain in such circumstances just because the scientist cannot, in principle, feel the same feeling the other person experiences, or perhaps does not at all. In good scientific fashion, one goes with the weight of evidence, not with skepticism based in untestable metaphysical possibilities. Doing the latter would be exactly like a scientist's rejecting another scientist's experimental data solely on the grounds of the metaphysical claim that he or she cannot be sure that the other person perceives at all, or perceives as we do, because we cannot experience their perception.

If science proceeds, then, by weight of empirical evidence in general and in the attribution of felt pain in particular and does not allow theses based in metaphysical possibilities of solipsism (e.g., lack of absolute certainty that anyone else perceives as I do), then it is equally a major logical error to deny felt pain to nonlinguistic beings a priori, regardless of what physiological, behavioral, factual, or theoretical evidence exists to vouch for such felt pain.

Certainly, that evidence is abundant in our experience with animals—so much so that ordinary experience, common sense, and language do not infer (or reason) that an animal is in pain but perceive it immediately. If a dog is run over by a car, is not unconscious, has a compound fracture jutting out of his skin and a crushed limb, is howling and whining and shivering, we automatically assume he is in pain. If someone asks, "But how do you know?" we assume that he is either demented or making a bad joke.

No one knows better than pain scientists that this powerful, unshakeable, common-sense response is strongly buttressed by myriad scientific evidence such as the following: that animals' pain physiology and neuroanatomy is essentially the same as humans' well down the phylogenetic scale; that pain biochemistry, including the emergence of endogenous opiates after trauma and the presence of such chemicals as bradykinin and substance P in painful areas, is similarly phylogenetically continuous; that pain behavior and signs of pain, while certainly different in some marked ways across species, is no more different than it is across human cultures and subcultures and is very similar in many ways (punch a Doberman pinscher, a tiger, a buffalo, a shark, and a gangbanger in the mouth and see the reaction; if you still doubt me, recall the guarding of limbs across species and such); that Darwinian evolutionary continuity makes the emergence of felt pain in humans alone highly suspect, especially given these similarities; that if animals did not feel pain, they could not serve as pain models for humans in pain and analgesia studies; that anesthetics and analgesics seem to have the same beneficial effects on animals as in humans, from quieting signs of suffering to accelerating healing; and that preemptive analgesia works the same in humans and (at least) in other mammals.

Indeed, let us recall that one eminent pain physiologist, the late Ralph Kitchell, co-editor of the American Physiological Society's symposium volume on animal pain, argued for the possibility that animals in general *feel* pain more acutely than humans. According to Kitchell, response to pain is divided into a sensory-discriminative dimension and a motivational-affective dimension (in Rollin and Kesel 1990). The former is concerned with locating and understanding the source of pain, its intensity, and the danger with which it is correlated; the latter is concerned with escaping from the painful stimulus. Kitchell speculates that since animals are more limited than humans in the first dimension, since they lack human intellectual abilities, it is plausible to think that the second dimension is correlatively stronger as a compensatory mechanism. In short, since animals cannot deal intellectually with danger and injury as we do, their motivation to flee must be correlatively stronger than ours. In a word, they probably hurt more.

There is no question in my mind that what we call language is unique to humans, and, very speculatively, something approximating language to a few other species, perhaps great apes and dolphins. That does not mean, however, as Descartes and our current Cartesians conclude, that language is the only sure way we can know that a being is in pain or feels fear, anxiety, distress, joy, sexual excitement, and other fundamental and basic modes of awareness. I argued in *Natural and Conventional Meaning: An Examination of the Distinction* (1976) against the traditional belief that there is a clear and unbridgeable gulf between the sort of meaning we find in natural signs (e.g., clouds mean rain or smoke means fire) and the sort of meaning we find in conventional (or manmade) signs (e.g., the word "cloud" in English means "visible condensed water droplets"). As the philosopher George Berkeley affirmed, nature is full of meaning, and science, in his metaphor, can be viewed as learning to read the language of nature. Animals, although presumably lacking language, find meaning in the world (e.g., a scent meaning prey) and impart meaning to other animals and humans (e.g., threats).

It is possible to suggest that a being with language can communicate better about the nature of pain than one who lacks language, but even if this is true, it does not mean that one cannot communicate the presence and intensity of pain without language through natural signs. Recall that language does not help us much in describing our pain to others; verbal reports are notoriously unreliable. Recall, too, that in addition to helping us communicate, language helps us prevaricate and conceal. The posture and whimpering of an injured animal or the groans of an injured person are, in my mind, far more reliable indicators of the presence and intensity of pain than are mere verbal reports. Let us further recall that the natural signs we share with animals are far more eloquent and persuasive signs of primordial states of consciousness such as love, lust, fear, and pain than is Shakespearean English. Words fail in the most fundamental and critical areas (as when a physician asks you to describe your pain).

It has sometimes been suggested that the possession of linguistic concepts is related to pain in the following way: Only a being with language, and the temporal concepts provided by language, can project ahead into the future or backward into the past. Much of our pain is associated with such projection: The pain of a visit to the dentist is surely intensified by the magnified recollections of previous pain, filtered through imaginative anticipations of horrific future scenarios informed by having seen the movie *Marathon Man,* wherein one's dentist turns out (literally) to be a Nazi war criminal. In the absence of concepts of past and future, animals cannot recollect or anticipate, being, as it were, stuck in the now. Thus, the claim is that their pain is considerably more trivial than ours.

Aside from the obvious objections—if animals have no access to the past, how can they learn (which they clearly do)? If animals have no concept of the future, how can a dog beg for food or a cat wait patiently for a mouse (which they clearly do)?—a much more profound issue is raised by this argument. If animals are, indeed, inexorably locked into what is happening in the here and now, as the argument suggests, we are all the more obliged to try to relieve their suffering, because they cannot look forward to or anticipate its cessation or even remember, however dimly, its absence. If they are in pain, their whole universe is pain. There is no horizon; they are their pain. So if this argument is, indeed, correct, then animals' pain is terrible to contemplate, for the dark universe of animals logically cannot tolerate any glimmer of hope within its borders.

In less dramatic and more philosophical terms, Spinoza pointed out that understanding the cause of an unpleasant sensation diminishes its severity and that, by the same token, not understanding its cause can increase its severity. Common sense readily supports this conjecture. Indeed, this is something we have all experienced with lumps, bumps, headaches, and, most famously, suspected heart attacks that turned out to be gas pains. Spinoza's conjecture is thus borne out by common experience and by more formal research. But this would be reason to believe that animals, especially laboratory animals, suffer more severely than humans, since they have no grasp of the cause of their pain. Thus, even if they can anticipate some things, they have no ability to anticipate the cessation of pain experiences outside their normal experience.

We further know that humans who cannot feel pain, even though they have the full nociceptive machinery, do not fare well as far as survival is concerned. Whether the inability to feel pain is a genetic anomaly or a result of diseases such as Hansen's disease (leprosy) or diabetes, such humans lose limbs, contract infection, and have truncated lives. Is it really plausible to suggest that all animals without language are permanently in that state? And if they are, how do they thrive?

One final argument against making the possession of language a necessary condition for feeling pain: The philosopher Thomas Reid pointed out, quite reasonably, that since babies are not born as linguistic beings, they must acquire language. Even if Noam Chomsky is correct that the skeleton for language is innate, it must still be actualized by experience of some language. This in turn entails the requirement that people be capable of experience before they have language or else they could not learn it (or actualize their innate capacity for it). But if nonlinguistic (or prelinguistic) experience is possible, surely one of the most plausible candidates for such experience is pain, first because it is so essential to survival and second because we have so much evidence (discussed earlier) that nonlinguistic beings, in fact, experience pain. For all of these reasons, then, including linguistic ability in the requirements for feeling pain or attributing pain to another represents a combination of bad science and bad philosophy.

I went on to argue that this definition leads to bad ethics among scientists in ignoring the treatment of pain in nonlinguistic beings and to a bad picture of science to society, something very undesirable at a historical moment wherein society has lost its old, utopian confidence in science and scientists. Presumably, some sense of the moral and political climate drove the IASP to modify its definition of pain in 2001 in a minimalistic way. In a note, the definition now affirms that "the inability to communicate verbally does not negate the *possibility* that an individual is experiencing pain and is in need of appropriate pain-relieving treatment" (emphasis added). This sounds far more like a concession to political reality than the embracing of a major conceptual upheaval.

In any event, the attitude revealed in the IASP's original definition is perfectly consonant with what we have documented about human pain and, given the situation with human pain, the reader can guess how cavalierly animals' pain was treated. The absence of discussions of felt pain in animals in veterinary and science texts has already been mentioned, as has the total absence of a literature on analgesia. It is surprising to members of the general public that veterinarians were as ignorant and skeptical about animals' consciousness, even their pain, as any scientist. To this day, and certainly in the 1980s, veterinarians called anesthesia "chemical restraint" or "sedation" and performed many procedures, such as castration of horses, using physical restraint—what was jocularly called "bruticaine"—or using paralytic drugs such succinylcholine chloride, a curariform drug that induces flaccid paralysis and is not an anesthetic. Indeed, one veterinary surgeon told me that, until he taught with me, it never dawned on him that the horse being castrated under succinyl hurt. This sort of absurdity also occurred in physiological psychology. I have already mentioned the psychological community's rejection of animals' consciousness. Yet the same community regularly performed stereotaxic brain surgery and brain stimulation using succinylcholine without anesthesia, because the psychologists wanted the animals "conscious."

I personally experienced the following illustrative incident. In the mid-1980s, I was having dinner with a group of senior veterinary scientists, and the conversation turned to the subject of this chapter—namely, scientific ideology's disavowal of our ability to talk meaningfully about animals' consciousness, thought, and awareness. A famous dairy scientist became quite heated. "It's absurd to deny animal consciousness," he exclaimed loudly. "My dog thinks, makes decisions and plans, etc., etc.," which he proceeded to exemplify with the kind of anecdotes we all invoke in such commonsense discussions. When he finally stopped, I turned to him and asked, "How about your dairy cows? . . . [D]o they have conscious awareness and thought?" "Of course not," he snapped, and then reddened as he realized the clash between ideology and common sense and what a strange universe this would be if the only conscious beings were humans and dogs—perhaps humans and *his* dog.

A colleague who was a doctoral candidate in anesthesiology in the mid-1980s was studying anesthesia in horses. The project involved subjecting animals to painful stimuli and seeing which drugs best controlled the pain response. When she wrote up her results, her committee did not allow her to say that she "hurt" the animals; nor could she say that the drugs controlled the pain. That was ideologically forbidden. She was compelled to say that she subjected them to a stimulus and to describe how the drugs changed the response.

Many rationalizations were ingrained in researchers and veterinarians that buttressed the formidable ideological denial of pain in animals. For example, it was dogma among surgeons that the whimpering, shivering, and crying that I saw as indicative of pain in postsurgical animals was not pain at all but aftereffects of anesthesia. When pressing for analgesia, I was told that the pain was necessary to keep animals still after surgery or injury. In actual fact, of course, animals are smart enough to avoid exertion when sick or injured. It is humans who keep working or playing. Furthermore, as we know from our own experiences of analgesia, it does not eliminate pain; rather, it raises our pain-tolerance threshold so that we do not suffer as much.

Still others affirmed that cattle did not need postsurgical pain control because they "eat right after surgery" and thus could not possibly be in pain. Because of such stoic behavior, some veterinarians still do spays (and, of course, castrations) on cattle with no anesthesia. The answer, of course, is that stoic behavior does not prove that the animals are not feeling pain. We need to recall that cattle are a prey species, and in nature, herds of cattle are always accompanied by circling predators, ever vigilant to signs of weakness or debilitation. Any cow, therefore, that does not behave normally when in pain will quickly be killed by a predator.

It was claimed that dogs did not hurt after abdominal surgery for anatomical reasons: Their viscera are suspended in a mesenteric sling. Similarly, one heard that dogs were alert and wagging their tails after surgery, so they surely did not hurt. Various researchers have done much to dispel such myths. The veterinarian Bernie Hansen has regularly pointed out that the presence of humans in a postsurgical ward significantly skews the animals' behavior and that one sees a different story when one videotapes the animals in the absence of humans. In one particularly dramatic videotape, Hansen shows a Malamute dog who had experienced major disk surgery, yet, in the presence of people, sat up putatively bright and alert and never even lay down to rest. The taping provided dramatic new evidence. When people were not present, the dog would involuntarily start to sink into a sleeping position. But his back hurt so much that any attempt to lie down would awaken him, as demonstrated by a pathetic series of cries and whimpers.

The federal legislation did much to eliminate agnosticism about, and denial of, felt pain in research animals and to force the use of analgesia even by those who remain agnostic, federal law being one of the few levers powerful enough to overturn ideology. Papers on analgesia and pain have proliferated, and in general the analgesia requirements are quite well enforced by Institutional Animal Care and Use Committees. Since most veterinarians in academe do research, they have communicated the need for and methods of pain control to their students, who in turn take this knowledge, plus the social-ethical imperative to control pain, into their jobs after they graduate.

Equally important, with the extraordinary augmentation of the emotional role that companion animals play in people's lives, public demand for pain control for their animals has become loud and forceful. This not only has forced veterinarians in practice to set aside their denial of pain; it has again led to increased academic attention to pain control. Once again, social ethics drives transcendence of ideology.

In addition, a huge market for pain control in animals suddenly emerged, and the drug companies were not slow to acknowledge it. Particularly relevant to this discussion is the story of Pfizer and Rimadyl, the trade name for carprofen, a non-steroidal anti-inflammatory drug used for analgesia in skeletomuscular problems. Originally developed as a human drug, carprofen showed no great advantages over other anti-inflammatories and thus was not marketed. However, someone at Pfizer thought of trying it on dogs, where it gave spectacular pain-control results. Pfizer began a successful advertising campaign showing older dogs unable to romp because of arthritis and other skeletomuscular pain and affirming that Rimadyl could control such pain. Shortly thereafter, I was approached by representatives of Pfizer who told me that the biggest obstacle to marketing the drug was veterinarians, whose ideology-based denial of animals' felt pain prevented them from prescribing pain control. In what was surely a first for a philosopher, I worked with Pfizer to help lay bare these ideological presuppositions and overcome them. In the end, it is rumored, Pfizer sold close to a billion dollars' worth of Rimadyl in one year soon after the drug was marketed.

One can argue that, in terms of rate of change, the control of animal pain probably proliferated far more rapidly than what we have indicated about human pain. I largely credit the federal law and the animal research community, who "recollected" common sense and common decency about animals' pain when faced with the law. With no law driving control of pain in babies, children, or the disenfranchised, change has been slower. However, aggressive social concern about pain has increased attention to it. Both human and veterinary medicine now specifically address pain management in the process of accrediting hospitals.

One need only look at the over-the-counter medications for sale in any pharmacy to realize that, at present, we are not a culture that makes a virtue of stoic endurance of pain and suffering. This is not only true of physical pain: Commercials relentlessly press mood-altering drugs, male erectile enhancers, and cures for the "heartbreak of toenail fungus" (I am not making this up). The Spartan ideal of stolid acquiescence while a fox disembowels you is a source of amazement in all but farm kids, athletes, and some military professionals. Pectoral implants and calf implants, simulating musculature in men without the hard work, are among the fastest-growing procedures in plastic surgery.

Although I cannot prove this claim, it seems fairly evident that the neglect of felt pain in human and veterinary medicine has drawn people to alternative medicine. Alternative practitioners, if nothing else, are generally highly sympathetic and empathetic. Whether their treatment modalities work or not, they project care and concern, which people sometimes forget is not a substitute for effective treatment. Purveyors of effective treatment, possessed by scientific ideology, may be guilty of lack of empathy and may focus only on the disease. The result is an extraordinary groundswell of support for alternative medicine, including modalities that have been shown not to work or that cannot possibly work (e.g., the practice of homeopathy in which medicine diluted to the point where not a single molecule of medication remains is claimed to have a "memory" that effects a cure) if modern science is true.

This may appear unintelligible to scientists—after all, how can people opt for what doesn't work over what works? The key point, though, is to remember what people mean by "what works." When ordinary people say assuredly that someone is a "good doctor" or a "good vet," they do not mean that they have studied the practitioners' cure rate or educational credentials. They mean that the practitioner is empathetic and seems to *care.* Thus, it is obviously not enough for scientific medicine to do well on double-blind clinical trials. It must also meet socio-ethical demand for empathy and control of pain and suffering. And this, of course, means that it must abandon scientific ideology's ignoring or bracketing of subjective states as irrelevant. It does not mean, in my opinion, trying uneasily to coexist with non-evidence-based alternative medicine.

One final issue needs to be discussed. Recall that the federal laboratory animal laws that forced what I have called the "reappropriation of common sense" on pain also contained a proviso mandating control of "distress." Beginning in 1985, however, the U.S. Department of Agriculture (USDA), in writing regulations interpreting the act, focused exclusively on pain, thereby upsetting many activists. In my view, this was extremely wise, though not necessarily intentionally so. The point is that the USDA has now begun to look at distress but is doing so after the acceptance of pain has become axiomatic. Had it demanded control of pain and distress from the beginning, little progress would have been made in either category, the dual task appearing far too formidable to allow for progress on either front.

The situation is quite different now. I recently attended a conference of experts on how to deal with "distress." The preliminary discussion illuminated a fascinating *Leitmotif* common to many participants. "While pain is tangible, very easy to get hold of," the argument went, "distress is far more amorphous and opaque." I was genuinely amused by this and altered my keynote address to acknowledge the source of my amusement. "Almost twenty-five years ago exactly," I said, "I attended a very similar conference on pain, sponsored by the same people. At that time, I argued that animals felt pain and that their pain could be known to us and controlled. . . . [An official with the National Institutes of Health] was there and said nothing but called the dean of my school to tell him that I was a 'viper in the bosom of biomedicine' and students should not be exposed to my ideas. The point is that felt pain was as remote and outlandish to scientific ideology then as distress seems to be today." I also pointed out that if five hundred million dollars were made available for distress research, it would not go begging and unclaimed. The distress issue, too, is simply reappropriating ordinary common sense regarding negative mental states or emotions in animals, such as fear, boredom, loneliness, social isolation, and anxiety, and then providing science-based clarification of these concepts and their operational meaning and criteria for identifying them. I am morally certain that in twenty-five years, distress, in retrospect, will look as transparent as pain.

13

Biotechnology

At about the same time that I was working on the laboratory animal laws during the late 1970s and early to mid-1980s, biotechnology was emerging as a major scientific modality and powerful tool for doing research and changing the nature of life itself. I was fortunate to get in on the ground floor of ethical discussion regarding a field that many feel will dwarf the computer in terms of changing our lives.

In 1985, I received a call from J. Warren Evans, a dean of agriculture at Texas A&M University, who asked me to keynote the first international congress ever held on the genetic engineering of animals, convened at the University of California, Davis. I was very excited by the challenge, as I knew very little about biotechnology but felt that it was an innovation that could rival—or, indeed, surpass—the computer in terms of shaping our lives and future. The event was a year away, which gave me time to educate myself in the area. I accepted and began to work on the talk. It turned out to be an important choice, as the talk and the paper I published based on it started a trail that led to my first book on ethical and social issues pertaining to genetic engineering on animals, *The Frankenstein Syndrome* (Rollin 1995b),

Portions of this chapter are drawn from Bernard E. Rollin, *The Frankenstein Syndrome: Ethical and Social Issues in the Genetic Engineering of Animals* (Cambridge: Cambridge University Press, 1995), and Bernard E. Rollin, *Science and Ethics* (Cambridge: Cambridge University Press, 2006).

as well as to numerous articles on many aspects of biotechnology and speaking invitations that continue today.

As I wrote the talk, I was goaded on by the familiar fear of making a fool of myself by not knowing the field, as well as by feeling the need for a "hook" that could capture the attention of the attendees, who most certainly were infected with the ideological denial of the relevance of ethics to science and the correlative lack of interest in a talk on ethics. I found the hook when I spoke to one of my colleagues, Fred Johnson, about the task I had undertaken. "Oh, the 'Frankenstein thing,'" he immediately remarked. A week after our conversation, I was perusing new acquisitions in our university library when I encountered the extraordinary, newly published *The Frankenstein Catalogue: Being a Comprehensive History of Novels, Translations, Adaptations, Stories, Critical Works, Popular Articles, Series, Verse, Stage Plays, Films, Cartoons, Puppetry, Radio and Television Programs, Comics, Satire and Humor, Spoken Musical Recordings, Tapes and Sheet Music Featuring Frankenstein's Monster and/or Descended from Mary Shelley's Novels* (1984), appropriately written by a man named Donald Glut. The book is precisely a comprehensive list and brief description of the works mentioned in the title. After recovering from my initial amazement that anyone would publish such a book, I was astonished anew by its content. It, in fact, lists 2,666 such works, including 145 editions of Mary Shelley's novel, the vast majority of which date from the mid-twentieth century. Putting these data together with my friend's remark, I experienced a flash of insight: Was it possible that the Frankenstein story was, in some sense, an archetypal myth, metaphor, or category that expresses deep concerns that trouble the modern mind? Could "the Frankenstein thing" provide a Rosetta Stone for deciphering ethical and social concerns relevant to the genetic engineering of life forms?

In the ensuing months, my hypothesis received succor. While visiting Australia, I met with an animal researcher whose field was teratology, or the study of birth defects—literally, the study of monsters. He had been extremely surprised to find that his work with animals had evoked significant public suspicion, hostility, and protest. "I can't understand it," he said. "There was absolutely no pain or suffering endured by any of the animals. All I can think of is that it must have been the Frankenstein thing." And in a cover story on the fortieth anniversary of the Hiroshima bombing in 1985, *Time* magazine invoked the Frankenstein theme as a major voice in post–World War II popular culture, indicating that the theme was society's way to express its fear and horror of a science and technology that had unleashed the atomic bomb.

The Frankenstein story gave me a key to unlock the issues of genetic engineering in particular and of biotechnology in general. I found three aspects of the story that could be applied to the social response to genetic engineering. The first was the ominous "There are certain things humans were not meant to do" (a line preferably delivered by Maria Ouspenskaya in an indeterminate, *mitteleuropaeische* accent). The second facet was exemplified in the monster's engendering catastrophic effects despite its inventor's altruistic intentions. The final aspect was the suffering of the creature, for in truth, in Mary Shelley's novel and in many of the films inspired by it, the creature suffers in many ways. (Recall our empathy for King Kong.) I also liked the Frankenstein story because it provided a powerful vehicle for delivering the message of scientists' moral responsibility for their actions. (Recall that, although Frankenstein was the name of the scientist, everyone thinks it was the name of the monster.)

I presented the talk to more than four hundred genetic engineers from dozens of countries on the first day of the conference. I was probably as nervous regarding that talk as any I had given before or have given since. After all, there was little literature to draw on, and my message raised questions about the enterprise. I did not feel any better when I learned that alcohol would be available during the dinner after which I was to speak.

I attended many talks that day in a futile effort to calm my anxiety. By and large, they were excellent, although the U.S. Department of Agriculture talk that focused on the meat inspection of genetically modified animals—"If the animal is a chicken with duck traits introduced genetically, is it to be inspected as a chicken or a duck?"—was unwittingly funny.

I vividly remember the dinner. I sat at a table with a wonderful group of genetic engineers who attempted to assuage my worries. One man from Thailand even gave me a silk handerkerchief for luck. I still have it. I began to read the talk—a miracle. People laughed at the jokes, nodded, smiled, even applauded once in a while. I finished to significant applause—more testament to the kindness and openness of the audience than to the brilliance of my speech. Then the nightmare began when I asked for questions. The first person to walk to the microphone was so drunk that he clung to the mike to help him stand. In a classic slur, he turned to the audience and asked, "Why are you clapping? You shouldn't clap. I didn't understand a shingle word he said. You shouldn't clap. I didn't undershtand anything." Inspired by adrenaline, I replied, "Before we go any further, sir, can you tell me your professional field?" He said he was a medical doctor. "Well, that explains your lack of understanding," I answered. "You're the product of a substandard education." The audience roared with laughter and applauded.

I hoped that would end the aggressive drunken questioning, but it did not. The next man who approached the microphone was even drunker. He was a very well known scientist who had developed the process for freezing embryos. I had heard him earlier that day and was impressed with his intellect. I hoped he would be friendly, but he wasn't. Although he was not slurring, the alcohol released his inhibitions, and he started a frontal attack: "You said science cannot proceed unconstrained [I had, indeed, said that], yet *you* proceed unconstrained. You demean me, my field, our work. You insult us all." Once again, the adrenaline inspired me: "You know, sir, if *you* proceed unconstrained, innocent creatures may suffer, dangers may arise for society. If *I* proceed unconstrained, all I do is insult some drunk who either didn't listen or didn't understand what I was saying. I worked on this speech for a year. . . . After all that work, after achieving my goal, I still get some belligerent drunk wanting to insult me and pick a fight. . . . So the appropriate response for me would probably be to get off the stage and kick your nuts down your throat. But I didn't do it, so I am very constrained." The audience laughed wildly, whistled, and applauded. My colleague, the brilliant genetic engineer George Seidel, who later cloned the first calves, was sharing a hotel room with the drunk. He told me that the man was still shaking hours later. "I told him not to start up with a philosopher when he's drunk and you're not," George told me later.

In any event, my approach to these issues is, and was, as follows: As noted earlier, I have articulated a Gresham's law for ethics. Recall that Gresham's law for economics asserts that bad money will drive good money out of circulation; in other words, if people are faced with the option of paying a debt with either of two currencies of the same face value, they will pay with the one that possesses less intrinsic value. A parallel phenomenon occurs in ethics: Given a new situation for which no consensus understanding of the moral problems involved exists, and given that the situation naturally demands articulation and discussion of such issues, the most shrill and dramatic articulations of these problems will tend to seize center stage. We in the United States have seen this occur with a variety of newly emerging social issues, such as the use of animals in research, concern with the environment, women's issues and radical feminism, diversity, and homosexuality. Social ethics, like nature, abhors a vacuum. In the absence of ethically informed expertise to counter and moderate the distortions inherent in such formulations, the distortions tend to dominate the social mind and drive the legitimate ethical concerns out of its awareness. This situation is typified by the "certain things are not meant for humans to do" rubric. This is, of course, what has occurred vis-à-vis genetic engineering in general and vis-à-vis the genetic engineering of animals in particular. Center stage has been occupied by lurid sound bites calculated to frighten and titillate: "Genetic engineering is playing God"; "Genetic engineering is against nature"; "Genetic engineering does not show proper respect for the gift of life"; "Genetic engineering breaches species barriers and violates species integrity." As empty of content and undefended as these assertions may be, they fill the ethical lacuna in social thought and become entrenched and difficult to counter, and they essentially define the universe of moral discourse for the society.

Much of the blame for this unfortunate state of affairs in the arena of genetic engineering must be laid at the feet of the research community. Part of the problem arises from its insularity and distance from the public. Even more of the problem comes from scientists' disavowal, in theory and practice, of responsibility for the ethical and social issues raised by new developments in science and technology. As I discussed earlier, science has deliberately distanced itself from social and ethical issues in theory and practice and runs afoul of ordinary common sense and public sensibilities. Regulating research on human and animal subjects and genetic engineering provide instructive cases in point. In addition, the way is paved for opportunists to define the issues in a manner to which it is difficult to respond and from which it is difficult to recover.

Scientists must recognize that science was not, is not, and can never be value-free or even ethics-free. When massive amounts of public money are funneled into AIDS research rather than into curing baldness or when the study of the relationship between race and intelligence is socially disallowed, the *subject matter* studied by science is determined by socio-ethical values. When biomedical research is performed on rats rather than on unwanted children and the control of pain in these rats is socially mandated, the *method of science* is determined by socio-ethical values. And when the degree of statistical reliability demanded in science fluctuates when one is testing the efficacy of a new human drug versus when one is testing a new survey instrument, one again sees the influence of ethics. The design of experiments, acceptable size of samples, and acceptable confidence intervals will vary greatly across different types of research because of moral concerns, even when similar sorts of questions are being asked. Thus, the very logic of science is modulated by socio-ethical concerns.

Similarly, genetic engineering of animals raises significant socio-ethical concerns that the research community must address or these issues will be erroneously defined by others. I have already mentioned such spurious issues that laypeople bring up, but it is worthwhile to briefly indicate why they are illegitimate. The average person—indeed, sometimes even the average scientist—will inevitably raise the issue of "playing God" when asked about the ethical issues involved in the genetic engineering of animals. I would argue that neither this nor any variation of this represents a genuine ethical issue. To be sure, the creation of new forms of life may be offensive or even immoral to certain theological traditions, but that does not mean that such activity represents an ethical problem in a secular society not governed by that tradition. If "playing God" in this area is intrinsically wrong, it is hard to see why damming rivers, eradicating smallpox, and building cities is not also wrong. As a matter of fact, numerous theologians from a variety of traditions do not see genetic engineering as inherently wrong.

One can similarly dismiss, at least on a rational level, the claim of various religious leaders, expressed in a statement from the National Council of Churches, that "the gift of life from God, in all of its forms and species, should not be regarded solely as if they [all the forms of life] were a chemical product subject to genetic alteration and patentable for economic benefit" (Crawford 1987, 480–481). Such a dictum contains no argument, or even a clear statement, of what is allegedly problematic; until these are forthcoming, the position cannot be taken seriously. The same is true of Jeremy Rifkin's claim that genetic engineering "desacralizes nature" (Rifkin 1985, 53).

And one can dismiss Rifkin's and others' jeremiads about the intrinsic wrongness of "violating species integrity" or "crossing species barriers." In fact, we know that species are not the fixed, immutable rigid building blocks of nature that Aristotle and the Bible believed them to be; they are, rather, "snapshots" of a dynamic natural process. Species evolve. Why, then, is it intrinsically wrong for humans to participate deliberately in that evolution, especially when we have been doing it since *we* evolved, unwittingly by serving as a selection pressure on other organisms and contrivedly through domestication and cultivation, preferential propagation, and the whole panoply of artificial selection? Indeed, it is estimated that 70 percent of grasses and 40 percent of flowering plants were "created" through human artifice, and vast numbers of animals have been drastically modified (witness the dog).

Theology and environmental philosophy probably provide the unseen skeleton underlying the objection about species integrity. In the case of environmental philosophy, which is a dominant mode of thought in contemporary society, much is made out of the point that species should not be allowed to vanish as a result of human activity. It is a psychologically small step, albeit a conceptually vast one, to move to the view that species ought not *change* at human hands, a position for which no adequate defense exists.

Another concern is sometimes voiced by those who allege the intrinsic wrongness of the genetic engineering of animals. Theological types in particular object to the "mixing" of human and animal traits. Presumably, this means the insertion of human genetic material into animals or the insertion of animal genetic material into humans. What, precisely, is intrinsically wrong with such an admixture? We have certainly inserted animal parts into the human body to treat disease—pigs' heart valves and skin, for example—and we routinely use animal products in the medical field. Suppose that an animal were found that contains genes to prevent cancer (sharks, allegedly, are tumor-free). Suppose, further, that this gene produced no untoward effects in humans; its only effect was to confer immunity against neoplastic disease. Why would such gene transfer be wrong in and of itself? Similarly, if the case were reversed and the gene were transferred in the other direction—from humans to animals to instill resistance to disease—it is difficult to see why this would be morally problematic. To be sure, when the human-growth-hormone gene was transferred to animals, it caused disease and suffering among animals; thus, such transfer was wrong because of its *effects*. But it still has not been shown that *in and of itself* such transfer is wrong. Earlier in the book, I provided an example of how bad ethics operates in society when I interacted with the creators of Dolly the cloned sheep and urged them to articulate the genuine ethical issues involved in cloning. They failed to do so, and the public said that cloning violated God's will.

Objections claiming that the genetic engineering of animals is intrinsically wrong have widened the gap in social thought in the absence of forthright articulation of genuine concerns by the scientific community. We have argued that none of these claims of intrinsic wrongness represent legitimate concerns. Nonetheless, genuine issues of risk to humans and to the environment grow out of the genetic engineering of animals that must be addressed and managed for the technology to be socially acceptable. The issues discussed above can be resolved if the biotechnology community undertakes such serious and genuine dialogue with the general public on all aspects of this technology, which I believe it must do to survive.

It is vital that discussion of such risks and their management not be restricted to "experts" but, rather, involve the public, perhaps through local community review. The public does not trust experts to articulate risks, to assess their likelihood, or to manage them: They have lived through too many Chernobyls, too many *Challenger*s, too many killer-bee escapes. In agriculture, the public has seen the unexpected consequences of DDT and the unanticipated contamination of groundwater from herbicides, pesticides, and fertilizers, not to mention the unexpected spillage of millions of gallons of hog manure in North Carolina during the summer of 1995, despite assurances from experts that it could not happen. Indeed, the public has a point: Scientists tend to be cavalier about risks in their area. Ask any university bio-safety officer. Scientists furthermore tend to minimize the danger of unanticipated consequences of new technology or believe that they can fix them with further new technology, whereas members of the public fear the unknown and tend to believe that technological fixes generate new and unanticipated consequences. Failure to involve the public in discussion of risk management is very likely to result in the rejection of genetic engineering. This has already occurred with the bovine somatotropin hormone used in dairy cows and with the Campbell Soup Company's genetically engineered tomato. *Jurassic Park* should provide a parable for genetic engineers. When the scientific community does not carefully enumerate, elucidate, and rationally discuss the full extent and magnitude of risks, ordinary people are drawn to the theologians and doomsayers who press the "Frankenstein thing."

Potential dangers emerging from the genetic engineering of animals obviously stem from the rapidity with which such activity can introduce wholesale change in organisms. Traditional "genetic engineering" was done by selective breeding over long periods of time, allowing ample opportunity to observe untoward effects of narrow selection of isolated characteristics. With the techniques that are currently available, however, scientists are doing their selection "in the fast lane" and thus may not detect the problematic aspects of what they are doing until after the organism has been widely disseminated. Another way to put the same point is that, with traditional breeding, an *enforced waiting period* is necessarily associated with attempts to incorporate traits into organisms. In the animal arena, especially, one can significantly change animals from the parent stock by selective breeding, but it will take many generations to do so, during which time one has many opportunities to detect problems with the genome one is creating or with its phenotypic bodily expression. To be sure, as occurred with the breeding of many purebred dogs, one may choose to disregard the untoward effects. But the point is that one could see the problems developing if one cared to do so. With genetic engineering, however, one can insert the desired gene in one effort, and the problems that emerge may be totally unexpected.

There are many instances of this, in fact, even in traditional breeding. One famous example concerns corn and grows out of the phenomenon known as pleiotropy, which means that one gene and its products controls or codes for more than a single trait. In this case, breeders were interested in a gene that controlled male sterility in corn so that one could produce hybrid seeds without detasseling the corn by hand, which is very labor-intensive. So the gene was introduced to provide genetic detasseling. Unfortunately, the gene also was responsible for increasing susceptibility to Southern Corn Leaf Blight, a fact of which no one was aware. The corn was widely adopted, and in one year a large part of the corn crop was devastated by the disease.

Similarly, when wheat was bred for resistance to a disease called blast, that characteristic was looked at in isolation and was encoded into the organism. The backup gene for general resistance, however, was ignored. As a result, the new wheat organism was very susceptible to all sorts of viruses, which, in one generation, mutated sufficiently to devastate the crop.

What we have, then, vis-à-vis the danger associated with genetic engineering, is what philosophers call an a fortiori situation. If such unanticipated consequences can and do occur with traditional breeding, where one necessarily proceeds slowly, how much more does the danger of unanticipated consequences loom when one is creating transgenic animals? When one inserts a sequence of DNA (a gene) into an organism, one cannot anticipate pleiotropic activities, in which the gene affects other traits in ways one did not expect. By the same token, one may have overlooked the need for more than one gene to get the desired result phenotypically. Any of these factors can produce a variety of conditions deleterious to the organism. The way to control this risk, then—whether one is doing traditional breeding or taking transgenic shortcuts—is to do a great deal of small-scale testing before one releases or depends on the new organism.

The second type of danger resulting from fast-lane genetic engineering of animals can be illustrated with reference to food animals. Here the isolated characteristic being engineered into the organism may have unsuspected harmful consequences to humans who consume the resultant animal. The deep issue here is that one can, of course, genetically engineer traits in animals without fully understanding the mechanisms involved in the phenotypic expression of the traits, with resulting disaster. Ideally, although this probably is not possible either in breeding or in creating transgenics, one can mitigate this sort of danger by being extremely cautious in one's engineering until one has at least a reasonable grasp of the physiological mechanisms affected by the insertion of a given gene.

A third general kind of risk that grows out of genetic engineering replicates and amplifies problems already inherent in selection by breeding—namely, the narrowing of a gene pool, the tendency toward the creation of genetic uniformity, the emergence of harmful recessives, the loss of hybrid vigor, and, of course, the greater susceptibility of organisms to devastation by pathogens, as has been shown to be the case in crops. So once again, we encounter a problem that already exists in traditional breeding. As we find the traits we consider desirable, we try to incorporate them into the organisms we raise—plants and animals. We continue to refine and propagate these animals and plants until a particular genome dominates our agriculture. In other words, we put all our eggs in one basket. The number of strains of chicken in the production of eggs and broilers, for example, has declined precipitously since large corporations have come to dominate the industry in the past fifty years. What this means in practical terms is that the industry stands and falls by what it considers the few superior genomes it has developed. If circumstances change, or if a new pathogen is encountered, wholesale devastation of the population will necessarily occur—and has occurred, for example, through Newcastle's disease and influenza. Loss of genetic diversity means loss of potential to adapt to new circumstances.

The way in which genetic engineering can accelerate this tendency is clear. Suppose a "superior" animal is created transgenically with great rapidity. Those who use this animal gain a clear competitive edge through increased disease resistance, greater efficiency in feed conversion, greater productivity, or whatever desirable trait has been created. To compete, other farmers replace their stock with this animal, because old strains are viewed as obsolete. The entire branch of agriculture tends toward a *monoculture,* with the extant gene pool severely limited. Over a period of time, however, untoward consequences of the new genome may emerge as susceptibility to disease, problems in reproduction, susceptibility to stress, or some other problem. A potentially disastrous situation forms because the best sort of response to the crisis has been lost with the loss of genetic diversity. Alternatively, social or economic circumstances may change so as to require change in agricultural practices or locale such that the extant genome does not fit well with the new circumstances. Once again, the presence of a limited gene pool militates against the sort of quick, reasonable, and efficacious response that a diverse gene pool would provide. In the end, then, the genetic engineering of animals runs the risk of accelerating the tendency toward monoculture that is already established in at least certain portions of animal agriculture (e.g., the chicken and egg industry).

A fourth set of risks arises from the fact that, in certain cases, when one changes the genetics of animals, one can thereby alter the pathogens to which they are host. This can occur in two ways. First, in genetically engineering an animal to provide resistance to a given pathogen, one could unwittingly create an environment in the animal that is favorable to a natural mutation of that pathogenic microbe, to which the modified animal would not be resistant. These new organisms then could be infectious to these or other animals or to humans. (Society already has witnessed such consequences as a result of its indiscriminate use of antibiotics in medicine and agriculture. Widespread use of these drugs killed off susceptible bacteria and, in essence, served to select for bacteria that were resistant to them.)

One possible example of this sort of reaction was discussed regarding the so-called severe combined immunodeficiency (SCID) mouse developed as a model for AIDS. These animals are genetically engineered to possess a human immune system and are then infected with the AIDS virus. Some researchers suggest that, in such mice, the AIDS virus could become more virulent and infectious by interacting with native mouse viruses, thereby taking on new characteristics—for example, they could become transmissible through contact with the airborne virus. It is for similar reasons that the National Institutes of Health, which has developed a different mouse model for AIDS, took extraordinary precautions to ensure that the experimental mice could not accidentally escape.

Even if one were to alter an animal genetically without specifically changing its immune system, one might inadvertently and indirectly alter the pathogens to which it is host by changing the microenvironment in which it lives. This, in turn, could cause these pathogens to become dangerous to humans or other animals. Thus, for example, in altering agricultural animals such as cattle through genetic engineering, one runs the risk of affecting the pathogenicity of the microorganisms that inhabit the organism in unknown and unpredictable ways. The more precipitous the change, the more difficult it is to estimate the effects of the pathogens.

A fifth set of risks is ecological, associated with the possibility of radically altering an animal and then having it escape into an uncontrolled environment. Although this might seem to be a minimal danger when dealing with intensively maintained and strictly confined swine, chickens, or laboratory animals, it could pose a real problem with extensively managed and loosely confined sheep or cattle, as well as with rodents or rabbits, which may escape despite ordinary precautions, and, most obviously, with fish. Experience teaches us that the dangers of releasing animals into a new environment cannot be estimated, even with species whose characteristics are well known. Witness the uncontrollable proliferation of rabbits and cats released in Australia and of the mongoose in Hawaii, as well as our inability to deal with the accidental release of killer bees and of imported snails in our waterways. Ignorance of what could happen with newly engineered creatures is even more certain.

A sixth set of risks is also environmental. By now, we are all familiar with the threat to global and regional ecosystems posed by agricultural expansion in Third World countries. Slash-and-burn techniques deployed to provide grazing land for cattle have led to desertification in some areas (Africa) and the dramatic loss of species in others (South America). What effect would genetic engineering have on these pernicious pursuits? The answer is not clear. It could be argued in favor of genetic engineering that our ability to adapt animals and plants genetically to indigenous conditions would halt such practices while allowing for economic growth. However, it is equally plausible to suggest that such technology would augment the plundering of the environment by foisting animals on all sorts of hitherto undisturbed areas, with unimaginable consequences. Once again, it is difficult to foresee such risks.

A seventh set of risks derives from potential military applications of such technology. It is not difficult to imagine the sorts of weapons that could be created using genetically modified animals as carriers to infect populations deliberately with human pathogens.

Finally, the patenting of genetically engineered animals poses socioeconomic risks. For example, many farmers' groups anticipate that small family farms will be forced to acquire expensive patented animals to compete with large corporations and could well be forced out of business. This, in turn, might strengthen the ever increasing tendency of large agribusiness to monopolize the food supply. We have ample evidence from the bovine growth hormone and elsewhere that the public will reject anything that endangers family farms. The extrapolation of these technologies to Third World cultures, where adequate regulation is unlikely and sociocultural disruption can threaten the social fabric and way of life, represents another risk in this category.

In June 1997, a team of researchers working as part of a Concerted Action of the European Commission and coordinated by George Gaskell of the London School of Economics, released the results of a survey of public attitudes toward biotechnology conducted in sixteen European Union countries. According to Gaskell (personal communication), the results shattered both the researchers' preconceptions and the conventional scientific wisdom about social responses to biotechnology. As reported in *Nature,* in a story titled "Europe Ambivalent on Biotechnology," the researchers found that "few [people] approve of the use of transgenic animals for research." In addition, they wrote:

> There is a striking mismatch between the traditional concern of regulators with issues of risk and safety, and that of the public, which centers on questions of *moral acceptability.* Although conventional wisdom suggests that the overwhelming social concern about biotechnology is risk, the survey confuted that presupposition. When the 17,000 people surveyed were asked about six different aspects of biotechnology—genetic testing (using genetic tests to detect heritable diseases); medicine production, using human genes in bacteria to produce medicines or vaccines, as has been done with insulin; crop planet modification, for example, moving genes from plant species into crops to produce resistance to insects; food production, for example, to make foods higher in protein or have longer storage life;

> transgenic research animals genetically modified for research, such as the onco-mouse; and xenotransplants, introducing human genes into animals to render their organs immunocompatible for human transplants. All were perceived as potentially useful, but the last two—the uses of transgenic animals for research and transplantation—were seen as *morally unacceptable.*
>
> The pattern of results across six applications suggests that perceptions of usefulness, riskiness, and moral acceptability could be combined to shape overall support [for biotechnology] in the following way. First, usefulness is a precondition of support; second, people seem prepared to accept some risk as long as there is a perception of usefulness and no moral concern; but third and crucially, moral doubts act as a veto irrespective of people's views on use and risk. The finding that risk is less significant than moral acceptability in shaping public perceptions of biotechnology holds true in each EU country and across all six specific applications. . . . This has important implications for policymaking. In general, policy debate about biotechnology has been couched in terms of potential risks to the environment and/or human health. If, however, people are more swayed by moral considerations, public concern is unlikely to be alleviated by technically based reassurance and/or regulatory initiatives that deal exclusively with the avoidance of harm. (Gaskell et al. 1997, 845; emphasis added)

Regrettably, the study does not enumerate or address the specific ethical concerns that rendered the creation of transgenic animals for research morally unacceptable. Below, I attempt to provide a plausible rational reconstruction of justifiable social moral concern about the production of transgenic animals for biomedical research and how this could be addressed.

Responding to the risks I have outlined is just as much a matter of prudence as of self-interest for those engaged in genetic engineering, because they are put at risk by many of the dangers enumerated and because any catastrophic outcomes will likely result in severe restriction of their activities and in massive public rejection of the technology. A purely moral challenge lies in the issue of the welfare of the animals to be engineered. Because human benefits can, and are likely to, exact a cost in animals' suffering, and there is no benefit to humans that militates in favor of controlling that suffering, the task of protecting such animals will be formidable. However, as I have discussed elsewhere, social concern for animal welfare has never been higher in the United States and abroad.

In agriculture, attempts to engineer animals largely have been based on increasing animals' efficiency and productivity. Based on the history and the development of confinement systems in industrialized agriculture, it is clear that if the pain, suffering, and disease of the animal do not interfere with the economic productivity, the condition is ignored. (Hence, the existence of the so-called production diseases endemic to—and, indeed, dominant in—confinement agriculture.) Most important, there are no legal or regulatory constraints on what can be done to animals in pursuit of increasing agricultural productivity, either in agricultural research or in industry. Given the absence of such constraints and the historical willingness of industrialized agriculture to sacrifice animals' welfare for productivity, the moral problem inherent in genetically engineering animals for production agriculture is obvious.

Most of the attempts that have been made thus far to engineer farm animals genetically have generated serious problems for those animals' welfare. For example, attempts to increase the growth rate and efficiency of pigs and sheep by inserting modified genes to control growth have achieved that result but have also engendered significant suffering, as reported by Vernon Pursel and his colleagues (1989). The desired results were to increase growth rates and weight gain in farm animals, reduce carcass fat, and increase feed efficiency. Although certain of these goals were achieved (in pigs, the rate of gain increased by 15 percent and feed efficiency increased by 18 percent while carcass fat was reduced by 80 percent), unanticipated effects, with significantly negative impact on the animals' well-being, also occurred. Life-shortening pathogenic changes in pigs, including kidney and liver problems, were noted in many of the animals. The animals also showed a wide variety of diseases and symptoms, including lethargy, lameness, uncoordinated gait, bulging eyes, thickening skin, gastric ulcers, severe synovitis, degenerative joint disease, heart diseases of various kinds, nephritis, and pneumonia. Sexual behavior was anomalous; sows were anestrous and failed to come into heat, and boars lacked libido. Other problems included tendencies toward diabetes and compromised immune function. The sheep fared better for the first six months but then became unhealthy.

There are certain lessons to be learned from these experiments. In the first place, although similar experiments had been done earlier in mice, mice did not show many of the undesirable side effects. Thus, it is difficult to extrapolate in a linear way from species to species when it comes to genetic engineering, even when on the surface the same sort of genetic manipulation is being attempted. Second, as mentioned, it is impossible to bring about simple one-to-one correspondence between gene transfer and the appearance of desired phenotypic or bodily traits. Genes may have multiple effects, and traits may be under the control of multiple genes. The relevance of this point to welfare is obvious and analogous to a point made earlier about risk: One should be extremely circumspect in one's engineering until one has a good grasp of the physiological mechanisms affected by a gene or set of genes. A good example of the pitfalls in terms of welfare is provided by attempts to engineer mice genetically to produce greater amounts of Interleukin-4 to study certain aspects of the immune system. This, in fact, surprisingly resulted in these animals' developing osteoporosis, a disease that results in bone fragility, which is clearly a welfare problem. Another example is an attempt to produce cattle genetically engineered for double muscling, which would then produce more meat per animal. Though a calf was born showing no apparent problems, within a month it was unable to stand on its own for reasons that are not yet clear. To the researchers' credit, the calf was immediately euthanized. Yet another bizarre instance of unanticipated welfare problems can be found in the situation where leglessness and craniofacial malformations resulted from the insertion of an apparently totally unrelated gene into mice.

Thus, welfare issues arise both in research on genetically engineered agricultural animals and, more drastically, in potential commercial production. The issues concerning research animals can best be handled with judicious use of anesthesia, analgesia, and, above all, early end points for euthanasia if there is any suffering. The issues associated with mass production of suffering genetically engineered animals must be dealt with in a different way. For this reason, I proposed the "Principle of Conservation of Welfare" to guide the agricultural industry (Rollin 1995b). This principle states that *genetically engineered animals should be no worse off than the parent stock would be if they were not so engineered, and ideally should be better off.* Genetically engineering resistance to disease (e.g., for Marek's disease in chickens) is a good example of the latter case.

The most profound moral issue, however, is raised by genetic engineering for biomedical research. Through the genetic engineering of animals, one can create "animal models" for human genetic diseases that do not naturally appear in animals and render them susceptible to study. The problem is that many, if not most, genetic diseases involve a great deal of suffering: The standard textbook of such diseases has more than three thousand pages. In most cases, the suffering attendant on these diseases cannot be controlled in humans. The issue, then—given that such animals will surely be developed as quickly as the technology allows—is how can one ensure that vast numbers of these animals will not live lives of constant pain, suffering, and distress? (I believe it is this concern that led Gaskell's subjects to reject transgenic animal models.)

A related issue also arises. Federal laws I was involved in drafting in the

1980s depend on local committee review of protocols screened for control of pain and suffering. Thus, a committee considering a fracture study will know the nature of the pain involved and mandate its control. As more research involves ablation, insertion, and modification of genes, the effects on the animals cannot be predicted. So how does one plan for the unforeseeable?

In sum, when considering genetic engineering of animals, animal welfare, which has been virtually ignored, raises far more profound ethical issues than the pseudo-issues that have received public attention. Animal welfare must become the subject of massive public attention. Economic and medical progress should not be achieved at the expense of limitless suffering by animal subjects.[1]

[1]I have gone on to apply the categories developed in this chapter to other emerging biotechnological modalities, including animal cloning, stem-cell technology, and human cloning. The interested reader can find these discussions in Rollin 2006c.

14

Animal Agriculture

Cowboys and Husbandry

During the early 1980s, although I was mostly too busy to think about anything besides learning biomedicine and veterinary medicine and articulating animal ethics, I still made time for self-doubt, the plague that God forgot to afflict the Egyptians with but left for the Jews. In particular, I worried about not doing "real philosophy," about not plowing the same ground as my peers, about not aspiring to leave CSU and get back to the East. This was not helped when I received a visit from one of my friends from graduate school, who said, "You have too good a mind to waste on animals and veterinarians." "What *should* I do?" I asked. "You should be scouring the philosophy journal for hot topics and saying something no one has said about those issues." "Whether I believe them or not?" I queried. "What does that have to do with it?" he retorted. "What counts is having your name on the right lips,'" he continued. "Sophia Loren's?" I joked. "No, no," he said and proceeded to name half a dozen trendy philosophers. The neurotic anxiety this engendered was quickly extinguished by a phone call to Arthur Danto, who assured me of the value of what I was doing.

Unquestionably, my life was changing. I was reasonably fit and strong. I was learning new fields and tapping unexplored issues. My wife had decided that, since she had almost flunked calculus as a college freshman, she would compensate by earning a doctorate in math at CSU in combinatorics and coding theory. She finished and never opened a math book again, proving for eternity that (1) she is far cooler than I am and (2) she is far brighter.

I have never encountered anything intellectual she couldn't master—and cogently criticize—in a flash.

In 1979, the greatest event of my life occurred when, on July 4, my son, Michael David Hume Rollin, was born. Fatherhood scared the hell out of me. My own father had walked out when I was five and my brother was one, leaving my mother and maternal grandmother to raise me at a time when coming from a "broken home" was shameful. All of my friends had fathers at home. The last time I saw my father was when I was nineteen; he showed up in Coney Island and asked whether I knew a kid named Bernie Rollin. Stung that he didn't recognize me, I said, "I think he works at the other end of the Boardwalk." I never saw him again.

I didn't have a model for being a father; for that matter, I had no clear model for being a man. One of my friends since the fifth grade recently remarked that I had drawn my model from western movies—clear-cut ethics: a willingness to fight for what is right without fear or, at least, without being paralyzed by fear. After a while, it dawned on me that I did have a model for being a father. I simply needed to attend to what I felt had been missing when I was a child: someone to teach me sports, to ride a bike, to protect me and make me feel secure, to teach me "guy stuff." By the same token, I knew what I hadn't missed: someone big to yell at me and punish me, someone to fear. I followed that notion, and my son and I became as close as any father and son can be while he grew up independent, competent, strong, and self-sufficient—like his father, a weightlifter and motorcyclist and, in addition, a black belt in karate, a musician, and a physician. He is a child psychiatrist driven by concern for the weak.

One of my early photos shows me on an Enduro all-terrain motorcycle with Mikey, age one, hung around my neck in a backpack. At four, he had a 50cc motorcycle with special training wheels attached. Since he was eight until the present, we have taken a one- to two-week motorcycle trip together every summer, all over the U.S. West. He rode on the back of my motorcycle until he was eighteen; after that, he had his own bike. From 1990 on, we made the trips on a Harley-Davidson, a wonderful key to entering new subcultures, including that of cowboys *and* Indians.

On one of our first trips, we went to the Navajo reservation in Arizona. I was stopped by a Navajo motorcycle patrolman; as it happened, he was the chief of police and was also riding a Harley. He politely told us that since the reservation was federally administered (though an independent nation), the law required riders to wear helmets. Though Mike wore one, I did not.[1]

[1]The interested reader should see "'It's My Own Damn Head'" (Rollin 2006b). The essay describes my objections to helmets.

As Mikey's face fell, thinking we had to leave the reservation, the chief smiled and said, "Notice *I'm* not wearing one. Have a good day!" In the twenty-plus years we have ridden together, even when Mike was a student at Stanford University and at the University of Colorado's medical school, we have had many adventures, most predictably from the Harley breaking down and our thereby meeting wonderful people. When applying to colleges, Mikey wrote his application essay about these trips. Interviewers never failed to focus on this (everyone is a biker at heart) and, indeed, he was accepted to every college to which he applied, including Harvard and Princeton.

One of our adventures took place on what is known as the loneliest road in the United States, a barren 100-mile stretch from Colorado to the Utah–Nevada border. We stayed at a motel. The next morning, when I pushed the Harley's starter button, nothing happened. Mikey was eleven or so and needed to push the 600-pound bike, the 250-pound father, and 50 pounds of luggage to a start repeatedly as we rode over 350 miles to a bike shop amid shouts of "Shame!" and "Child abuse!"

Mikey is one of the brightest people I know. I took him with me everywhere: to my classes, on trips to lectures, even to department meetings. After one two-hour meeting, when he was about seven, he approached the department head. "Dick," he said, "wasn't the question that needed deciding A or B?" "Right," said Dick. "And wasn't A impossible?" he asked. "Right again," Dick said. "Then why did it take two hours for them to choose B?" When he was five, he asked me what philosophy is. I said that philosophers worry about questions such as "What is the number 1?" He wrinkled his brow and said, "It is something that is not something else," thereby articulating the Russell–Whitehead–Frege view and leaving me speechless. He was not only smart; he was smart enough to know when to keep quiet. While I was working on my book on animal consciousness, I asked him whether the dog thinks. "Sure," he said. "Well," I asked, "since she doesn't have language, she can't think in words, so *how* does she think?" "How should I know?" he replied.

Needless to say, he grew up sharing my concern for animals. Mikey almost never cried—even when he broke his arm while learning to ride a bicycle. Yet one day when he was little, as we drove to Cheyenne, Wyoming, I saw tears silently roll down his cheeks. "What's the matter, honey?" I asked. He pointed to a bilevel cattle truck and said, "Those animals are hot and scared and pooping on each other. That's not right." The image of his tears stayed with me and fueled my work in agriculture.

That I got involved with animals used in research and teaching is not all that surprising. I team-taught biology. I studied science. I understood research. Totally amazing was my increasing involvement in agriculture, to the point that I have been listed in one scholarly directory as an "animal scientist." When I got to Colorado, I didn't know hay from straw or foals from ponies, and when my wife asked me why farmers plow at night, I replied, "Because it's cooler." I was unaware that only by working in the daytime at city jobs could they keep the farm going.

This involvement was unplanned. Like my involvement in the veterinary program, my connection with agriculture just happened. It initially occurred because so many of my veterinary students were cowboys who also were involved with rodeo. In fact, CSU had an annual vet school rodeo. This was a perfect issue to engage these students. As the rodeo approached, I "casually" mentioned that a future veterinarian's engaging in rodeo was roughly equivalent to "orthopedic surgeons picking fights in bars." This riled the cowboys. "What do you mean?" they wanted to know. "Well you're supposed to be curing animals, not hurting them," I replied. "Look at calf-roping for God's sake. You are jerking a baby animal to a stop at twenty miles an hour."

The next week, they came in and asked to continue the discussion. "Would it satisfy you if we made some changes?" they asked. "Whoa," I said. "You don't need to satisfy *me.* You need to satisfy yourselves." "OK, OK," they said. "What if we modify calf roping?" "How?" I asked. "What if we use breakaway ropes?" "What does that mean?" I asked. "Rope attached to strings so that we can rope the calf, but the string breaks when they pull it." "Sounds reasonable," I said. I did not fully grasp the significance of the idea until a cowgirl took me aside after class. "You don't understand what they've done," she said. "In our culture, breakaway ropes are used only in women's events." There began my love and respect for cowboys and ranch people. I would witness that honesty and integrity myriad times over the next thirty years.

A similar event took place a few years later when I was invited to address the CSU Rodeo Club about the new ethic for animals in relation to rodeo. When I entered the room, I found some two dozen cowboys seated as far back as possible, cowboy hats tilted down over their eyes, booted feet up on chairs, arms folded defiantly, and arrogantly smirking at me. With the quick-wittedness for which I am known, I immediately sized up the situation as a hostile one. "Why am I here?" I began by asking. No response. I repeated the question: "Seriously, why am I here? You ought to know—you invited me." One brave soul ventured, "You're here to tell us what's wrong with rodeo." "Would you listen?" I asked. "Hell, no," they chorused. "Well, in that case, I would be stupid to try," I said, "and I'm not stupid." A long silence followed. Finally someone suggested, "Are you here to help us think about rodeo?" I asked them whether that was what they wanted. "Yes," they said. "OK," I replied. "I can do that."

For the next hour, without mentioning rodeo, I discussed many aspects of ethics: the nature of social morality and individual morality, the relationship between law and ethics, the need for an ethic for how we treat animals. I asked them about their position on that last question. After some dialogue, they all agreed that, as a minimal ethical principle, one should not hurt animals for trivial reasons. "OK," I said, "in the face of our discussion, take a fifteen-minute break, go out in the hall, talk among yourselves, and come back and tell me what *you guys* think is wrong with rodeo from the point of view of animal ethics."

Fifteen minutes later they came back. All took seats in the front, not the back. One man, the president of the club, stood nervously in front of the room, hat in hand. "Well," I said, not knowing what to expect or what the change in attitude betokened, "what did you guys agree is wrong with rodeo?" The president looked at me and quietly spoke: "Everything." "Beg your pardon?" I said. "Everything," he repeated. "When we started to think about it, we realized that what we do violates our own ethics about animals." "OK," I said. "I've done my job. I can go." "Please don't go," he said. "We want to think this through. Rodeo means a lot to us. Will you help us think through how we can hold on to rodeo and yet not violate our ethic?" To me, the incident represents an archetypal example of successful ethical dialogue, using recollection and, again, judo not sumo.

In any event, the students went home and told their families and friends about what I was teaching. One student, who was from a powerful ranching family, insisted that I be invited to the animal convention of the Colorado Cattlemen's Association. He was persistent, and I got a call from the group. "You're invited at your own expense," they said. "You'll have ten minutes to speak." I was angry. "You're responding to pressure," I said. "You don't really want me, so I'm not coming. When you really want me, you will damn well pay my way and give me a reasonable amount of time."

By 1980, the vet course was garnering much attention, even being written up in the *Chronicle of Higher Education.* I began to know some of the animal-science faculty, mostly ranch people. One of them, Ed Pexton, now deceased, asked me whether I could teach a course that would help animal-science students understand emerging animal ethics and philosophy, as well as develop their reasoning ability and speaking and writing skills. I had already done some guest lectures for the faculty and very much enjoyed the students, who in turn were very interested. I agreed and taught the course for the first time in 1982. As I expected, I loved the students—at that time, mostly ranch kids. They were honest, straightforward, and open to new ideas and, at the same time, articulate in defense of their way of life. I have never had a bad group among those students. They are timeless in attitudes and values.

Two students stand out from that group. One was Mark Haake, who came from a dairy farm near Denver. He was an active class participant and an A student. At the end of the term, fifteen-page term papers were due. As the students passed the papers up to me, I noticed that one was in a binder and was as thick as a small-town phonebook—master's thesis length. "Whose is this?" I asked. Mark raised his hand. "This was supposed to be fifteen pages," I said. "If I was gonna do it, I was gonna do it right," he replied. He and I have stayed friends, and I have been out to his farm on numerous occasions.

One Sunday afternoon, I received a call from Mark. He was upset. "A lady from Denver just knocked on my door and is screaming at me," he said. "She saw my calf hutches [igloo-like houses that dairy calves are kept in to avoid spreading disease]. She's yelling and crying that she won't let them be raised for veal." (At that time, veal calves were raised in tiny crates in which the animals were confined and kept anemic and immobile so their meat would be pale and tender.) "She says she's going to bring [television] reporters down to film this 'atrocity,'" he continued. "Question for you is: Should I try to educate her or kill her?" "Killing her will probably mess up your summer plans." I said. "Try to teach her." Three hours later, he called back and said proudly, "Well, I explained the hutches to her. She's still yellin' about bringing the TV people. Only now she wants everyone to see how well we care for our calves. She's bringing a whole bunch of school kids."

About ten years later, in the early 1990s, CSU's veterinary student demographic had diminished from 85–90 percent cowboys and cowgirls to about 20 percent. (Now fewer than 5 percent are cowboys and cowgirls, which is a real shame.) One of the worst urban students was a woman who had a degree from Wesleyan University, the Vatican for political correctness. She berated the cowboys for "raising flesh" and me for not being politically correct. "If you were at Wesleyan and said some of the things you say," she told me obnoxiously, "we students would hold a candlelight vigil at your house." I asked her whether the vigil would be held during the day or at night. "Night—why?" she asked. "Because candles are great targets at night," I said. In any event, she kept harassing the most archetypal cowboy in the class about the incongruity between being a vet and "raising flesh." Before Thanksgiving, he came to see me. "Doc, I got two choices with that woman," he said. "I either bring her home for Thanksgiving and show her how we care for animals or I'll kill her. I'll try bringing her home first." After Thanksgiving, she was still an opinionated motor mouth, but her opinions had done a 180 degree turn. She incessantly talked about the excellent care ranchers provide for their livestock.

In 1982, I started teaching the world's first Ethics of Animal Agriculture course for CSU's Department of Animal Sciences. Once again, as in veterinary medicine, a few liberal intellectuals in the department saw the need for such a class. Today, I hold an appointment in animal sciences and work as closely with that department as with veterinary medicine. One of my students in that class was Melissa Miller, a member of a prominent agricultural family in Colorado who was both highly knowledgeable and highly analytical. At the end of the first week of class, she asked to see me in my office. As soon as she sat down, she burst into tears. "I can't do it." she cried. "I just can't do it." "What?" I asked. "I just can't spy on you." Spy on me? It turned out that her master's adviser had asked her to sit in on my class and report back if I was teaching vegetarianism. I couldn't help laughing. "Why spy on me? I offered the faculty the chance to team-teach the class." "Yes," she said, "but they fear your intellect and that you will mop up the floor with them if they try to argue with you." "In that case," I said, "keep reporting to them. Maybe they'll learn something."

I had my revenge shortly thereafter. A new hire in the Department of Animal Sciences was John Edwards, a beef specialist and livestock judging coach—the best in the United States—who was about my age. He taught the introductory animal science class with three hundred or so students and asked me to lecture on animal ethics. We did not meet until I arrived in his classroom for the lecture. He chatted a while and introduced me. I was still annoyed about the Melissa incident, so I began my lecture by saying, "As near as I can tell, the faculty in this department are a bunch of ignorant shit kickers, and this guy is no exception." I thought Edwards would burst; then he started to laugh. At the end of the two-hour class, he invited me for a beer, still laughing. We have been close friends ever since and have stayed in each other's homes after he was hired away by Texas A&M and, later, became president of the Limousin Association (for cows, not cars).

Melissa Miller and I also stayed friends. After she graduated, she became the first female beef extension specialist in Colorado's history. She was posted in Kiowa, a High Plains town midway between Denver and Colorado Springs. One day in 1982, Melissa called to invite me to address the Stockman's Seminar in Kiowa on animal ethics. At that time, I had never spoken to ranchers, just to their kids, and I was still smarting from the obnoxious invitation from the Colorado Cattlemen described earlier. "Are *they* inviting me?" I asked. "Or are *you* inviting me?" "Same thing," she said. I was shortly to find out that there was a major difference. A date was set in the spring. Melissa told me that I was to speak in the high-school cafeteria and to ask anyone for directions to the high school when I got to Kiowa, since there were no addresses. I agreed. On the appointed day, I put on my tie and blazer and drove to Kiowa. (By the way, I look ridiculous in a blazer or suit but always wear them to speak out of respect for my audiences. When I lecture at CSU, I usually wear Harley T-shirts.)

I arrived in Kiowa at the dinner hour. It looked like a ghost town. There was no one to ask where the high school was. After a while, I spotted the sheriff's car, parked, and walked toward it. The sheriff rolled down the window. I noticed immediately that he was the most non–Jewish looking man I had ever seen: lots of lines and angles and muscles in his face, his eyes covered by mirrored sunglasses. He made Clint Eastwood look rabbinical. "Officer," I said, "can you direct me to the high school?" He slowly removed his shades. "You the speaker?" he asked. "What speaker?" I stammered. "That animal rots [rights] feller," he replied. Oh, my God! The word was out. My mind jumped to Spencer Tracy in *Bad Day at Black Rock.* He pointed me toward the high school, his face an expressionless mask.

Things did not get better as I entered the high school and confronted 150 unsmiling ranchers and their wives. "Hi," I said idiotically. No one responded—just stared. Fine—to hell with them. I'm not here to be loved. My dog loves me. I chatted with Melissa, and time passed. She stood up and introduced me—as "the man who teaches animal rights in the vet school." I had just begun to entertain the thought that this was not the most politic introduction when the audience began to boo, hiss, catcall, and stomp their feet. And it continued. Stunned (nothing like this had ever happened before), I glanced at my watch, seized by an inexplicable desire to know how long they would boo. The ruckus continued for one minute and thirty-eight seconds, roughly the time it takes to read a typewritten page out loud. During that period, my shock turned to indignation, and then to fury. Sons of bitches. I was not going to take this crap from them. But what to do?

I sketched a plan in my mind. As the booing waned, I asked, in a cold, dead voice, "Are you finished yet?" A few yelled, "No" and continued to boo. I asked again in fifteen seconds. Same result. After another minute, they grew tired of the game, and the cafeteria grew quiet. I stared at them without saying anything. The room grew even quieter. Finally, I spoke. "You guys have read my stuff—is that why you're booing?" "No," they said. "Well, you've heard me speak before, and that's why you're booing?" "No," they shouted, "and we don't want to hear you tonight." I continued, "Have your sons and daughters been in my classes and carried my message here, and *that's* why you're booing?" Again they answered no. My eyes narrowed. "Then you can't be booing my ideas, because you don't even know what they are. So what could it be? I bet you're looking up here and seeing this hippie, commie, Jew bastard, faggot professor and *that's* why you're booing." They cheered. "OK, that's what I thought," I said. "If that's the case, I'll take you outside one at a time and kick your fucking asses. Who's first?" I looked at a stocky man in the first row. "How about you, fatso? I heard you booing?"

I should relate the phenomenology of what I was experiencing. While part of me was doing this song and dance, another part was sort of on the ceiling, above the fray, watching what was happening and quietly wondering whether I should be doing it. As angry as I was, that part was quickly suppressed.

At any rate, the room was now silent. I remember thinking, idiotically, that it seemed as if the silence was a positive phenomenon, a thing, not the absence of sound. Perhaps I could slice it and sell it—fresh Colorado silence. They stared at me openmouthed. I kept ranting. "Where I grew up you learn early that you don't take shit. If you take it once, you take it forever. You guys aren't even paying me for this talk—even if you were, I couldn't put up with this crap." My eyes scanned the room. They were listening. "Do I have your attention?" They nodded. I said, "Good. Now I'm going to ask you two questions. If the answers turn out right, we may have a profitable evening. If they don't, I'll go back to Fort Collins, and you guys can go out and lynch somebody or whatever you do for recreation." After a moment, someone said, "OK, ask your questions."

I said, "First of all, do you guys believe in right and wrong?" "Hell, yes," they replied. "This is Kiowa." "So far so good. Second question: Would you do anything at all to an animal to increase profit and productivity? In other words, if you could increase feed efficiency by torturing a cow's eye with hot needles, would you do it?" "Hell, no," they chorused. "Good," I said. "So we're just arguing about price." It was as if someone had introduced a vacuum cleaner into the room and sucked out the hostility. I started my lecture at quarter after seven and finished at nine thirty. "Time for a break," I said, eyeing the coffee and cookies. No one offered me any, so I invited questions. The first was "Tell us what's wrong with ranching from an animal-welfare point of view." "How the hell should I know?" I shot back. "I'm just a hippie, faggot, commie, Jew-bastard professor. You tell me." And they did. They told me everything I would have told them, plus a number of issues I had never heard of before. This was my first encounter with the honesty and common sense that characterizes this population. Indeed, when they listed knife castration as a welfare issue, I gave them an out, pointing out that many veterinarians believe that animals don't feel pain. One man pulled out his Buck knife and said, "If you think it don't hurt, how'd you like yours cut off with this? If it don't hurt, why the hell are they bellowin' and struggling?"

The evening continued with rapid-fire discussion and no dead time. No cookies for me. Eventually, the custodian said, "Have a heart folks. I can't go home until I lock up the high school." I looked at my watch—almost five hours had passed. I still had a three-hour drive. Enough. I walked over to Melissa to say goodbye, chatted for a few minutes, then left. As I walked toward my car in the dimly lit parking lot, I noticed five men following me. Awash as I was in adrenaline, I assumed they were taking me up on my challenge. So be it. I took off my jacket and tie and glasses, placed them on the roof of the car, and put my back up against the car. "What the hell do you guys want?" I snarled. They were all forty to sixty years old, and one man was clearly the leader. "We came to apologize, Doc," he said, extending his right hand. Coney Island experience kicked in. If I shake hands with him, I lose one weapon—my hands—that I can't afford to lose. I was about to turn my back when it occurred to me that perhaps he meant it. If he did, not shaking would be ignoble, graceless, so I stuck out my hand, and we shook. "We're sorry, Doc. We had no call to boo you before you even said anything," he said. "Thanks for not walking out on us. We learned a lot from your talk." After I shook each man's hand, and said, "No problem. See you guys next time." I drove off, and when I was far out of town, I stopped the car, shook like a leaf, and cried like a baby. And the story is not over. I'll finish it later.

I have never had another incident quite as dramatic, and eventually my reputation became such that I was greeted as a friend. On one occasion, my small son and four students accompanied me to Laramie, Wyoming, where I was to speak at the "Summit," an annual conference for ranchers at the fairgrounds. The audience was cold and surly until I was done. Then an immaculate man in western attire, probably eight-five years old, stood up with the aid of a pair of canes and said, "Thank you for eloquently putting into words how I have tried to live my life." I even got a positive story in the Laramie local paper, the *Boomerang.* I became so comfortable with these people that I would tease them. For example, since cowboy humor is very similar to New York Jewish humor, I would often tell them they were the lost tribes who, as Bugs Bunny put it, "took a wrong turn at Albakoyke [Albuquerque]."

I have addressed some fifteen thousand ranchers since my first talk, all the way from northern Alberta to southern New Mexico, from California to Nebraska. I have found them to be warm, open, tough, independent, open-minded, and kind people who, unlike M.D./Ph.D.s hear what you say, not what they expect you to say. To help cement my image, I often went to give talks on the Harley, my little boy on the back. Ironically, he became the "go to" person at Stanford University on western ranching, a topic about which students were insatiably curious.

Another good story concerns the cowboy "poet" and comedian Baxter

Black, of whom one of my cattle veterinarian friends once said, "It's a damn good thing he's funny, because he's not worth shit as a veterinarian." A few years after I started teaching the vet class, I received an unexpected call from Black during which he mocked my course and animal ethics, finally desisting when I offered him the opportunity to come to the class and debate me. I assured him that, to be fair, I would tie half my mind behind my back. (Yes, I originated that phrase well before Rush Limbaugh.) That ended that. There is no way a cheap-shot artist will engage in genuine discussion. A few years after that, I was invited to address the Bull Test Seminar dinner, a big event in Worland, Wyoming. (A bull test is a meeting that centers on finding the best bull genetics.) I found out that Black would be the after-dinner speaker. I must have appeared uncomfortable, because my host asked why that bothered me. I told him the story and said that, while I criticize some aspects of ranching, Black obsequiously lavishes praise on them. My host put his arm on my shoulder and said, "Don't worry, Doc. He's a paid entertainer. We understand that a friend tells you what you *need* to hear, not what you want to hear. You're a good friend." That story encapsulates why I am proud to call many of these people my friends.

One of my longtime cowboy friends is a man named Barney Cosner who introduced me to the issues of rodeo, fairs, and livestock shows. When I met Barney in the early 1980s, he was livestock manager of the Texas State Fair and invited me to speak to the Fair and Rodeo Association's annual meeting of managers, held that year in Jackson, Wyoming. Barney is a man of courage, ethics, and integrity. In my speech to the group of open, friendly people, most of them from a cowboy background, I talked about emerging societal ethics for animals and warned the audience of what would soon be unacceptable: anything that hurt animals for fun, notably calf roping and steer tripping (the latter is illegal in all but a few states). I enjoyed the meeting greatly and had a very pleasant dinner with a man I liked immediately, Charles W. ("Chuck") Sylvester, manager of the large and prestigious National Western Livestock Show and Rodeo in Denver.

Through my friendship with Chuck, I had an experience that really showed me how much I had been accepted by cowboys for myself and not as a "wannabe." (I see Chuck a few times a year for dinner, at his annual party, and at the stock show, and I supported his ill-fated but noble run for governor as an independent write-in candidate in 2006.) I got a call from Eric Mills, a witty crusading animal-rights activist from San Francisco who has fought to improve rodeo in California. Eric had taken my son to an animal-rights demonstration against crated veal when Mikey was about six and given him a sign to carry. (Thus, my son has done one more demonstration than I have, demonstrations not being my style.) I was amused by Mikey's enthusiasm and even more amused when a passing yuppie playfully grabbed his sign to tease him. I barely prevented Mikey from taking out his kneecap with a side kick.

Eric told me that he had received a call from a Denver activist saying that National Western was putting on a Mexican rodeo. Mexican rodeos are atrocious, particularly because they involve horse tripping, in which a competitor ropes a horse's legs at a full gallop. Horse tripping is now illegal in most states. (I was later to work with the American Association of Equine Practitioners president, the excellent Jay Merriam, another man I am proud to call a friend, to eliminate these spectacles.) I told Eric that even though I had no firsthand knowledge of what the National Western was doing, I would guarantee that, knowing Chuck Sylvester, there would be no animal-abusive Mexican rodeo and told him to call Chuck and use my name. I was correct. What was planned was a rodeo with a Mexican flavor (mariachis, dancing, and the like) but nothing abusive (besides the ubiquitous calf roping present at all rodeos and the source of my major critique of rodeo). Eric confirmed this with Chuck, and Chuck was touched by my willingness to assure a critic about his decency.

Chuck and I worked together over many years. When my cowboy friends elected me to the National Western Stock Show Association, he helped me establish the association's Animal Care and Use Committee to ensure proper treatment of the animals at the show. The committee has done good work that has ranged from appointing a group of retired veterinarians to do plainclothes patrols of the show to ensure that the animals are receiving adequate food and water and are handled properly and gently to ensuring that a draft horse on which children sit while their pictures are being taken does not have to stand on concrete and hurt his feet and legs. I was surprised when Chuck asked me to stay overnight at his ranch in Wyoming and accompany him when the U.S. Bureau of Land Management (BLM) toured the land he was leasing from the government. The tours ostensibly are done to ensure that the land is properly managed and grazed. Under President Bill Clinton, the BLM managers were responsive to environmentalists' demands that ranchers be prevented from grazing their cattle on public land, and the tours often turned into bureaucratic bullying and browbeating. I asked Chuck what value my presence would have. He just smiled and said, "You'll see."

I spent a pleasant evening and morning at his beautiful ranch, talking to a group of his neighbors. At breakfast before the tour, I asked the dozen or so ranchers present a question I had asked many times before, a litmus-paper question for identifying the husbandry ethic—"How many of you have spent more on a sick animal than the animal is worth?" (I knew the answer; indeed, my students with ranching backgrounds had taught me that the only time they had even been punished or yelled at by their dads was when they had gone to a dance or movie without caring for the animals first.) The answer was: everyone in the room. One woman, a fifth-generation rancher, thought I was critical of doing that and said, with an edge, "What's wrong with that, Buster?" (Buster?) "Nothing by my lights," I replied, "but if I were an agricultural economist, I would tell you that one does not spend twenty dollars to produce a widget that one then sells for ten dollars." "Well, that's your mistake, Buster," she said. "We're not dealing with widgets. We're dealing with living things we're responsible for." You can see why I was so willing to help Chuck. Ranchers are the last large group of people practicing husbandry, or what my colleague Temple Grandin has called the "ancient contract" with animals, a highly symbiotic relationship that endured essentially unchanged for thousands of years. Ranching depends on large, extensive grazing areas. Much of that land is under federal control by the BLM. If ranching were removed from public land, there would be virtually no husbandry agriculture. The BLM of late is not kind to ranchers, and its officials were coming to check on the condition of Chuck's leased land.

We were to meet the BLM people near the firehouse in Jeffrey City, Wyoming. Chuck, who is politically savvy, had invited dozens of rancher friends and a husband-and-wife cowboy-and-lawyer team who specialize in suing the BLM, as well as me. I still had no idea why I was there. It became clearer when we got to the firehouse. Seven or eight BLM people showed up in Jeeps led by a man I will call Jack Murphy, a pink-and-white Irishman who did not like ranchers. He had expected only Chuck and the adjacent landholder; he was greeted by about sixty people in dozens of trucks. "What is this?" he asked, turning red. "Just some friends," Chuck said. "This is public, isn't it?" Murphy began to hand out index cards, asking us all to write down our names and affiliations. Since I did not look like a rancher—I have been described as looking like a cross between a rabbi and a biker—his gaze focused on me. I began to get the idea. I filled out the card—B. Rollin, CSU, Distinguished Professor. Murphy turned pinker as he read it. "CSU," he said. "Long way from here." "Yup," I said. "You in agronomy?" "Nope," I replied. "Range management?" "Nope." "What are you in?" "This and that," I said, enjoying the moment. "What does that mean?" he stammered. I said, "Vet med, animal science, and philosophy." "Ph-Ph-Ph-Philosophy?" he said. "Wh-What's your interest?" I put a brawny arm on his shoulder and said, "I deal in conflict resolution and want to see how you handle these people."

We spent the next six hours bouncing over rangeland while Murphy pointed out degradation I could not detect even as he pointed it out. Finally, he stopped us all at the pièce de résistance, a minuscule stream about three feet wide, and pointed to it accusingly: "Look at this riparian area. The banks are eroded. I had to show this to the head of the Sierra Club last week. I was mortified. He was horrified. I'm going to have to fence this off so cattle can't do more damage." The woman who had called me "Buster" got emotional. She said to Murphy, "I am a fifth-generation rancher here. My family's blood, sweat, and tears are in this land. This Sierra Club fellow, he is maybe here one time. Doesn't my interest count more?" "No," said Murphy. "I protect the land for all, and you people cause me great embarrassment."

I hate bureaucrats—especially bureaucrats who brandish their authority as a cudgel. I hated Murphy and walked away before I said something I might regret. I walked about a mile in a spiral. Suddenly something struck me as I examined the ground. I rushed back to the spot where Murphy was winding up his chastisement. I raised my hand; he acknowledged me. "Mr. Murphy, I'm a city boy, so forgive my ignorance," I said as he eyed me suspiciously. "Are you saying that cows did this damage?" "Of course," he replied. I gave him a gunfighter look. "Well, I just walked a spiral for about a mile, and if it was cows, there would be cow shit, right? All I saw was horseshit." I watched him pale as it dawned on him where I was going. "Chuck runs a few horses but keeps them fenced in by his house. He doesn't run horses out here. In fact, only the BLM runs horses out here." Murphy turned deep red and blustered, "We only run about thirty." I said, "Gee, Chuck and I counted over ninety this morning alone near his house." "Impossible," Murphy said. I smiled—with my mouth but not my eyes. "I guess we've got a factual dispute here. As a matter of fact, I have a friend in Lander [where Murphy was based], a wildlife biologist who counts antelope for the oil companies. I could have him come out and count horses." "Great idea," said one of Murphy's lackeys. "No," he shouted, looking daggers at the underling, who reddened and said no more. "Why not?" I asked. "Be-Be-Because it will stress them." "Yeah, sure," I said. Applause broke out from the ranchers. I later heard that this was the first time Murphy had dealt fairly with ranchers. Chuck just smiled at me. I had earned my bed and breakfast.

I once went to Billings, Montana, to lecture on rodeo to the Northern Rodeo Association. I was so well received that the association asked me to give the lecture again when I was done so they wouldn't miss any points. On another occasion, I was invited to Rocky Mountain College in Billings to talk to a group of ranchers about animal ethics. When they asked me how much time to allot, I said, "As much as you can give me so we can have dialogue." Imagine my surprise when I was scheduled for eight hours, with an hour for lunch. Despite my trepidation, we went two hours over. In the middle of the afternoon, one woman asked if we could break so she could go to the bathroom. The group said, "You go pee; we don't want to stop."

If you are wondering why I have such an excellent relationship with ranchers, this is a good time to explain. It is my contention that western ranchers, from northern Alberta to the Mexican border, from Kansas to California, are the last large group of people in agriculture practicing "animal husbandry." Husbandry is the traditional essence of agricultural success and, sadly, is now almost extinct.

The traditional account of the growth of human civilization out of a hunter–gatherer society invariably invokes the rise of agriculture: the domestication of animals and the cultivation of crops. This allowed as predictable a food supply as humans could create amid floods, droughts, hurricanes, typhoons, extremes of heat and cold, fires, and other vagaries of the natural world. Indeed, the use of animals enabled the development of successful crop agriculture, with the animals providing labor and locomotion, as well as food and fiber. This is what eventually resulted in the "ancient contract" with animals. Humans selected animals that were congenial to human management and further shaped their temperaments and production traits through breeding and artificial selection. These animals included cattle, sheeps, goats, horses, dogs, poultry and other birds, swine, ungulates, and other animals capable of domestication. As people grew more effective at breeding and managing animals, productivity increased. And as humans benefited, so did the animals. They were provided with the necessities of life in a predictable way. This gave rise to the concept of husbandry, the remarkable practice and articulation of the symbiotic contract.

"Husbandry" is derived from the Old Norse words "*hus*" and "*bond*"; animals were bonded to one's household. The essence of husbandry was care. Humans put animals into the best environments possible for their survival, the environments for which they had evolved and been selected. In addition, humans provided sustenance, water, shelter, protection from predation, such medical attention as was available, help in birthing, food during famine, water during drought, safe surroundings, and comfortable appointments. Eventually, what was born of necessity and common sense became articulated in terms of a moral obligation that was inextricably bound up with self-interest. In the biblical story of Noah, we learn that even as God preserves humans, humans preserve animals. The ethic of husbandry is, in fact, taught throughout the Bible: The animals must rest on the Sabbath even as we do; one is not to seethe a calf in its mother's milk (so we do not grow insensitive to animals' needs and natures); we can violate the Sabbath to save an animal's life. Proverbs tells us that "the wise man cares for his animals." The Old Testament is replete with injunctions against inflicting unnecessary pain and suffering on animals, as exemplified in the strange story of Balaam, who beats his ass and is reprimanded as the animal speaks through the grace of God.

The true power of the husbandry ethic is best expressed in the Twenty-third Psalm: "The Lord is My Shepherd; I shall not want. He maketh me to lie down in green pastures, He leadeth me beside the still waters, He restoreth my soul." We want no more from God than what the good shepherd provides to his animals. Indeed, consider a lamb in ancient Judea. Without a shepherd, the lamb would not easily find forage or water; it would not survive the multitude of predators—lions, jackals, hyenas, birds of prey, wild dogs, velociraptors (just checking to see that you are paying attention)—the Bible tells us prowled the land. Under the aegis of the shepherd, the lamb lives well and safely. In return, the animals provide their products and sometimes their lives, but while they live, they live well. Even slaughter, the taking of the animal's life, must be as painless as possible, performed with a sharp knife by a trained person to avoid unnecessary pain. Ritual slaughter in antiquity was a far kinder death than bludgeoning; most important, it was the most humane modality available at the time. The metaphor of the good shepherd is emblazoned in the Western mind. To this day, ministers are called shepherds of their congregations, and the word "pastor" derives from "pastoral." When Plato discusses the ideal political ruler in *Republic,* he deploys the shepherd-and-sheep metaphor: The ruler is to his people as the shepherd is to his flock.

Animal husbandry can be characterized as putting square pegs in square holes, round pegs in round holes, and creating as little friction as possible in doing so. Ranchers still practice and believe in husbandry. Ranching is basically unchanged structurally from the nineteenth century: Cattle graze on vast ranges and get to express their *telos* more fully than any other agricultural animal. The modern rancher may differ from his nineteenth-century predecessor, perhaps, by riding fence with a motorcycle, but even that is largely unchanged and can be done on horseback. More than 90 percent of the fifteen thousand ranchers with whom I have spoken heartily endorse the notion of rights for animals I have discussed—a greater percentage of them, in fact, than of the general public. This is because husbandry *must* work with the animals' natures and does not override them with technology. The biggest animal-welfare issues in ranching are so-called management practices—castration without anesthesia, hot-iron branding without anesthesia, dehorning without anesthesia. Every rancher answers the question "If God came down and said that these practices were banned, would you go out of business?" the same way: "Of course not." But it is easier to get them to admit that these practices are wrong than to get them to adopt alternatives.

I—and animals—have benefited greatly from my friendship with the Colorado Cattlemen's Association and Colorado Cattle Feeders Association. Out of that relationship, and my relationship with the Colorado dairy industry, came the passage of the strongest "downer cow" law in the United States. (Downer cows are animals that are unable to walk because of illness or injury and are sometimes dragged to a truck and shipped to slaughter and dragged out at the destination.) I was lecturing to the Colorado Cattlemen in the 1980s at a meeting. Among other issues, I was discussing downer cows. "What do you guys think of that?" I asked. I was told, "It ain't right. We should eat our mistakes, not ship them." One large man stood up and said, "I'm Dr. Don Klinkerman, a sale barn vet. I think you're full of shit." Music to my ears. "Care to debate that, pal?" I asked, twirling my imaginary six guns. "Nope," he said. "I need to think about it." Five years later, he called me. "I thought about it," he said. "Want to debate?" I asked. "No," he said. "I decided you're right. We shouldn't allow shipping of downers."

He enlisted dairy farmer managers, a major source of downers due to hypocalcemia ("milk fever") and traditionally the source of opposition to stopping the practice. I already had developed a good relationship with the dairy people—I am the official Colorado Dairy Welfare Extension Specialist—and they were very open and supported the bill. I told him I would be happy to help. He said he would call me if he needed me. I eventually got a call; he was experiencing hostility from the sale barn vets, as sale barns made some money from downers. I said I would do what I could and called one of my colleagues at CSU, the large-animal veterinarian Cleon Kimberling, a legend across the West. Dr. Kimberling made some calls; the pressure ended and the bill passed.

The most appropriate story to conclude this chapter occurred in 1997, after the passage of North American Free Trade Agreement (NAFTA), designed to loosen trade barriers among the United States, Canada, and Mexico. The U.S. Department of Agriculture (USDA), part of whose job is farm-animal health, was accustomed to preventing Mexican cattle from crossing the U.S. border, because Mexican cattle often have tuberculosis and brucellosis, which wasn't present in the U.S. herd. When NAFTA passed, they could no longer keep these animals out. In its trademark heavy-handed way, the USDA decided that the appropriate response was to use hot-iron branding on the faces of Mexican cattle so they could be readily identified by a large, clearly visible "M" and carefully watched for disease.

I was made aware of this by the famed animal activist Henry Spira, who had successfully organized the first massive animal-rights demonstration in 1989 against sexual-behavior experiments on cats done by the Museum of Natural History. He rallied Manhattan office workers to protest outside the museum during their lunch hour on beautiful spring days. The protest was immense and eventually forced the museum to stop invasive research. I knew Henry quite well from 1978 until his death and liked and respected him. He was the person who called public attention to the infamous Draize eye irritancy test done on rabbits to ensure the safety of cosmetics. Henry had gone to Revlon with a professionally made poster showing rabbits having their eyes irritated and the slogan "How Many Rabbits Must Revlon Blind for Your Beauty?" He told cosmetics executives that he would put the ads in every subway system in the world unless they funded the Center for Alternatives to Animal Testing at Johns Hopkins University to research alternatives to using animals. The industry contributed, and the center made great progress under the leadership of Alan Goldberg. (I was honored a few years ago to receive the Spira Award from the center at an International Congress on Alternatives in Berlin.)

Henry called me to ask where he could get a branding iron. I was surprised but assured him I could get one and asked why. He then told me about his campaign against the USDA's face branding. Although Henry lived in the most modest circumstances, taking only something like twenty thousand per year in salary from his organization, he spent great amounts to protect animals. He always had in reserve the fee for a full-page advertisement in the *New York Times.* He sent me copies of the anti-USDA ads he had already run. As with everything else Henry did, they were classic. For example, one ad showed a child with a USDA face brand and the slogan "Good Thing USDA Isn't in Charge of Child Care." In another, he described the face-branding atrocity and gave the Secretary of Agriculture's home telephone number, resulting in thousands of (urban) phone calls to that hapless bureaucrat. Anyway, he wanted a branding iron as a prop. He also told me that investigators from People for the Ethical Treatment of Animals had video footage of a face-branded cow enveloped in smoke from her own burned face and that some animals, branded too close to the orbital, had had their eyes boiled out. The USDA also had Mexican veterinarians spay the females on the Mexican side of the border with no anesthesia or analgesia and close the wound with metal "hog clips" that had gotten caught in slaughterhouse equipment and sent deadly shrapnel shooting in all directions. I also knew that the USDA, in the early 1980s, had been convicted of cruelty in a New York State court for face-branding dairy cattle when it was buying up dairy cows to stabilize the price of milk and needed permanent identification to keep the farmers from recycling the cows into dairies.

At this time, my book *Farm Animal Welfare* (1995) had appeared. The book grew out of a research project I had done on farm-animal welfare and had originated as a USDA report. I thought, having essentially introduced USDA officials to the farm-animal-welfare issue, I might be able to reason with them. I told Henry that I could probably get them to stop the face branding. I called contacts at the department and was told, in essence, to butt out because this was a done deal. I was distraught. I already had concerns about branding on the rump—but *face* branding? I tried every trick in my arsenal. In my presence, Jim Voss, dean of veterinary medicine at CSU, even called the bureaucrat who had signed the face-branding order, who was a former veterinary school dean, but got nowhere and cut the conversation short by saying, "You're just another mealy-mouthed bureaucrat." After slamming down the phone, he remarked, "That's the end of a twenty-year friendship." I began to call rancher friends who were also horrified. I thought about starting a petition drive among them.

A few days later, I received a call from the Colorado Cattlemen's Association, which had heard about my concerns and invited me to talk to the board of directors. I agreed, put on a suit, and went to Denver, very tense. It didn't help when I began to speak and they began to tease me. "You seem nervous today, Doc. You're usually such a cocky little bastard." ("Little," of course, is a relative term.) I responded by saying that this was a very troubling issue: bad for the animals, a black eye to ranching. "Relax," they said. "We've already decided to back you. See those phones over there? We've got the California and Washington State cattlemen on them. They'll back you, too. What we need from you, being that you are a wordsmith, is to stay for lunch and help us write the statement we'll give you." I was amazed. In contrast, the National Cattlemen's Association supported the USDA. I stayed and helped them write a brief, to-the-point statement opposing face branding. The secretary typed it onto letterhead, and I grabbed it and took off, making a brief stop in the men's room. At the adjacent urinal was a very large man who, I had been warned, was the biggest redneck in the group. He turned to me and said, "Thanks for taking this on, Doc. I'm eighty-four, and I declare that if I saw someone branding an animal on the face, I'd have to kick the shit out of him."

I drove about five miles and stopped dead. I had forgotten to ask what I could do with the written statement. Could I give it to Henry to use in an ad? Could I threaten the USDA with it? I went back to the association's headquarters and asked the executive director. He said that it was a board decision, so I needed to go back to the boardroom. I did, and the chairman of the board said, "You again? What now?" I explained. He looked me in the eye and said, "Doc, we talked the talk; you walk the walk. It's your document now. We trust you." He called for a break and, as he walked me back to my car, said, "You haven't changed a bit." "How do you know?" I replied. "I don't know you." "Oh, but I know you," he said. "How?" I asked. He replied, "Remember that night in Kiowa? Remember the guy who came out to apologize? That was me." He shook my hand.

I called the USDA. My contacts' reply was "We already told you. It's a done deal." I let them know that I had new information, to which they replied, "Give us a week to ask for new comments, and then it will be rescinded." It was. Henry called to thank me and to offer a full-page ad thanking the Cattlemen's Associations of Colorado, Washington, and California, but they said no thanks. The National Cattlemen's Association (a much more bureaucratic group) left me a voice mail the day of my visit to the board saying, "Keep your nose out of our business." I called back knowing who had left it, although he was too gutless to leave his name. I told him he wasn't big enough to tell me where to put my nose.

It is incidents such as that one that led one eighty-year-old rancher in rural Colorado to stay after I had finished my talk and, when everyone else had left, look me in the eye and say, "I got you figured out, Doc. . . . Way I figure, you were born too late. You should have lived a hundred years ago and been a gunfighter. You love getting us all riled and then taking us on and getting us to agree. Closest thing you can do that's like gun fighting." I can't disagree.

15

Industrial Agriculture

If my work in agriculture had ended with dealing with ranchers, it would have been easy. But in the early 1990s, I was called on to turn my attention to industrial agriculture, popularly known as "factory farming," which contained a far more serious and difficult set of issues.

I became aware of industrial agriculture in broad outline in the 1980s but was not familiar or knowledgeable enough about it to include a discussion of it in *Animal Rights and Human Morality* (Rollin 1981). I was not comfortable writing about areas in which I did not have firsthand knowledge, and my students were by and large cattle people. While the cattle industry had intensified after World War II when the "Green Revolution" led to an abundance of cheap grain, and people realized that they would earn far more money if they put the grain into cattle, feedlots were recognized to be the least problematic of confinement units. The social nature of cattle was respected in the large pens in which they were kept, and they could move freely. There certainly were, and still are, welfare issues in feedlots—notably, poor drainage that leads to the animals' standing in mud (and, in winter, frozen mud) and a lack of shade and shelter from prairie sun, wind, and weather. But these problems did not approach the gravity of confined systems for producing pigs, poultry, eggs, and veal. Since the majority (some 85 percent) of feedlot operators come from ranching backgrounds, and thus were imbued with the husbandry ethic, they were not hostile to my message. In fact, I gave the keynote speech at two annual general meetings of the Colorado Cattle Feeders Association and had good relations with that organization.

My knowledge of confinement agriculture grew sharply in the 1990s through my relationship with John Patrick Jordan, one of the first friends I made at CSU outside the Philosophy Department. Pat, as he was known, held a doctorate in science and had a broad range of interests, from agriculture and veterinary medicine to ethics and philosophy. He was also a man of enormous energy. He directed CSU's Agricultural Experiment Station, which had a decent budget and sponsored research relevant to agriculture in Colorado, which in Pat's mind included philosophy, history, and sociology. He put me on a CSU committee charged with awarding small grants for research.

All of the other committee members were senior scientists. I was the token humanist representing the College of Liberal Arts to meet a legal requirement. Twice a year, we met and received our assignments of submitted protocols, which we reviewed for a month, and then reconvened to make the awards. The committee did not know what to do with me and finally gave me two protocols. One was on mycorhyzoids (root funguses), because mycorhyzoids are important in production, food production is an ethical issue, and I was in philosophy. The other was on music therapy, which was the only submission from my college. I recall spending an inordinate amount of time mastering the protocols so I would not disgrace myself or my field. When we came to the music-therapy protocol, which involved a request to fund an organ to try to teach autistic children to speak, I was very critical of it, as no evidence had been cited to support any connection between organ music and the acquisition of language; nor was there even a reasonable hypothesis regarding a connection. Clearly, the researcher wanted money for an organ. I articulated my objections and concluded by saying that the proposal, though from my college, was neither conceptually nor empirically well founded and should not be funded. I was shocked when the committee's chairman looked directly into my eyes and said, "I don't know about you, but I for one want to leave no stone unturned to try to help those poor children, and I'm surprised you don't." Worse still, all of the other members were nodding and looking at me as though I were Scrooge. They unanimously voted to fund the proposal and ignored my rejoinder "Why don't you hire a witch doctor?" *Mirabile dictu,* all but me were accomplished scientists.

Thus, Pat was instrumental in helping me realize that science is not value-free; it is not the ideal crystalline structure I had been taught in philosophy of science classes. (It is, rather, a human and value-laden enterprise.) In the late 1980s, Pat was tapped to become a U.S undersecretary of agriculture in charge of the Cooperative State Research Service, which, together with the Agricultural Research Service, performed and funded research in agriculture with hundreds of millions of dollars.

In 1991, the U.S. Department of Agriculture (USDA), in part because of Pat's urging, sponsored an international conference on farm animals' welfare in Wye Woods, Maryland, and invited speakers from all over the world, including Ruth Harrison, the British journalist who exposed the ills of factory farming in her pioneering *Animal Machines* (1964), which so agitated the British public that Parliament was forced to charter the famed Brambell Commission to examine confinement agriculture. I was invited to speak and delivered a paper on farm animals' welfare. On hearing the many papers by others, and caught up in the spirit of conference, I asked Pat how much of the USDA's research money went toward farm animals' welfare. The answer, which he researched for me, was none of it. I said that this was unconscionable, given the suffering of animals and the fact that the welfare of farm animals was already a major issue in Europe. He agreed and hired me to write a manuscript explaining the philosophical and societal context of farm-animal-welfare issues and describing the researchable issues in each industry that needed to be studied.

The resulting manuscript was accepted by the USDA in 1993, and fifteen million dollars were allocated for research into the welfare of farm animals. Unfortunately, the program lasted only a few years: Political pressure from the industry on the USDA's new secretary forced its cancellation. But I was bitten by the bug. Whereas at most one hundred million animals were used in research, nine billion to eleven billion animals were produced in confinement agriculture. I published my reports as *Farm Animal Welfare* (Rollin 1995a). In writing that book, I had visited many confinement facilities and had been most deeply affected by seeing gestation crates for pregnant sows, two-by-three-by-seven-foot cages with concrete slat flooring in which a sow spent her whole productive life. I saw the animals go mad from stress and boredom in these sow stalls—pigs are at least as smart as dogs. Having forced the research community to "reappropriate common sense" about animals' pain and distress via legislation, I made a resolution that I would work to end sow stalls.

Recall the story I told about ranchers spending more on calves than is economically warranted. I have a parallel anecdote about industrialized agriculture. It was told to me by Glen Rask, one of my colleagues in the Department of Animal Sciences at CSU. His son-in-law had grown up on a ranch but could not return to it after college because it could not support him and all of his siblings. He reluctantly took a job managing a feeder pig barn (pigs being grown for slaughter) at a large swine factory farm. One day, he reported to his boss that a disease had struck his piglets. "I have bad news and good news," he said. "The bad news is that the piglets are sick. The good news is that they can be treated economically." "We don't treat," the boss said. "We euthanize" (by dashing the baby pigs' heads on the side of the concrete pen). The young man could not accept this. He bought the medicine with his own money and reported for work even on his day off to treat the animals. They recovered, and he told the boss, who said, "You're fired." The young man pointed out that he had treated the pigs on his own time and with his own money and was thus not subject to firing. He did, however, receive a written reprimand. Six months later, he quit and became an electrician. He wrote to Rask, "I know you're disappointed that I left agriculture, Dad, but this ain't agriculture."

Industrial agriculture contrasts sharply with husbandry. The singular beauty of husbandry is that it is at once an ethical and a prudential doctrine. It was prudential in that failure to observe husbandry inexorably led to ruination of the person keeping animals. Although this ancient contract with domestic animals was inherently sustainable, it was not, in fact, sustained with the coming of industrialization. Husbandry was born of necessity, and as soon as necessity vanished, the contract was broken. The industrial revolution portended the end of husbandry, for humans no longer needed to respect their animals to ensure productivity. In symbolic advertisement of the breaking of our sustainable contract with animals as industry replaced husbandry, in the mid-twentieth century academic departments of animal husbandry in the United States became departments of animal sciences. Indeed, animal sciences textbooks characterize the field as the application of industrial methods to the production of animals. The values of productivity and efficiency replaced the values of husbandry, to the detriment of animals, sustainability, the environment, agriculture as a way of life, rural communities, stewardship, and a respectful, moral stance toward the living things on which we built our civilization.

One of my colleagues in animal sciences, a beef production specialist (as mentioned, sectors of the beef industry are the only remaining bulwarks of husbandry), has repeatedly affirmed, "The *worst* thing that ever happened to my department is betokened by the name change." If a nineteenth-century agriculturalist, for example, had tried to raise a hundred thousand egg-laying hens in cages in one building, they all would have died of disease spread in a month. Today, such systems dominate animal agriculture. Why did this occur?

I must stress that the new approach to animal agriculture was not the result of cruelty, bad character, or even insensitivity. It developed instead out of perfectly decent, prima facie plausible motives that were a product of dramatic and significant historical and social upheavals that occurred around the time of World War II. At that point, agricultural scientists and government officials became extremely concerned about supplying the public with cheap and plentiful food for a variety of reasons. First, after the Dust Bowl and the Great Depression, many people in the United States had soured on farming. Second, reasonable predictions of urban and suburban encroachment on agricultural land were being made, with a resultant diminution of land for food production. Third, many farm people had been sent to foreign and domestic urban centers during the two world wars, thereby creating a reluctance to return to rural areas that lacked excitement. Recall the early-twentieth-century song that says, "How are you gonna keep 'em down on the farm after they've seen Paree?" Fourth, having experienced the specter of literal starvation during the Depression, the American consumer, for the first time in history, was fearful of an insufficient food supply.

When these considerations of loss of land and diminution of agricultural labor are coupled with the rapid development of a variety of technological modalities relevant to agriculture during and after World War II, and with the burgeoning belief in technologically based economies of scale, it was probably inevitable that animal agriculture would be subjected to industrialization. This was a major departure from traditional agriculture and a fundamental change in agricultural core values; industrial values of efficiency and productivity replaced and eclipsed the traditional values of way of life and husbandry.

Between World War II and the mid-1970s, agricultural productivity—including animal products—increased dramatically. In the hundred years between 1820 and 1920, agricultural productivity doubled. After that, productivity continued to double in much shorter and ever decreasing time periods. The next doubling took thirty years (1920–1950), the subsequent doubling took fifteen years (1950–1965), and the next one took only ten years (1965–1975). As Robert E. Taylor points out in *Scientific Farm Animal Production* (1992), the most dramatic change took place after World War II, when productivity increased more than fivefold in thirty years. Fewer workers were producing far more food. Just before World War II, 24 percent of the U.S. population was involved in production agriculture; today, the figure is well under 2 percent (1.7 percent, in fact). Whereas in 1940 each farm worker supplied food for eleven persons in the general population, by 1990 each farm worker was supplying eighty persons. At the same time, the proportion of a family's disposable income spent on food dropped significantly, from 30 percent in 1950 to 11.8 percent in 1990, and is even lower today.

There is thus no question that industrialized agriculture, including animal agriculture, is responsible for greatly increased productivity. It is equally clear that the husbandry associated with traditional agriculture has been radically truncated as a result of industrialization. No husbandry person would ever dream of feeding sheep meal, poultry waste, or cement dust to cattle, but such "innovations" did, in fact, take hold and are entailed by an industrial efficiency mindset.

For our purposes, several aspects of technological agriculture must be noted. First, as just mentioned, the number of farm workers has declined significantly, yet the number of animals produced has increased. This has been made possible by mechanization, technological advancement, and the consequent capability to confine large numbers of animals in highly capitalized facilities that are expensive to build. Of necessity, less attention is paid to individual animals. Second, technological innovations have allowed the environments in which animals are kept to be altered. Whereas in traditional agriculture, animals had to be kept in the environments for which they had evolved, we can now keep them in environments that are contrary to their natures but congenial to increased productivity.

When I first began to think about these issues, I was troubled by a vexatious question: When people developed these confinement systems, and assuming that they were normal people with normal concern for the well-being of their animals, why did they not see the now obvious consequences for animal welfare? Did they not care? We can only speculate—but, I think, with reasonable accuracy. Recall that the only model the originators of confinement agriculture had to base their thinking on was traditional agriculture. In traditional agriculture, as the discussion thus far implies, productivity of the individual and welfare of the individual animal are closely connected—indeed, inextricably connected. I believe that the early confinement agriculturalists illegitimately extrapolated this connection to industrialized agriculture. Only now they mistakenly assumed that productivity of the entire confinement operation ensures the welfare of the animals in it. The logical error, of course, is that productivity is now being deployed as an economic measure of the entire operation, whereas welfare needed to be predicated of individual animals. In confinement egg production, for example, it is well known that when hens are crowded together in cages, each hen will produce fewer eggs. But the whole operation is still highly productive, because hens are cheap and cages are expensive. Thus, productivity *per cage* is no measure of the welfare of the animals therein.

Let us approach this point in a different way. Consider creating a definition of animal welfare. A report by the Council of Agricultural Science and Technology (CAST) issued in 1982 stated, "The principle [*sic*] criteria used thus far as indexes of the welfare of animals in production systems have been rate of growth or production, efficiency of feed use, efficiency of reproduction, mortality and morbidity." In other words, the welfare of an animal was to be determined by how well the animal fulfilled the human purposes to which it was being put, not by how the animal felt. So in this view, an animal has positive welfare if it is productive.

The most charitable interpretation one can give to such a view is, as mentioned, that it is implicitly rooted in husbandry. Under husbandry, if an animal was productive, it was well off, because both productivity and well-being depended on satisfying the animal's *telos*. But in industrialized agriculture, this close connection was severed, for an animal could be productive without being well off. A whole host of errors are at work here. First, there is a huge logical error. One cannot logically go from "All A is B" to "All B is A"—that is, it does not follow from "all dogs are animals" that "all animals are dogs." Similarly, it does not follow that if all well-off animals are productive, all productive animals are well off.

The reason it doesn't follow involves another logical error: When animal scientists consider productivity, they look at the aggregate economic return across an entire operation. When we look at welfare, we are looking at least at the fundamental import of an individual animal's subjective experiences. So we come to an apples-and-oranges objection. To return to the example of the egg-laying chickens, just because we produce a lot of eggs per cage doesn't mean that each of the chickens in the cage is doing well. Furthermore, some forms of successful production can actually occur when animals are not well off. Today's dairy cow is bred to produce tremendous amounts of milk but is burned out metabolically in a few years. Thus, its productivity is no assurance of its well-being. Or consider a production operation that makes pâté de foie gras, a process that involves force feeding geese whose feet are sometimes nailed to a floor. No one could argue, however productive each animal is in developing a fatty liver (which in any other context is defined as a disease) or however productive (economically) the operation is, that the animals' welfare is ensured.

Or let us take a fanciful example. Many people eat a great deal when they are depressed and unhappy. Imagine cannibals raising people for food and selecting for people who put on the most weight. Let us suppose that the best weight gainers are the depressed and miserable. Surely, no one would argue that because the people farm was productive, the people were well off.

The concept of welfare is far more sophisticated than all this, and I discuss it in detail shortly. For now, however, I return to the issue at hand—namely, why industrialized confinement agriculture is worse for animals than the agriculture of husbandry. The basic approach of confinement agriculture, as mentioned, is to treat animal production as an industry, with the industrial values of efficiency and productivity reigning supreme. This means raising vast numbers of animals, limiting the space needed to raise these animals, moving them indoors into "controlled environments," and installing lower-cost replacements for labor (i.e., replacing humans with mechanized systems). One can tell a priori that this is inimical to husbandry, for husbandry required naturalistic environments, relatively few animals, and a workforce that was knowledgeable about the animals (i.e., the good shepherds).

Confinement agriculture is responsible for generating suffering in animals on at least four fronts that were not a significant part of husbandry agriculture—disease, scale, deprivation, and deskilling:

1. Disease: Veterinarians acknowledge the existence of so-called production diseases—diseases that would not be a problem or, at worst, would be a minor problem if animals were raised traditionally. Production diseases are, in fact, the vast majority of diseases that veterinarians treat in industrial agriculture. One example is liver abscesses in feedlot cattle. Beef cattle are typically raised in pastures and are "finished" by being fed large amounts of grain in feedlots, where a large number of animals are crowded into relatively small spaces for the last few months of their lives. That much grain is not a natural diet for cattle: It is too high in concentrate (calories) and too low in roughage. Although a certain percentage of feedlot cattle get sick and may die, the overall economic efficiency of feedlots is maximized by the provision of such a diet because profit comes from the weight gained by the cattle. Fatty liver in geese, as we just saw, is another example. The idea of using a method of production that *creates diseases* that are "acceptable" would be anathema to a husbandry agriculturalist. Well over 90 percent of what feedlot veterinarians treat are production diseases. A veterinarian colleague of mine calls this "the shame of veterinary medicine," since vets should be working to eliminate pathogenic systems, not treating their problems.

Indeed, the issue of diet causes other problems. In husbandry agriculture, animals ate natural forage. In industrialized agriculture, the quest for "efficiency" has led to feeding cattle poultry waste, newspaper, cement dust, and, most egregiously, bone or meat meal, which is something herbivores would not naturally eat. Mad cow disease (bovine spongiform encephalopathy) resulted as a human health problem because cattle were fed animal products.

2. Scale: The huge scale of industrialized agricultural operations—and the small profit margin per animal—militates against the sort of individual attention that typified much of traditional agriculture. In traditional dairies fifty years ago, one could make a living with a herd of fifty cows. Today, in some areas, one needs literally thousands. In the United States, dairies may have ten thousand cows. People run swine operations with thousands of pigs, employing only a handful of unskilled workers. A veterinarian sent a case that speaks to this point to me for commentary in the ethics column that I write for the *Canadian Veterinary Journal*:

> You (as a veterinarian) are called to a 500-sow farrow-to-finish swine operation to examine a problem with vaginal discharge in sows. There are three full-time employees and one manager overseeing approximately five thousand animals. As you examine several sows in the created gestation unit, you notice one with a hind leg at an unusual angle and inquire about their status. You are told, "She broke her leg yesterday and she's due to farrow next week. We'll let her farrow in here and then we'll shoot her and foster off her pigs." *Is it ethically correct to leave the sow with a broken leg for one week while you await her farrowing?*

Before commenting on the case, I spoke to the veterinarian who had experienced this incident. He explained that such operations run on tiny profit margins and minimal labor. Thus, even when he offered to splint the leg at no cost, he was told that the operation could not afford the manpower that separating this sow and caring for her entailed. At this point, he said, he realized that confinement agriculture had gone too far. He had been brought up on a family hog farm, where the animals had names and were provided individual husbandry and injured animals would have been treated or, if not, euthanized immediately. "If it is not feasible to do this in a confinement operation," he said, "there is something wrong with confinement operations."

3. Deprivation: Physical and psychological deprivation in confinement through lack of space and inability to move freely, lack of companionship for social animals, boredom, and austerity of environments has brought another new source of suffering for animals in industrialized agriculture. The animals evolved in adaptation to extensive environments; when they are placed in such truncated environments, deprivation is inevitable. This was not a problem in traditional, extensive agriculture. From a public point of view, this is the most notable gap in confinement agriculture. Paul Thompson has commented that the average American still sees farms as akin to Old MacDonald's Farm. Cows, in the public mind, should be in pastures; lambs should be gamboling in fields; pigs should be happily cooling themselves in a mud wallow.

4. Deskilling: Workers in confinement facilities no longer need to be "animal smart" or good husbandry people. "The intelligence is in the system," one industry person told me. Today, the largest obstacle to establishing more husbandry-oriented systems is finding good husbandry workers. When average people encounter high-confinement operations, their reactions are memorable. Confinement production of swine serves as a good example. Such operations are usually described in terms of the number of sows in the facility. One operation I visited had three hundred thousand sows spread out in a number of buildings. Each sow lives her entire productive life indoors, regardless of the weather, in what is called a gestation crate or sow stall. A gestation crate is essentially a small pen made of concrete slatted flooring surrounded by heavy bars on each side and at the top. According to the official recommendations of the National Pork Producers Council, which speaks for the industry, the "crate" should measure two and a half feet wide, seven feet long, and three feet high. To get more crates into a building, these enclosures, in actual practice, often tend to be two feet wide.

Each sow can weigh up to six hundred pounds and, in some cases, is longer or wider than the enclosure, so she must lie bowed and uncomfortable. The slats on the floor are covered in excrement; her feet and legs, which are evolutionarily adapted to soft loam, are broken down in the crate. She cannot stand up, turn around, or make significant postural adjustments. Although she possesses bones and muscles, she cannot exercise them. It is generally accepted that swine are far and away the most intelligent of farm animals: Miniature swine raised as pets have consistently triumphed over dogs in obedience contests. With this truncated, sterile, solitary environment, the sow goes mad, compulsively chewing the cage bars and demonstrating stereotypical compulsive behavior that the industry absurdly calls "vices." This locution is misleading and downright inaccurate, for it suggests that the pigs are somehow to blame for the aberrant behavior they display under confinement conditions that violate their *telos.* As Ronald Kilgour and Clive Dalton (1984, 150) note, "Pigs are easily bored and housing and management should be planned to provide for their inquisitive nature. This will prevent most vices, which are the result of boredom."

In general, the behavior of domestic swine is not far removed from that of their wild counterparts. Many cases are known in the United States of groups of domestic pigs that have become feral populations and display the entire behavioral repertoire shown by wild swine that were never domesticated. Moreover, controlled studies show that pigs born and reared in confinement, descended from generations of other animals born and reared in confinement, will display "natural" pig behavior when placed in extensive conditions. For example, they will head directly for a mud hole and wallow. The most exhaustive study in this area was performed at Edinburgh University in the early 1980s by Alex Stolba and David Wood-Gush (1981), who placed domestic pigs in a "pig park," essentially a large enclosure replicating conditions under which wild swine live. On the basis of such work and other research into swines' preferences, one can get a sense of the full range of pig behavior and begin to understand the most serious areas of deprivation in confinement.

A summary of "natural" swine behavior and preferences can serve as a guide to identifying problematic areas in the agricultural confinement rearing of swine. In Stolba and Wood-Gush's pig park—consisting of a pine copse, gorse bushes, a stream, and a swampy wallow—small populations of pigs consisting of a boar, four adult females, a sub-adult male and female, and young pigs (about thirteen weeks of age) were studied over three years. The researchers observed not only the behavior patterns of the animals but also how the pigs used the environment in carrying out their behavior. They found that pigs built a series of communal nests in a cooperative way. These nests displayed certain common features, including walls to protect the animals against prevailing winds and a wide view that allowed the pigs to see what was approaching. These nests were far from the feeding sites. Before retiring to the nest, the animals brought additional material for the walls and rearranged the nest.

On arising in the morning, the animals walked at least seven meters before urinating and defecating. Defecation occurred on paths so that excreta ran between bushes. Pigs learned to mark trees in allelomimetic fashion (i.e., by copying others). The pigs formed complex social bonds with one another, and new animals introduced to the area took a long time to be assimilated. Some formed special relationships. For example, a pair of sows would join together for several days after giving birth and would forage and sleep together. Members of a litter of the same sex tended to stay together and to pay attention to one another's exploratory behavior. Young males also attended to the behavior of older males. Juveniles of both sexes demonstrated manipulative play. In the fall, 51 percent of the pigs' day was devoted to rooting.

Pregnant sows chose a nest site several hours before giving birth; the site was a significant distance from the communal nest (six kilometers in one case). Nests were built, sometimes even with log walls. The sow would not allow other pigs to intrude for several days but might eventually allow another sow with a litter, with whom she had previously established a bond, to share the nest, though no cross-suckling was ever noted. Piglets began exploring the environment at about five days of age and weaned themselves at twelve to fifteen weeks. Sows came to estrus and conceived while lactating.

One of Wood-Gush's comments is telling: "Generally the behavior of . . . pigs, born and reared in an intensive system, once they had the appropriate environment, resembled that of the European wild boar" (1983, 197). In other words, there is good reason to believe that domestic swine are not far removed from their non-domestic counterparts. Thus, comparison of behavioral possibilities in those in confinement with those in the rich, open environment that pigs have evolved to cope with seems a reasonable way at least to begin to assess the adequacy of confinement systems to pigs' welfare. If confined environments generate behavioral disorders in the animals, this is additional reason to believe that there are problems with these environments. We are thus in a good position to measure current systems against all aspects of the swine *telos,* physical and behavioral.

Virtually every expert with whom I have discussed the swine industry sees the confinement of dry sows as its major welfare problem. This view is echoed in books and articles dealing with swine welfare. The experts perceive the confinement of sows as problematic in two ways. First, it is truly a welfare problem. Plainly, many of the needs of the animals are not met in austere confinement systems. To be sure, as Colin Whittemore points out, confinement is not the only issue: "We are not suggesting excessively restrained pigs are happy—undue restraint is an important loss of welfare. But [our] work shows that restraint is not the only thing. By all means, let the pigs out, but don't think that solves all the welfare problems" (quoted in Clanton 1990, 62). The second sense in which sow stalls are highly problematic is equally important, as we shall see. The emerging social ethic for animals and the attitudes connected with that ethic simply will not accept sow stalling, regardless of the scientific evidence. The animal scientist Joseph Stookey stated this point beautifully in a personal communication:

> Such issues as sow stalls are destined to be resolved by moving in the direction toward systems which the public finds acceptable. Obviously the public is concerned about restricting the freedom of movement of animals and the public would prefer that such systems (such as tethers [used mostly in Europe] and sow stalls) be abolished. This is a response that has nothing to do with "welfare" from the pig's perspective (though they would argue that is the very essence of their concern)—they simply find stalls offensive from their own personal perspective and would like to see them abolished. No amount of scientific evidence would ever convince the public that such systems are not cruel.

This statement is exceptionable for two reasons. First, "cruelty" is not the issue. Second, I believe the notion that the public response has "nothing to do with 'welfare' from the pig's perspective" is overstated. Nonetheless, Stookey points out the indisputable fact that public perception should be of fundamental moment to the future of the industry. As agriculturalists often remark, "Perception is reality." Stookey continued, "If . . . sow stalls continue to [be] an acceptable practice in the swine industry, I believe the days are still numbered before the public outcry will take over the legislation and force the government to ban the stalls. In the long run, the industry could be worse off and may lose credibility by not moving in a direction that satisfies the public."

The confinement of sows has been banned in Sweden since 1988, and the European Union has affirmed that the practice must be phased out within a decade. In the United States, a number of states have banned sow stalls by legislation of referendum, and, as I later describe, I convinced Smithfield Foods Company, the world's largest pork producer, to phase them out.

It is hard to overestimate the horror with which ordinary people view sow stalls. Many people immediately respond by saying indignantly, "I wouldn't keep my dogs this way." One former confinement producer has publicly told the story of taking his eight-year-old daughter to see his sow barn for the first time. Much to his amazement, the little girl began to cry. When he asked her why, she replied, "This is not the way God meant us to keep animals." To his great credit, he completely redid his operation to make it welfare-friendly. This is why, ironically, I am so amused when people in the confinement swine industry say, "We gotta show the public where their food comes from." I invariably point out that if you show the average person where bacon comes from, he or she probably won't eat it.

During my career, I have encountered two other swine producers who were led to "recollect" the tradition of husbandry and voluntarily changed to open systems. In one case, the producer told me that he could not look the animals in the eyes when he was keeping them in crates. He moved to open outdoor pens with mud wallows for the sows and is still making the income he made before. His secret? He hired three generations of an Iowa husbandry family to make the system work. Unlike workers in confinement systems, his workers are, as he says, "pig smart." This, in fact, leads to the fourth major problem created by industrialized agriculture: In confinement systems, the intelligence is in the mechanized system. The workers are often illiterate migrants with no background with animals and no inherent husbandry-based concern for them.

The second story is quite dramatic. I was scheduled to give a keynote speech on ethics and animal welfare to the swine producers of Ontario, Canada. Tim

Blackwell, the chief swine veterinarian for Ontario, had asked me to speak, and I could not say no to him. Not only was he the editor of my ethics column in the *Canadian Veterinary Journal,* a column that he had built into a stunning success, but he was also a tireless fighter for animals' well-being. Fifteen years earlier, he had led a large campaign to produce "humane" pork. He was also a cherished friend and, at six foot six, a charismatic and benign Cuchulain.

By then I had delivered more than three hundred lectures to all kinds of audiences, but I had never spoken to pig producers. I had known similar fear the first time I spoke to western cattle ranchers, but that fear vanished when I realized that virtually all of them were solid believers in the ethic of animal husbandry and care. To them, ranching was more a way of life than a way to make a living. Consequently, they cared deeply about how they managed an animal, even if it meant losing money or sleep treating a sick creature. But the group I was about to address were *the* pig people. They had converted to high-confinement, highly intensive, highly capitalized, highly industrialized production methods that replaced husbandry with industry and traditional agricultural values with an emphasis on efficiency and productivity. This had occurred in the 1970s and 1990s, so it seemed that a whole generation of swine farmers had failed to absorb the ancient biblical agricultural values of animal care and stewardship.

Most small pig producers had been relentlessly eliminated by competition from large corporate entities (up to hundreds of thousands of sows per operation) that were run by accountants and executives who viewed their primary obligation as being to investors, not to animals. The few small producers who remained, including those I was going to address, had converted to confinement systems. What could I say to these producers? What here could I touch? With cowboys, I could appeal to the husbandry ethic. What could I use here? I finally decided that the only choice I had was to try the same tactic and hope that an ember of the husbandry ethic still burned in these producers, even after a generation of industrialization.

Tim woke me up from my neurotic musings. I had gone over this a hundred times. It was too late to think up a different strategy. In any case, two hundred people were waiting for me. The meeting was being held at a fairground. People were seated outdoors at picnic tables and would eat lunch at the end of the morning session. As always, my fear began to dissipate as I started speaking and was replaced by a rhythm generated by content and form. Because I am nearsighted, I removed my glasses. In this venue, I could not see the facial expressions of those in the audience, a crucial requirement for gauging their reactions and making adjustments in my talk. But given the picnic-table setup, people were spread out. I was more or less tethered to the podium with a wired microphone.

As I recall, I had an hour and a half for my speech, with a half-hour for questions and discussion. I began in my usual fashion—with a few jokes, a few anecdotes, autobiographical comments about being a Brooklyn kid lecturing to farmers and ranchers. People laughed in the right places. So far so good. I continued as I had planned, discussing the differences among social ethics, personal ethics, and professional ethics. Professional ethics, I said, is the responsibility of important subgroups of society to govern themselves in a way that accords with social concerns so they are not regulated by others who do not understand the pressures of their profession. I said that society was becoming increasingly concerned about the treatment of animals—in research, in zoos and circuses, and in agriculture. This was due to many factors: urbanization, media attention to animals, the relentless ethical searchlight illuminating hitherto disenfranchised elements of society. But most of all, it was due to the supplanting of an agriculture of husbandry—the practice of reciprocity and symbiosis between animals and people—by an exploitative agriculture in which animals do not benefit from being domesticated by humans. I reminded them that biblical injunctions to care for animals and respect their natures had served us well until the 1950s. I also reminded them of the Twenty-third Psalm. I beseeched them to look into themselves, examine what they were doing and see if it accorded with their own ethics. Then I quit.

At first, no one applauded. Oh-oh, I thought. Silence—my perennial nightmare. But then the applause began and grew. I still could not see faces, but Tim moved toward me, grabbing my hand. "You've done it, you son of a bitch; you've done it." "Done what?" I asked. "Touched their hearts. Can't you see the tears in their eyes?" Stupidly, I replaced my glasses and saw that he was right. One man climbed atop a picnic table and began to speak. "This was it," he shouted. "This was the straw that broke the camel's back. I have been feeling lousy for fifteen years about how I raise these animals and so, in front of my peers, so I can't back out later, I am pledging to tear down my confinement barn and build a barn I don't have to be ashamed of. I am a good enough husbandryman that I can do it right, make a living, and be able to look myself in the mirror." This was Dave Linton. Tim whispered to me, "If Linton says it, he means it."

A year and a half went by. Periodically, I received progress reports from Tim. Linton had broken ground. Linton was building. Then Tim called. "Do you have time to visit Dave Linton's new barn? He would like you to—it's attracting a lot of attention. The Canadian Broadcasting Company has done a story on it." I said I would. Tim took me to the Lintons' place. With eyes dancing, Dave and his wife spoke about the new barn while serving us what is arguably the best strawberry-rhubarb pie in the universe. Finally his wife said, "Enough talk, Dave—let the man see for himself." We walked to the barn and opened the door. There was sunshine. "The roof is hydraulic," Dave explained. "On nice days, we retract it so the animals are, in essence, outdoors. And look: no stalls, no crates." Indeed, in place of the crates were huge pens, lavishly supplied with straw, with fifteen or so animals to each pen. The sows lay around on beds of straw chewing it as a cowboy chews tobacco. "They look," I groped for words, "non-neurotic. Happy. That's it. Happy." Tim said, "I've been a pig vet for twenty years, and this is the first time I've seen sows smile." "And," I marveled, "the air is sweet—at least, as sweet as it could be." The three of us shook hands. Linton was effusive. "I'm a religious man," he said. "God has already paid me back for doing the right thing." I asked him how. "When we had the old barn, my son dropped out of school and did nothing but play videogames," he said. "I couldn't interest him in the business or even get him to set foot in the barn. Since I built this one, I can't get him out." The key point is that there are alternatives to sow stalls. After all, we raised pigs for thousands of years without stalls. In fact, Tim Blackwell and I recently made a film entitled *Alternative Housing for Gestating Sows,* in which we showed a number of different loose housing (non-crate) pen systems. What was notable was our discovery that these systems not only work well but also cost half as much to build as full confinement systems, giving the producers a clear financial benefit.

Although sow stalls, or gestation crates, are far and away the most dramatic and obvious problem in confinement swine production, there are many other welfare problems. One of these is farrowing crates, devised to prevent sows from crushing piglets, a common phenomenon under extensive conditions. Generally, a sow spends about a month in a farrowing crate, from directly before giving birth until weaning of the piglets. Since the point of crates is to restrict the movement of sows so they cannot turn around, and since the crates are about the same size as gestation stalls, the same welfare problems relating to restricted movement vis-à-vis gestation crates arise here. Farrowing crates have also been correlated with some pig diseases, including dystocia (difficult labor), agalactia (faulty secretion of milk following birth), and wasting disease.

The farrowing crate raises other welfare problems. Most important, perhaps, is the frustration of normal maternal behavior, an extremely powerful instinct. Sows will continue to try to make nests, even in farrowing crates. As Stookey and Patience have noted, "The fact that nest building is so innate and that the sow continues to build the nest even in the absence of any material, suggests that the behavior has tremendous biological significance. No doubt survival of wild pigs is dependent upon a nest at farrowing" (1991, 67). Thus, in my view, the primary research issue concerning farrowing crates is the development of a system that protects the piglets yet is also friendly to the sow. Such a system is needed for both intensive and extensive pig rearing. I have consulted for the Pig Improvement Company, the major company that supplies swine genetics, which believes that the issue can be solved by changing pigs' genetics to favor maternal instincts and not just productivity. Indeed, many of the welfare issues in confinement agriculture have come from relentless selection for productivity alone.

Confinement rearing of sows leads to welfare problems beyond those that grow out of boredom, frustration, isolation, and inability to move. Sows kept in confinement appear to have more reproductive problems, such as delay of estrus and failure to become pregnant after mating. Confined sows are more vulnerable than unconfined sows to foot and leg problems, including fracturing. Pig farmers who have experience with both free and confined sow operations have told me that fracturing is far less common in sows that are allowed to move. Since activity is known to increase bone strength, it may well be that the immobility of confined sows renders them susceptible to leg breakage. Generally, slatted floors lead to more injuries than unslatted floors. Sows are evolved for soft loam, so concrete floors harm feet and legs. Providing straw for bedding and chewing alleviates problems but is difficult in total confinement. Urinary tract disease appears to be more common in confined sows, probably because the animals lie in their excrement and because they drink less and urinate less; thus, the urine is concentrated and bacteria are allowed to act longer in the urinary tract. It is reasonable to attribute these problems to lack of activity.

Finally, as in the case of the sow with a broken leg, the combination of total confinement, automation, and the large scale of swine operations results in minimal inspection of the individual animals. Thus, disease and injury may go undetected until they are quite advanced, especially in sows. Further, as we saw, the minimal labor force in many operations makes treatment difficult or impossible. Unquestionably, automation tends to be inimical to stockmanship or careful husbandry. Kilgour echoes this point when he asserts that good stockmanship is especially important in large intensive units in which, through automation, people are replaced by mechanical devices.

A number of significant welfare problems are associated with piglets in swine production. Between day one and ten after birth, piglets are subjected to a battery of invasive procedures, including vaccination, ear notching or tattooing for identification (in some cases), teeth clipping, tail docking, and castration of males. Producers usually argue that these procedures are minimally invasive, but common sense says otherwise, especially when all of them are taken together. Even if the producers are correct, public opinion is not likely to be on their side.

Teeth clipping and tail docking are management procedures. Incisor, or "needle," teeth are clipped to prevent lacerations of sows' udders and abrasion of the faces of piglets during competition for teats. The handbook of the Universities Federation for Animal Welfare, *Management and Welfare of Farm Animals,* argues, reasonably, that teeth clipping should not be a routine procedure; it should, instead, be done "as needed"—that is, where there is early evidence of damage from the teeth. Given the lack of surveillance of individual animals in large, intensive operations, however, the degree of scrutiny demanded by this alternative is implausible. It is simply more economical to clip routinely.

Docking of tails, a procedure that grew out of intensive systems, is done to prevent tail biting, which, once begun, generally increases and spreads to biting other parts of the body. A victim of tail biting gradually ceases to react to being bitten, a kind of learned helplessness. Infection often ensues and can become systemic. Pigs have always had a tendency to bite tails. Under extensive conditions, pigs have the space to get away from one another; it is only in confinement that tail biting becomes a serious problem. The producers' response has been to amputate the distal half of the tail, a surgical solution to a problem that has been induced by humans and that arises from keeping the animals in a pathogenic environment. Tail biting is referred to as a "vice," as if the pig is *bad* for doing it.

I do not consider surgical solutions to problems caused by humans morally acceptable. One ought to change the environment to a healthier one, not mutilate the animal. Animals that tend to bite tails can be grouped together, as they do not generally show this behavior when they are so grouped. Uncomfortable factors need to be eliminated, such as high levels of ammonia, carbon dioxide, or humidity in the atmosphere or low barometric pressure. Stocking density should be kept down. Better husbandry, provision of straw, and the opportunity to root all decrease tail biting. It thus appears that boredom is relevant to tail biting. As other stereotypical behaviors do, then, tail biting provides a clue to conditions that need improvement.

Castrating piglets is clearly painful. As in beef cattle, castration in pigs is performed to diminish aggression and to prevent the development of adult male sexual pheromones, which give pork the "boar taint" most consumers dislike. Most producers agree that intact males grow better, faster, and more efficiently and produce learner and more meat. It can be argued that, given the age (five to six months) at which most males attain market weight (about 250 pounds), few of the animals have reached sexual maturity. Thus, the need for castration, which is expensive and painful, is obviated, especially since a pheromone test is available to detect boar-tainted carcasses. In Europe, uncastrated males are the rule. The main obstacle to eliminating castration seems to be resistance from meatpackers based on fear that consumers will reject boar meat and the packers' lack of confidence in the pheromone test.

A major issue in piglet welfare arises out of early weaning. Although pigs left to their own devices will wean at twelve to fifteen weeks of age, industry practice weans piglets at three to four weeks of age. As Andrew Fraser and Donald Broom remark in *Farm Animal Welfare and Behaviour* (1990, 367), "Such early weaning must have considerable effects on the piglets, leading to poor welfare, but only a few have been assessed." We know now that early weaning leads to aberrant behavior, including compulsive belly nosing and sucking, which is presumably an attempt to suck and find milk. Anal massage is a similar deviant behavior. Piglets showing this behavior chase and inflict injuries on other piglets. Other aberrant oral behavior, such as sucking on walls and bars, may also be a result of early weaning. A recent study showed that relocation of piglets to a nursery may be a major stressor that augments the stress of early weaning. The study suggests that mixing groups of early-weaned piglets in the farrowing crate (a familiar environment) is less stressful than relocating them to a nursery.

Increasing numbers of swine producers are operating with an "all in–all out" approach to avoid the mixing of pigs, since mixing leads to stress and aggression. When pigs leave the nursery (at about six weeks old), they go into a grower–finisher pen in groups of fifteen to twenty. One facility I visited placed them in an eight-by-twenty-five-foot pen They remained together for the next five or so months until they had reached market weight. Groups of fifteen to twenty allow the pigs to establish a stable hierarchy. At the early stages of finishing, the pen seems to provide adequate space, but by the time the pigs attain market weight, they appear to be quite crowded. Given the ethic we have discussed, I believe that the public would consider the pigs too crowded.

Austere environments in grower–finisher pens represent another welfare problem that may augment tail biting. It is true, as producers argue, that pigs have one another to interact with as a check against boredom, and they do play a great deal. Typically, though, the animals are not given toys (such as bowling balls) as an additional deterrent to boredom, because such devices can damage pens. This lack may well lead to boredom-based tail biting and aggression. Research should be undertaken to enrich the environment in ways that do not work against the system. Providing straw would be a step toward an enriched environment. Access to the outdoors and to soil, as discussed with regard to sows, might also represent an enriched environment for finishers kept indoors.

Access to the outdoors raises feed costs. However, such access might counter some of the untoward effects of indoor finishing, such as high humidity, poor ventilation, and problems with respiratory disease. In numerous pig facilities, workers must wear respirators; obviously, such a situation is harmful to human and animal welfare.

Another problem appears to be lighting, which is both short in duration and low in intensity. Pigs are kept in limited lighting to avoid aggression, yet studies show they will work to obtain light. Research into optimal lighting should be undertaken, and systems should be devised to meet those needs. Light cycles have major physiological consequences.

The amount of space per pig is important. Equally important is the *quality* of space. Space in grower–finisher pens should take account of the need or desire of pigs for separate dunging and lying facilities, for eating without harassment by others, and for ways to avoid attack. The provision of "hidey-holes" for pigs has been shown to reduce untoward effects of aggression.

Foot and leg problems associated with problematic flooring are another area of concern. Slippery floors can cause lameness, abrasions, strains, and foot injuries.

Being highly intelligent and sensitive animals, pigs are very responsive to stressors. Handling is thus relevant to productivity. Indeed, in two separate studies, Paul Hemsworth and colleagues (1986) and H. W. Gonyou and colleagues (1986) have shown that pigs that receive positive handling and interaction are easier to manage, have faster growth rates, and have better reproductive success than pigs that receive negative handling.

In research and on farms, those who handle pigs often rely on "macho muscling" methods, which produce significant stress. It is far better, as the National Pork Producers Council's *Swine Care Handbook* states, to employ workers with knowledge of pigs' behavior for handling. Hotshot (electrical prod) use should be minimal; most pigs can be handled and moved without these methods by "pig smart" people. The establishment of seminars in handling of the sort done by Temple Grandin would benefit both animals and producers.

Transportation, too, is a major stressor for an animal that is kept in confinement all its life and then is suddenly moved outside, loaded, and transported. Grandin has shown that pigs raised in environments that have some stimulation (suspended plastic tubing) move and load more easily than those raised in barren environments, presumably because they have learned to deal with some variety. Grandin (1991) points out that restricting sensory input makes the nervous system more reactive to stimulation. This is important, because loading has been shown to be a greater stressor than transport. Mixing of pigs during transport is also a significant stressor, as is poor, rough driving. Ignoring the stresses of loading, handling, and transport can lead to bruising, carcass blemishes, Pale Soft Exudative (PSE) syndrome, and malignant hyperthermia syndrome, all of which harm both producers and animals. Research into "idiot-proof" systems of loading, handling, and transport would therefore be of great value.

Continued, sophisticated research into swine behavior and cognition should be supported. I believe that the better we understand the "mind of the pig," the more we will be able to grasp the subtleties of making production systems animal-friendly. Good research may be expensive, but we need a research scalpel, as it were, not a bludgeon.

I have gone into great detail on the swine industry, particularly sow stalls, to clearly illustrate the welfare problems brought about by the dominance of industrialized agriculture. But the swine industry is only one example of the problems that occur in all areas of confinement agriculture: egg production, poultry production, veal production, dairy, and some aspects of beef. The reader who is interested in an in-depth understanding of the wide range of issues in these other areas of confinement agriculture should consult *Farm Animal Welfare* (Rollin 1995a) or *The Well-Being of Farm Animals: Problems and Solutions* (Benson and Rollin 2004). Here it suffices to point out some of the most egregious problems in other areas of confinement agriculture and to contrast industrialized agriculture with the cow-and-calf part of the beef industry and the extensive sheep industry, the last vestiges of husbandry still operating on a significant scale.

The first full confinement systems were developed for egg production in the 1930s and, largely through the negotiations of People for the Ethical Treatment of Animals (PETA) with chain restaurants, have recently become an object of concern on the part of the public. Today's chicken produces 275 eggs per year, compared with the chicken of the 1930s, which produced about 100 eggs per year. As many as six or even more hens can be forced into a small cage, with chickens standing on top of chickens. As noted earlier, this increases productivity per cage. Crowding leads to increased aggression and absence of escape, so the industry "de-beaks" the animals with a hot blade to prevent them from pecking at one another, a procedure that in turn produces neuromas that create chronic pain. The hens are unable to display virtually all of their natural behavioral repertoire: social behavior, nesting behavior, dust bathing, stretching and flapping their wings, exercise, pecking at the ground. Unwanted male chicks are often killed by suffocation.

In addition, the industry routinely practiced "forced molting." Egg laying is naturally cyclical. The ovary becomes less active, and the diminution of sex hormones leads to new feather growth, which forces out the old feathers. At the end of this rest period, when feather regrowth is complete, the laying cycle resumes. But waiting for the cycle to proceed naturally is not cost-effective, because the quantity and quality of the eggs diminish, so producers have learned to induce molting. This requires subjecting the animals to sufficient stressors to inhibit ovulation so the cycle can begin more rapidly. (Stress can inhibit reproductive capacity in all animals.) Producers accomplish this by withholding food and water, which is a significant stressor for the birds, since it is known that the demand for food and water is "inelastic," or fundamental. Happily, this practice is being phased out.

The standard forced molting procedure involves removing food for up to twelve days and water deprivation for up to three days. Obviously, such an intentional stressor is quite traumatic for the animals, given the strength of the need for food and, especially, for water. In addition, the protocol usually involves withdrawing daylight, another stressor to which the animals are unaccustomed. Indeed, this approach to artificially manipulating the egg cycle is so significantly adverse to welfare that the British codes of practice since 1987 categorically recommend against using it.

Broilers (meat chickens) are not raised in cages, but ten thousand to twenty thousand are raised in one building, leading to extreme crowding in which monitoring individual animals becomes impossible. Whereas broilers used to reach market weight in five months, genetics and nutrition allow them to reach the same weight in seven weeks. But in breeding for fast growth, no attention was paid to musculoskeletal considerations, leading to a host of injuries and diseases. Weak animals sit in soiled litter, which again produces disease and sores. Because these animals have been selected for their voracious appetites, breeder broilers must be kept under severe food restrictions. Capture and transportation to slaughter are highly stressful.

As the intensification of agriculture has grown, the old image of a dairy as a small herd of contented cows lounging in idyllic green pastures has come to be less and less typical of the industry. Some cows never see pasture; today's dairies can contain ten thousand cows. Whereas husbandry and individual attention was the key to success in traditional dairies, diminished labor has tended to make this degree of attention impossible. Today's cow is genetically derived to produce, on average, nineteen thousand pounds of milk per year per cow; in the 1950s, the quantity was five thousand pounds. Unless one is a superb manager, the metabolic demands of very high production can lead to "burnout" as well as to high degrees of mastitis, particularly when the cows are given the growth hormone exogenous bovine somatatropin to further increase production. Foot and leg problems—lameness—are a huge problem in today's dairies because of flooring, diet, sanitation, and waste disposal. "Downer" animals resulting from hypocalcemia are a problem that has garnered media coverage when such animals are shipped for slaughter. Despite empirical evidence showing that mastitis is not improved by tail docking (the theory is that the tail flings manure, leading to infection), many dairymen still dock cows' tails without anesthesia and leave the cows unable to chase flies. In some dairies, branding and dehorning may be performed without anesthesia. The welfare of calves, particularly early separation from their mothers, is another welfare issue. A recent concern about "cows' comfort" in the industry may signal an attempt to restore husbandry, although it is hard to see how a limited labor force can do justice to six thousand or ten thousand animals or more per dairy.

Even when the U.S. public knew nothing whatever about agriculture, it was widely known that eating veal was ethically problematic. News reports abounded of the scandal of "white veal." People who otherwise didn't worry about the ethics of what they ate foreswore veal. When I lectured at the USDA in the 1990s, a significant part of my audience (more than half) affirmed that they would not eat veal.

The so-called white veal industry is an offshoot of dairy farming. It provided a way to turn unwanted bull calves into money. The calves are isolated, placed in small pens called crates, and fed an iron-deficient diet to keep the meat pale. Lack of exercise ensures that muscles don't develop so the meat is tender. When removed from the crate, the animals have trouble standing. No play or social behavior is possible; many normal behaviors are thwarted.

The vast majority of the fifteen thousand western ranchers I have addressed over the past twenty years will not eat veal for ethical reasons. I have yet to address a group of cattle ranchers who find the production of white veal acceptable. Indeed, if I were to transcribe the remarks generally made by the ranchers about veal into a typescript, one might assume that one was reading the opinions of extreme animal-rights advocates. (I actually have such a transcript, based on a seminar I gave in Worland, Wyoming.)

The strong antipathy toward white veal production in the public is arguably a function of emotionalism, sentimentality, the "Bambi syndrome," the fact that calves have "big soulful eyes," and the like. But such a claim can surely not be made about ranchers. In their case, the distaste for veal production is a result of their understanding of cattle's *telos* and their belief that nothing could be further from accommodating that *telos* than the raising of white veal. Happily, the confinement veal industry is virtually dead, killed by antipathy as consumers have become educated. The industry has announced the phasing out of crates.

The beef industry has two distinct parts: cow-and-calf production and feedlots. The cow-and-calf component, peopled by the individuals discussed in the previous chapter, has remained essentially unchanged for hundreds of years and is not industrialized. Although this part of the industry is most famously associated with the U.S. West, there are husbandry-based cow-and-calf producers in the Southeast and Midwest, as well. All have in common an ethic of husbandry for the animals and stewardship for grazing land. (If they do not preserve the land, they lose their livelihood.)

Beef cattle in principle could be raised strictly on rangeland, as they were for most of the history of beef production and as is now being done in South America. The result is animals that spend their entire lives in pastures and yield "grass-fed beef." The practice of feeding grain to cattle to fatten or "finish" them over roughly the last few months of their lives developed after World War II, when the United States experienced a grain surplus due to greater efficiency in grain production. It was the realization that, in effect, converting grain to beef was more profitable than selling it as grain that led to the rise of feedlots. With the price of grain soaring today, in part due to biofuel, we can anticipate a resurgence in grass-fed beef. There is now an association of such producers.

The major welfare problems associated with cow-and-calf producers are management practices that are sanctified by tradition—hot-iron branding, castration without anesthesia, dehorning without anesthesia. Branding is a cultural event—a big party—and people take pride in their brands. One rancher told me that his two sons, a surgeon and an attorney, come home to help at branding, but not at Christmas. Nonetheless, cowboys know that branding is morally questionable because they have too much common sense to embrace scientific ideology's audacious agnosticism about animals' pain. They also, on some level, know that these practices are not essential to ranching. Recall that all agree with me when I ask, "If God came down and said you can no longer use painful management practices, would you go out of business?" They always say, "Hell no!" Most rationalize these practices by saying they cause only short-term pain that is outweighed by the animals' living lives dictated by their *telos.* There are viable alternatives to these practices, anyway: Not castrating is an alternative to castrating, and animals grow better with testes; identification, which also helps ensure the safety of the food supply, can be done by using retinal images instead of branding; and animals can be bred for hornlessness.

Feedlots are generally acknowledged to be the animal-friendliest confinement units. A lot is a large dirt pen filled with animals. There is plenty of room to move, exercise, and socialize. The welfare problems with feedlots also represent productivity problems, since feedlots do not rely on high technology. These problems include poor drainage, lack of shelter from wind and shade from sun, and limited behavioral opportunities. Thus, fixing them has some economic incentive. This point notwithstanding, the industry has been slow to change. In my experience, most feeders have backgrounds in cow-and-calf production and still very much possess the ethic of husbandry.

Beginning in the mid-1980s, I sought alternatives to some of the standard practices in the beef industry—notably branding and castration without anesthesia. It dawned on me that perhaps castration could be accomplished immunologically; some people had pioneered in such work. I suggested this to some of my colleagues in animal sciences—notably, Tom Field, a ranching expert, and Garth Boyd, a beef extension specialist. They generously shared their time and resources to try immunological castration. We conjugated a foreign protein to gonadotropin-releasing hormone (GnRH), a hormone that is vital to spermatogenesis, in the hope that it would elicit an immunological reaction from the body that might halt the spermatogenic cascade. Even my seven-year-old son was involved in the project, weighing the cattle. Later, some graduate students got involved and attempted to do the weighing, only to be told by Garth, "Mikey is doing great. I want the same eye on the scale for all readings." (Mikey and I never forgot that, and Garth is still a dear friend.) We had some success in suppressing bulls' behavior, particularly the mating urge, but the semen remained viable, which ranchers would not accept. Also, the grading system graded our immuno-castrates as bulls, thereby allowing the packers to pay less for the animals. And my wife put the final nail in the coffin when she pointed out that no American man would eat meat injected with something that shriveled its testicles.

One of the graduate students working on the project was Gary Teague of Texas A&M. One day, as we were moving young bulls through a chute, Gary declared that I needed to be anointed a "real cowboy." He proceeded to do this by taking a handful of warm bullshit and rubbing it on my bare arm. As everyone cracked jokes about how I usually dispensed bullshit, I washed it off. A few minutes later, I began to talk in a thick Texas accent, aping Teague's: "Gary, ah fill funny. Ah cain't tawk; ah cain't reason; ah cain't think. Ah believe ahm turning into a Texan."

In the end, the best alternative to castration is not castrating. Ranchers castrate to make the animals more docile and to keep them from breaking fences to impregnate females that belong to others or from simply doing so in mixed-range conditions. A significant literature has developed in the twentieth century to show that castration without anesthesia hurts the animals, stresses them, makes them more susceptible to disease, and affects weight gain. In addition, there is incontrovertible evidence that if one markets young bulls up to thirteen months of age, there is no difference in tenderness, taste, or palatability. Furthermore, at that age the bulls don't fight, are leaner, and can, in fact, reach market weight a few months before steers (castrates), thereby saving the cost of feed. One man did this quite successfully under the brand name Dakota Lean. In sum, as one rancher in Casper, Wyoming, said, "Doc, we ranchers are dumb shits. We cut off the animals' balls without anesthetic, get dinged by the public for being inhumane. Then we put their balls in their ears [i.e., use growth hormonal implants]. And to add insult to injury, the ears don't work nearly as well as the balls."

In 1996, in response to a rancher's challenge, I formed a company with two CSU colleagues, Bruce Golden and Ralph Switzer, to develop identification of animals using images of the retinal blood vessel patterns, which are unique and unchanging in each cow. Our company is called Optibrand.

Despite its certainty and inexpensiveness, retinal identification (the retinal pattern can't be altered) has not caught on with ranchers, although it has been used by packers for "trace back" (following the source of the product back to its origin—for example, in case of disease). Ranchers claim they cannot use retinal identification to sort their cattle from others' cattle on mixed ranges. But I repeatedly point out that, once permanent retinal identification has been obtained, they can use other methods, such as paint or colored tags, to recognize their cattle. No one can rustle them because the permanent ID is stored in a database.

Since we made no headway in replacing branding with retinal identification, we looked for other answers. For more than twenty years, I have taught veterinary ethics with Tony Knight, the longtime head of the Clinical Sciences Department at CSU and a cattle veterinarian. A few years ago, a group of fifteen veterinary students from ranching backgrounds wanted to continue our course with an eye toward helping ranch communities. We continued for three additional semesters. We realized that a local injection of lidocaine might help alleviate the pain of branding. The students found a rancher willing to try and devised a hypodermic setup to inject many sites with lidocaine at once. Amazingly, there was no literature on this. Not surprisingly, the blocked animals showed fewer signs of pain, and the procedure was cost-effective. I see no excuse not to replace branding with electronic identification, and if people insist on branding, they should pursue research into anesthesia and analgesia.

Not surprisingly, as societal awareness of food-production practices has increased exponentially, and as referenda against confinement agriculture have continued, agriculture has begun to think more about change. And the beef industry has begun to rethink its painful but traditional management practices.

16

Changing Industrial Agriculture

European society has been far more concerned than U.S. society about industrial agriculture, perhaps because agriculture there is more visible. In any case, there was an unbroken chain of social concern from Ruth Harrison's *Animal Machines* (1964) and the Brambell Commission to a very dramatic event in Sweden, orchestrated by the veterinarian Kristina Forslund, with Astrid Lindgren, author of the Pippi Longstocking books and, until her death, essentially the Swedish national grandmother.

Kristina is a brilliant, forcefully charismatic woman who befriended Astrid. She is also a large-animal veterinarian and a member of the faculty at the University of Uppsala, Sweden's only veterinary school. As she tells it, she was driving in the country with Astrid, who was then in her eighties, and they passed some low, windowless buildings. Astrid asked what they were. When Kristina told her they were a confinement pig farm, Astrid said, "Impossible! Where are the pigs?" When Kristina explained, Astrid demanded to see inside. She was horrified. This was not like the husbandry-based pig farms of her youth. She told Kristina that this was unacceptable. Kristina informed her that all of animal agriculture had moved in that direction. This deepened Astrid's resolve, and she and Kristina began to write legislation to reverse the trend and ultimately presented the bill to the Swedish Parliament.

One cannot understand what happened without knowing the place of Astrid Lindgren in Swedish society. She was venerated, a mainstay of everyone's childhood through her stories. It was culturally impossible to say no to her. So in 1988, a law phasing out high confinement in a series of steps passed the Swedish legislature "virtually unopposed," as the *New York Times* put it. Sow stalls and battery cages were phased out, and cattle were granted "in perpetuity the right to graze." In 1995, Kristina invited me to Sweden. I traveled with her husband, also a large-animal vet, and watched him use anesthesia and analgesia in castration. I spoke to pig farmers, who did not mind the reforms as long as everyone was back at the same starting gate. Swedish agriculture adapted and did not collapse.

Meanwhile, the European Union and member countries were phasing out sow stalls, confinement veal, and battery cages for hens. A literature had developed on alternatives to high confinement. I became convinced that we could do it as well, despite protestations from U.S. agriculture that Europe was Mars (i.e., an alien, deviant, touchy-feely place). When I visited my first sow barn, I was shaken. I resolved that I would do my best to eliminate sow stalls. Through what I knew of Europe and from Tim Blackwell, a swine vet, I was convinced that it could be done. Plus, pigs had been raised without stalls for ten thousand years. I learned much from Tim, both from long conversations and from the ethics column he has edited and that I have written for the *Canadian Veterinary Journal* since 1990. Tim sent me numerous cases concerning confinement agriculture, and about swine in particular, which greatly increased my knowledge in the area. Before I met him in 1990, Tim had worked diligently to try to eliminate sow stalls from swine production in Ontario, only to be stymied by supply-chain issues. A few years ago, I urged him to make a film about group housing that worked both for pigs and for the producers. He did so, showing five different such systems, including Dave Linton's. The best thing about the film was the producers' avowal that they were making just as much money as they had with sow barns, but the pen barns that had replaced them cost 50 percent less to build. Thus, their profit margin increased. We now had an economic argument in favor of eliminating sow stalls.

A very interesting spinoff from the column related to a major problematic practice in industrial agriculture that occurred in 2000. One of the cases Tim had sent me concerned the use of antibiotics in animal feed to promote growth. (No one is sure of the mechanism, but it definitely works.) The problem with such use (first anticipated in the 1940s with the onset of antibiotic use) was that, particularly in large quantities, it would, by basic principles of evolutionary biology, drive the evolution of antibiotic-resistant pathogens (germs, to you!). This is how this happens: When you feed antibiotics by the barrel to animals (or overuse them in human medicine), you kill the germs that are susceptible to that antibiotic. What are left are germs that are resistant to that antibiotic; thus, infections from these germs are more difficult to treat. Since agriculture used many antibiotics that also were used for human disease, this, in essence, was breeding for resistance to germs and diseases.

I affirmed this in the column and incurred the wrath of a feedlot veterinarian in western Canada who (surprise!) supplied many of the antibiotics to feedlots. He wrote a nasty letter accusing me of a variety of evils, and I responded by cutting him to ribbons. Some months later, I received a call from the head of the World Health Organization's committee on antibiotic resistance and livestock, asking me to serve on the committee in Geneva. I pointed out my limited knowledge of the issue and reminded him that I was a philosopher. "No problem," he said. "You can do the opening ethics talk." "But why me?" I asked. "Because you're obviously not afraid of who you make angry," he said. "I read your discussion in the *Canadian Veterinary Journal.*"

I was worried about my ignorance in the area, so I read compulsively and engaged in dialogue with knowledgeable colleagues. Pfizer was kind enough to send me cartons of books, making no attempt to influence what I said. (I had worked with Pfizer to publicize the canine analgesic Rimadyl when the company discovered that I was right about veterinary training and the ideological denial that animals felt pain.) I delivered my speech, arguing that rationality dictated ending the practice of antibiotic use for growth promotion because of the dangers to human health. I also cited figures showing that the effect on food prices would be negligible and that any mother would pay that amount as insurance against her child's getting a resistant infection. The speech was published as a paper in the *Journal of Agricultural and Environmental Ethics* (Rollin 2001).

The response was amazing. I have already related the story about the U.S. Food and Drug Administration veterinarian who was "offended" by my talk. In addition, many drug-company executives were there. As soon as I was done, up jumped one of them, looking, as one of my friends puts it, like "oil dipped in slime"—gold cufflinks and all. With heavy sarcasm, he intoned, "You obviously don't care about the Third World." "How do you deduce that?" I asked. "In fact, in my talk I specifically said that since I care about the Third World, I do not think we should afflict them with all the problems of confinement agriculture. Better to help them become sustainable." "Well," he said, "if you cared about them, you wouldn't try to limit antibiotic use. We can't feed the Third World without antibiotics." I smiled. "Excuse me, sir," I said. "You have antibiotics now, ad libitum. Are you feeding the Third World?" (See what I mean about God making them dumb?)

Over lunch, I had a conversation with the Swedish minister of agriculture. He told a fascinating story that buttresses all I have said about "technological sanders." In the mid-1980s, the Swedish public had passed a referendum banning the use of antibiotics in animal feeds. The cattle industry was distraught. It tried various probiotics, which increase benign bacteria and crowd out bad ones, and zinc oxide, to no avail. As some leaders sat around wringing their hands, one man mused, "You know, when I was a little boy I worked with my grandfather with cattle. We had no antibiotics. He made sure we cleaned the premises thoroughly between loads of cattle." The others muttered the proverbial "That's so crazy it just might work." It did, and food prices *dropped* because the cost of antibiotics was gone. As a way to forgive bad husbandry, antibiotics are technological sanders.

I have continued to talk to large numbers of people in all areas of agriculture. I have a particularly good relationship with the Animal Science Association, having done numerous talks and papers for the organization. I also have a wonderful relationship with the dairy people of Colorado. Historically, there is no area of agriculture that was more dependent on good husbandry. M. F. Seabrook (1980) showed—and, traditionally, dairymen knew as a matter of common sense—that gentle and kind treatment of the dairy cow was a, if not *the,* major variable that correlated with milk production. Although most dairies today represent some form of confinement, dairymen are not far removed from the husbandry ethic of their parents. The result is that they have been receptive to my message in Colorado. I have already mentioned their pioneering effort on downer cows. The majority of dairymen in Colorado have also repudiated tail docking, an unfortunate practice that has no scientific basis at all.

I began to be known in agriculture outside ranching. The second Council of Agricultural Science and Technology (CAST) report on the welfare of agricultural animals, published in 1997, cited me by name as the person in animal welfare who had the most influence on and credibility with the animal science and veterinary communities.

I spoke to many animal sciences departments in which, by and large, there was little knowledge of ethics or animal welfare but quite a bit of interest. That interest grew over the years as societal concern with animal ethics increased. The first talk I gave to an animal sciences department in about 1981 or so attracted one person—the department head—who had had his arm twisted by the dean of veterinary medicine. By the 1990s, however, things had changed. One year, I was invited to speak at the annual meeting of the Animal Science Association and given a room that held twenty-five people. We had to move to the grand ballroom to accommodate the five hundred who showed up. Another year, I was introduced at the Animal

Science Association by a very hostile moderator—an equine extension person who announced that I was a radical not worth listening to. It was a rather stupid move on his part, because it created instant sympathy for me. But just to make sure, I began my speech by saying that this was high praise from an ignorant shitkicker and by telling him to stop me if I used too many big words.

The most ridiculous experience I ever had lecturing to an animal sciences department was at the University of Illinois. I was the Something Something Distinguished Lecturer, which meant that I gave fourteen talks in two and a half days. Thirteen of the fourteen were great. Illinois is a first-rate school with wonderful students and faculty. The fourteenth was a noon talk to animal sciences faculty and graduate students. Almost everyone was polite and engaged, but I noticed two forty-something-year-old men with blond crewcuts whispering and nudging each other with elbows. They were clearly hostile; I dubbed them the "twin Nazis" and ignored them—for a while. When their whispering and nudging showed no sign of abating, I said, "Gentlemen, if you have something to say, say it to the whole group. I'm almost done with my talk, and if you don't question my assumptions or refute my logic, you must accept the conclusion." That elicited a response. "No, we don't," one of them said. "This is America. We don't have to accept anything we don't want to. It's a free country." The other nodded in agreement. The students were so embarrassed that they sent a delegation to the office I was using to apologize and to ask me not to judge the department by "those two" extension faculty members.

My work with animal sciences reached a culmination in 2003, when I was asked to keynote the plenary session of the annual meeting of the American Society of Animal Science/American Dairy Science Association. It was, in fact, their first joint meeting with the Mexican Animal Science Association, and I was to speak to an audience of about three thousand. I was both honored and anxious and worked hard to craft a paper that would, on the one hand, move their thinking forward while, on the other, not create blind rage. The paper focused on emerging social ethics for animals and particularly on the loss of husbandry. Gratifyingly, it was very well received. (In fact, it was published in the *Journal of Animal Science* [Rollin 2004].) The most common question I received was how to restore husbandry to highly industrialized agriculture. Virtually no one in the audience defended the claim that this ought not be done.

I have always been loath to turn down speaking invitations. As Chaucer said, "Gladly do I lerne and gladly teche." I love to teach and often teach more courses than required, hold extra classes, and do numerous guest lectures in classes my colleagues teach. I never charge a lecture fee to student groups. There is no high like exciting people intellectually. On a more pragmatic level, one never knows what will come out of a talk. Harley people say, "Shit happens." This is true. But unexpected good things also happen. Case in point: I received a call from a colleague asking me to talk to the Chipotle restaurant chain during the winter break between semesters. It was an eleventh-hour invitation; it would take place during vacation; I had never heard of Chipotle; I had planned to take time off; I wasn't being paid. So naturally, I did it.

The people who attended were wonderful. I soon learned that the Chipotle restaurant chain was a unique company; as much as possible, it bought humanely raised meat and tried to save family farms. My talk on emerging societal ethics excited them; I was in turn excited by their attempt to promote eating with conscience in a non-heavy-handed way. I visited Chipotle's corporate headquarters, met the workers and founders, and began to speak regularly to various departments of the company. Even more important, many of the chain's senior staff became personal friends, particularly Ann Daniels, a former buyer for McDonald's. She is smart, savvy, and knowledgeable about all aspects of the business.

Chipotle was originally owned by McDonald's but was wisely given free rein in corporate policy and established a niche similar to that of Whole Foods Market in the grocery business, serving excellent food and appealing to young people concerned with animals, the environment, and healthy eating. In 2006, Chipotle went public and opened at about \$24 a share. (It peaked in 2008 at more than \$160 a share, an eloquent marker of social thought.) In 2007, I was honored to find my biography printed on Chipotle's drink cups under the rubric "People We Are Proud to Know."

One day that I was scheduled to speak to Chipotle employees in Vail, Ann called and asked whether I was comfortable with two executives from Smithfield Foods coming to my talk. "Why not?" I replied. Ann and I were to have dinner with them and met them at the hotel's restaurant. (They had taken the corporate jet.) One of them broke the ice by saying, "We hope you're not talking about ethics." Wow—that needed to be pursued. "Why do you hope that I'm not talking about ethics?" His reply: "Because we don't listen to ethics." (This was too good.) "What do you listen to?" I asked. "We only listen to the bottom line," he answered. I put a heavy arm on his shoulder: "Hey, buddy, if you don't listen to ethics, you won't have a bottom line." The other executive grasped the point instantly (thank God).

We conversed through dinner; they attended my lecture, and then we chatted some more. I focused on pig gestation crates, or sow stalls, and urged their elimination. I explained the new social ethic for animals. Before they left, the senior executive took me aside and told me that he was close to the chief executive of Smithfield and would convey the argument. He also gave me his word that Smithfield would try, on an experimental basis in a few facilities, a pen system for sows. I felt good. This was the first time a senior person in the industry had admitted that there was an issue with sow stalls. The usual line was "They're much better off in confinement—no predators, environmental control, blah, blah, blah."

I promptly forgot about Smithfield's promise. But in February 2007, I got an astounding phone call from one of the two Smithfield executives. "Well, we listened to you," he said. "We're about to announce that we're phasing out sow stalls." He told me that the company had done focus groups, consumer surveys, and so forth, and all confirmed what I had said. I was delighted. The Smithfield executives asked me whether I would comment on their decision to the *Wall Street Journal.* I said I would, and less than five minutes later, the *Journal* reporter called. I told her that Smithfield's decision to eliminate sow stalls from its own farms, as well as from the farms of its contract growers, was a "major step forward." Then she asked about the timetable—ten years for Smithfield's farms and twenty for those of its contract growers. "Doesn't that seem long to you?" she asked. I said that, if it were up to me, it would be faster. "But you can't turn a steamship on a dime," I said and asked her to stress the latter part of the statement. When the story came out, I was portrayed as a "critic of Smithfield" who had complained about the time it would take to phase out the sow stalls. I was furious. I had been interviewed in some thirty countries and never been so egregiously misquoted. (Not that I would have known in Poland or Sweden.) The quote would surely sour my credibility with Smithfield and with the industry in general. The reporter knew what I had said and had distorted it for a more sensational story.

I began to make phone calls. I began with the *Journal*'s editor-in-chief, who was gracious and put me in touch with the editor of the letters to the editor. She could not have been kinder. It turns out she knew my work and realized how the story could hurt that work. I wrote a letter rectifying the misquote. Smithfield beamed; everyone was happy. I had dodged a major bullet. Within days of Smithfield's announcement, Maple Leaf Foods, Canada's biggest pork producer, announced that it also would eliminate sow stalls.

I am not naïve enough to think that I was the major—or even a major—influence on Smithfield. Many other things got their attention: the voter referendum to eliminate sow stalls that passed overwhelmingly in Arizona; proposed voter referendums in other states; legislation in Oregon moving to eliminate sow stalls; the success of Chipotle, Whole Foods, and other enterprises that emphasize humane animal production; increased U.S. social concern with the treatment of farm animals; increased media coverage of farm animals—and, last but not least, the advent of the Pew Commission, on which I was privileged to serve.

Anyone who watches public television will recognize the Pew Foundation or Pew Charitable Trusts as a stalwart supporter. Pew is the Sun Oil Company foundation and has assets of more than five billion dollars. In 2005, Pew, after dialogue with the Johns Hopkins Bloomberg School of Public Health's Center for a Livable Future, agreed to fund a commission that would look into the problems raised by confinement agriculture, or industrial agriculture factory farming—call it what you will—and make recommendations. The problem areas were identified as human health, animal health, antimicrobial resistance, air and water quality, animal waste disposal, food safety, animal welfare, and social issues such as migratory labor and community coherence.

The commission—officially named the National Commission on Industrial Farm Animal Production and later renamed the Pew Commission on Industrial Farm Animal Production—was carefully chosen. The commissioners included a former governor of Kansas; a former secretary of agriculture; the dean of a veterinary school; the dean of a school of public health; the former director of the National Catholic Rural Life Conference; a high-level executive at Cargill; and various academics (including me) with expertise in public health, nutrition, agriculture, and ethics. Although its recommendations were to not be released until the spring of 2008, the commission made the confinement agriculture industry nervous from its inception. Some of the industry's less responsible voices labeled it "vegetarian activists" and so on, and an agriculture lobbyist attended all of the commission's meetings. The industry was worried about its recommendations, particularly because the group was very credible and because of the connection with Johns Hopkins, the most prominent public-health school in the United States. Although I cannot prove this claim, it seems obvious to me that the commission made the industry more attentive to the issues we were examining. It began its work in March 2006 and held ten meetings across the country, gathering information, listening to a diversity of opinions, and garnering pubic input on issues relevant to its mission. The commission issued the final report in April 2008.[1]

Serving on the commission was a powerful educational experience. I toured livestock operations and talked to producers, regulators, and the

[1]The full report is available online at http://www.PCIFAP.org.

public. Most of the people on the commission did not have a background in agriculture but were quick learners. They were also incredibly bright and deeply morally committed. Although we worked fourteen-to-sixteen-hour days, it was always fun and exciting. The commission's staff was run by Robert Martin, a seasoned attorney from Washington, D.C. The whole sense was of a family working for a common cause in mutual respect—if such families exist.

The agriculture industry was nowhere near as enamored of the group as I was. From the beginning, the industry's running dogs (such as the Center for Consumer Freedom, which also defended the tobacco industry) attempted to malign it in various ways. (For example, Bob Lawrence, director of the Center for a Livable Future, was characterized as a "vegetarian activist" because he had once advocated "meatless Mondays" to improve health.) Every time the commission met, it was accompanied by lobbyists. However, the agriculture industry was also helpful and open, particularly in regard to getting commission members into animal facilities.

My personal gripe with the industry was its mantra about basing animal welfare solely on "sound science." On one occasion, an industry representative said at a commission meeting that, although the people she spoke for were "nervous" about the commission, they were comfortable with what it was doing as long as it was all based on "sound science." My response was at least to attempt to show her that animal welfare is at root an *ethical* notion—what do we owe animals and to what extent? Only when this is decided is science deployed. Her response was "Huh?" I tried restating the idea: "Science can tell us how to raise pigs in confinement. The question society and the commission is asking is '*Ought* we raise pigs in confinement?' and science, sound or otherwise, can't answer that." Her response, again, was "Huh?" In any case, because much of the little scientific research that is done into animal welfare is supported by industry, and since there are few sources of funding outside industry, such research is likely to be "sound" from an industrial point of view but otherwise inherently suspect.

In April 2008, I went to Washington to give a public briefing on animal welfare on Capitol Hill. A few weeks later, I attended the presentation of the commission's final report. (I urge the interested reader to look at the final report at www.pcifap.org.) Our recommendations included phasing out highly intensive agriculture in a decade and returning to husbandry. The public and media response has been overwhelmingly positive. More than seven hundred stories have run in the press, and virtually all have been supportive. The report explained that, although animal products may seem quite cheap at the cash register, this is misleading because many of the costs of production have been "externalized," or charged to society in an indirect way. These costs include health care to treat problems caused by confinement agriculture; environmental despoliation; loss of family farms and rural communities; human health issues; and costs to animals' well-being.

Other factors have also served to bring attention to the agriculture industry—most notably, the referenda mentioned earlier against sow stalls and the direction the Humane Society of the United States (HSUS) has taken under Wayne Pacelle to press for referenda and state legislation and to maximally use existing laws to the benefit of animals. Also highly relevant have been the number of law schools (more than 130) teaching animal law and the number of lawyers of prominence focusing on animal law. At the Harvard Law School's Future of Animal Law Conference held in March 2007, registration quickly reached the maximum limit of 350 and more than 250 people were turned away. I am gratified to see many bright people turning to the law to help protect animals' interests. The Animal Legal Defense Fund (formerly Attorneys for Animal Rights) has been a pioneer in this area under the leadership of the indomitable Joyce Tischler, who founded the group and wrote the earliest papers on animal enfranchisement.

My biggest—and most stressful—project involving agriculture began in 2007.

A few years ago, the HSUS was searching for a new executive director. I was approached by a headhunting firm but realized that I had neither the desire nor the requisite diplomatic and fundraising skills to do the job. Wayne Pacelle, a graduate of Yale University who is deeply committed to animal welfare, took the position. Unlike his predecessors, he uses the HSUS's considerable resources directly to benefit animals. As I do, he sees the legal system as the best vehicle for elevating animals' welfare, and I saw his organization's legal people at the major conferences on animal law held at Harvard Law School and at Lewis and Clark Law Schools in Portland, Oregon, where I lectured. In particular, Wayne tries to use existing laws in creative ways; he also makes use of citizen-driven petitions to charter referenda in states that allow them, a procedure I suggested more than twenty-five years ago.

In the spring of 2007, Wayne announced that he would create referenda (laws introduced to voters by citizen petition) to abolish sow stalls (gestation crates), veal crates, and battery cages for laying hens. Specifically, he would launch the initiative in California—and in Colorado. Members of the agricultural community in Colorado were quite upset and met with me shortly after the announcement. They asked how to deal with this. I responded that I had predicted this sort of thing for many years and that they could preempt it by making improvements in animal welfare of their own. That was deemed unacceptable, so I moved on to other issues.

As it happened, I was scheduled to speak in July on a panel for executive directors of state veterinary associations held in Washington, D.C., by the American Veterinary Medical Association (AVMA). Sharing the podium with me were Gail Golab, a progressive voice on animal welfare within the AVMA, and Wayne Pacelle. At the seminar, Wayne approached me and said laudatory things about my work. I responded, in my Dale Carnegie way, by asking, "Then why are you screwing me in my own state?" I pointed out that I had worked with people in Colorado agriculture for twenty-five years and had persuaded them to do some very good things—to pass the strongest "downer animal" bill in the United States to prevent the shipping of nonambulatory animals, to condemn the U.S. Department of Agriculture's face branding of Mexican cattle, to renounce the tail docking of dairy cattle. With the pressure of a referendum, I said, I feared they would move to the right, and all of my reminding would be lost. Wayne acknowledged this and said, "If you can broker an agreement between us and them, I'll abandon the referendum." I agreed, as did the agriculture community and twenty members of the Colorado Livestock Association (CLA), the umbrella group for agriculture, and I met with Pacelle in August in Denver.

It is relevant to the story that Wayne is an exceptionally handsome man (some refer to him as a "metrosexual"). After he passed a copy of a bill based on his proposed referendum to the CLA, we met for the first and only time in Colorado. Wayne was resplendent in a beautifully cut charcoal suit and a pink tie; the agriculture people wore jeans, western shirts, hats, and boots. The funniest part of the meeting was when Wayne sat down, smiled, and said, "Let's have a discussion." Twenty pairs of arms immediately folded across the agriculture people's chests with the perfect synchronization of Rockettes. The semiotics of this was not lost on me.

For the next six months, I carried each party's position to the other and tried to mediate. As some agriculture leaders were to tell me later, Wayne behaved with grace and consistency. Agriculture, however, needed to garner acquiescence from a diverse and sometimes socially naïve constituency. This was frustrating, to say the least. The CLA's leadership was unfailingly rational and cooperative but needed to respect its constituency. The main players from the CLA were Bill Hammerich, from a cattle feeder background, and Ivan Steinke, representing pork. Both were unfailingly intelligent and kept their eyes on the prize, mindful that some of their constituents were less so.

Despite my twenty-five years of work with the agriculture community, some people met my involvement with suspicion. Fortunately, senior people within the ranks of beef, dairy, and swine recalled my work and (somewhat) silenced the paranoids. The major obstacle to mediation came from the egg producers, who refused to negotiate. In all fairness, they would suffer the greatest costs, since eliminating cages for laying hens would cost them millions of dollars and they would become vulnerable to competition from egg producers in states that did not have laws against battery cages. The swine people benefited from input by Smithfield and from Ivan's wise and diplomatic leadership. The dairy people, in turn, were influenced by Bill Wailes, head of the Department of Animal Sciences at CSU, who was himself a dairy producer and one of the nicest, most progressive and intelligent people I ever met in agriculture, or anywhere. (He was the person who honored me by saying I could teach any course in his department without a co-teacher if I felt capable of doing so, an extraordinary declaration of trust.)

It was slow going. Agriculture people by nature can be independent and averse to intrusion. But a compromise gradually emerged. Wayne and his adviser, Paul Shapiro, an extraordinarily bright and well-informed young man, were as patient and dialectical as anyone could have been, earning the trust of the CLA. By Christmas, we had tentatively reached an agreement that eliminated sow stalls and veal crates. Wayne graciously accepted omitting the restrictions on egg producers from the agreement. He understood that a desire for unity could force the other agriculture elements to unite behind the egg producers, even though few personally liked battery cages, and he accepted the compromise. But, as the cliché says, the devil is in the details. The governor's office, which did not want a constitutional amendment on animal housing (that is what Colorado referenda do), got involved, introducing another complication into an already complex situation. There were numerous fits and starts, but both Wayne and the CLA's leaders remained committed to compromise.

As mediator, I must have made three hundred phone calls and started to develop a phobic reaction to the many fits and starts and stumbles I encountered along the way. Case in point: The Farm Bureau, notoriously not the brightest bulb in the agricultural chandelier, allegedly announced at its annual meeting in New Orleans that, in essence, Colorado would take no crap from Wayne Pacelle and the HSUS and would throw the sons of bitches out of the state. Fortunately, I was able to convince Wayne that the CLA leaders were as irate as he was about these ill-advised remarks, and the Farm Bureau retracted them.

The deadline for filing the consensus legislation was Friday, February 29, at noon. On Thursday, we encountered a potentially deal-breaking obstacle. Fortunately, thanks in large part to Wayne's commitment to the process, I was able to effect one last compromise, and consensus was reached at 11:55 A.M.—five minutes before the deadline. The consensus legislation went through the legislature easily. I hope I never have to do that again. The governor signed the bill on May 14, 2008.

What this story reveals is a major theme in my life's work: that even in issues as divisive as animal welfare, rational people can negotiate compromise. The deal established was the first of its kind in U.S. history, and I hope it will not be the last. In the end, it vindicates my deep belief that animal welfare, like other highly controversial issues in our society, can be resolved in bloodless and democratic ways by intelligent people of good will.

In November 2008, the HSUS's proposal to eliminate sow stalls, battery cages, and veal crates was put to the California voters as a referendum (Proposition 2). Despite millions of dollars spent by agriculture, particularly the egg industry, to frighten voters about increased food costs, threats to human health, and even racism, Proposition 2 passed two to one and would have passed even in the less liberal parts of California—that is, even if Los Angeles and San Francisco had not been counted. There is a powerful message here. It is widely believed (even by the agriculture industry) that such referenda will pass anywhere in the United States, even in agricultural states such as Iowa. Animal advocates will surely seize this low-hanging fruit, either in state-by state campaigns or through federal legislation during the administration of President Barack Obama.

I am not surprised. I saw the same bipartisan public moral commitment regarding the laws for animal research, and I have predicted the emergence of the new "social ethic for animals" since the late 1970s. Husbandry, and the fair contract it represents with animals, is not dead in the public mind. The increased public awareness of the deleterious aspects of confinement agriculture, brought to social attention by the Pew Commission's report, will surely give impetus to societal concern. Water and air pollution, antibiotics used for growth promotion and to cover up bad husbandry, dangers to human health, production diseases for animals, destruction of small farms—all have shown the public that vaunted "cheap food" is not so cheap. We may not pay at the register, but we pay in other ways.

As I told the Animal Science Association in a recent speech, this is not a rejection of the work of animal scientists. It is a challenge to vector into their work the additional considerations well characterized by the Pew Commission. The cost of food at the register may go up, but currently Americans spend less than half, on a percentage-of-income basis, for food than Europeans do. And slight increases in food costs are a small price to pay for the decent treatment of animals and of the environment and for the preservation of human health.

17

Odds, Beginnings, and Ends

The preceding chapters describe the major areas in animal welfare that have occupied my attention over the past thirty years, including the use of animals in research, animal agriculture, animals in teaching, veterinary ethics, animal law, animals' pain, animals' minds and consciousness, biotechnology, the construction of a philosophical basis for the moral status of animals, animals' distress, and issues surrounding companion animals. But these are by no means the only issues I have engaged. As one of very few people doing what I do, I get many strange issues to work on. In this chapter, I talk about some of the fascinating opportunities I have enjoyed.

Big Business

For most people, the term "agribusiness" calls to mind huge feedlots and multinational corporations, but business figures in agriculture in a variety of ways. One of the most interesting is livestock showing, a popular rural activity totally unknown to me as I was growing up in Brooklyn. Competitive livestock shows, often found in conjunction with county and state fairs, were originally intended to fulfill two functions. First, they provided a mechanism for improving the genetics of cattle, sheep, pigs, goats, chickens, turkeys, rabbits, and so on. People who saw these showcases of the "best" animals were drawn to improving the genetics of their own livestock. Equally important, young people who raised such animals virtually from birth to maturity were taught good husbandry and care of the animals, as well as the sense of responsibility I cherish in my agriculture students. Children would dote on the animals, groom them and train them, and, eventually, after a show season, sell them for market. While invariably a painful experience, children learned to deal with the reality of livestock production. Activists have complained that these shows viciously "teach children to kill their best friend." More appropriately, I have described them as teaching children that animals are entitled to the best possible care while they are alive, even though, as food animals, they are destined for slaughter.

Unfortunately, in the past few decades, money and ego have polluted this pristine educational well. For one thing, when I gave the keynote speech at a conference on the ethics of livestock showing in Las Vegas that had been specially convened because of a series of revelations concerning appalling cheating at livestock shows, none of the more than five hundred people attending, by and large 4-H, Future Farmers of America, and other livestock teachers and leaders, could articulate the purpose of livestock shows just outlined.

Far worse, the initial purposes were lost to scrambling for big money. Amazingly, at the Denver National Western Livestock Show in the 1990s, the winning steer received five hundred thousand dollars, and the winning *goat* received seventy thousand dollars. This has occurred because corporations such as McDonald's bid on the steer and then publicize the purchase. With that kind of money at stake, as well as parents' egos (*vide* Little League and soccer), cheating was inevitable. Cheating took many forms, from illegal use of clenbuterol, an asthma medicine with anabolic muscle-building properties, to injecting beer under the skin of cattle to fill out their contours, running lambs incessantly on treadmills to increase the size of their rear-end muscles, injecting vegetable oil under the skin to create the same effect (with the oil later going rancid and creating gangrene), and dyeing animals' coats and passing them off as a different breed. All of this is often performed by professional cheaters, known as "fitters." A good fitter can make well over a hundred thousand dollars a year, according to a veterinary student who worked as one.

The incidents that precipitated societal concern about livestock showing, which in turn gave rise to the conference, were well publicized and generated some efforts to ban showing altogether. In one case, the winning steer at a major show was found full of clenbuterol, which would have gone into the food chain as the animal was butchered. In a second incident, a pig was "drenched" and killed by a young man trying to increase its weight. (Drenching means forcing water with a hose into the animal.) Finally, at the Oklahoma State Fair, a young person was caught beating his lamb with a two-by-four to cause the hindquarters to swell. The woman who ran the fair, a veteran show person, could not conceal her emotion when she told me about it.

The Las Vegas conference was quite productive, generating suggestions that ranged from taking away the big money to distributing calves at random so rich people can't buy fancy genetics and judging by husbandry, not appearance. Interestingly, the Colorado Cattlemen's Association opposed livestock shows because it saw them as "cow beauty contests." The association is quite correct: Traits that win shows do not guarantee the quality of an animal's carcass or its temperament; the latter is the case with dog shows, as well. The cattlemen support carcass shows to make them relevant to the industry and preclude cheating. I must confess, I cannot judge a beautiful cow. They are all beautiful to me.

A year later, we held a second conference, in Dallas. The keynote speaker was a man who had studied livestock showing for his doctorate. As he gave his speech, an extraordinary thing happened: He kept talking about "livestock winning" being a way of life in Texas. As he repeated that phrase, I deduced from the context that he meant "livestock showing." When I called it to his attention, he blinked in surprise at his Freudian slip. I later found out that Texas (where he came from) was as obsessive about livestock showing as it was about high-school football and cheerleading. Barney Cosner, whom I discussed earlier, was the director of the Texas State Fair when he banned fitters from the show. That very evening, he had his life threatened in the parking lot. Later, he tried to ban extremely short tail docking in lambs in Wyoming (such docking can cause rectal prolapse) and again was subjected to an angry mob. (I was there.) I wish this story had a happy ending, but it does not. One of my students surveyed thousands of young people involved in livestock showing both before and after the scandals. There has been no improvement. In fact, cheating has increased.

From the time that I began to work on animal issues, I encountered the same response: These alleged animal ethical issues are really economic issues. (I am still confronted with this claim regularly.) My early answer, that deciding issues strictly by appealing to economics (cost, profits) was itself an ethical position—namely, that economic considerations are of greater value than animal suffering—did not seem to sway people enough to get them to see that appeals to economics were not ethically definitive. The need for a more effective response did not become acute until I was invited to keynote an International Air Transport Association conference. Transporting animals by air can cause suffering, harm, and death. I was warned that those in attendance would be hardheaded businessmen who were not open to moral suasion. They would not see ethics as relevant to business. As a result, I knew I needed a powerful approach to make them think in ethical terms.

I began by saying that, before getting into animal issues, I wanted to use my first encounter with businessmen to test my economic solution to poverty along the U.S.–Mexican border. As eagerly and enthusiastically as I could, I pointed out that there were many unwanted children in that area. They agreed. "Suppose we send a few video filmmakers down there and make a large batch of child pornography films," I continued. "Video cameras are cheap; we don't need to pay the kids much. We could make very hard-core videos and sell them by the thousands to perverts here and abroad. If we charge fifty dollars per video and sell a thousand, that's a fifty-thousand-dollar return on an investment of a few hundred. Since we could produce an indefinite number of videos . . ." I watched as their faces contorted. Finally, they began to make protesting noises. I paused. "You can't do that," they said. "It is wrong." "I thought ethics has no relevance to business," I retorted. They got the point. Much progress was made in the ensuing twenty-five years in increasing the welfare of animals transported by air.

Some fifteen years later, I was twice invited to address the group of businessmen involved in transporting live seafood. To my astonishment, they were very cognizant of both ethics and animal welfare, and we made much progress in discussion. I still correspond with some of them, and the literature on the issues has proliferated. All of this work reinforced my belief that people have deep concerns about animal welfare. The issue is getting them to "recollect."

United Airlines

I had another interesting interaction with big business in the mid-1980s. During the Arab oil crisis of the late 1970s, United Airlines could not afford to train pilots in jumbo jets because fuel cost too much. The airline negotiated with the pilots' union to consider flight simulators, methods of training that had been used in World War II. The union agreed to consider that approach, with flying actual planes as the yardstick to measure the simulation. In the end, the union agreed that simulation training, while not as good as real experience, was well above threshold.

What did this have to do with me? Having acquired simulation companies, United hoped to apply its expertise in that area to biomedical research—in particular, as a modality to replace animal use, as well as to make money. Working with a United executive, I formulated a suggestion. Emergency-room doctors and nurses need to be trained in intubating newborn babies who are not breathing—that is, inserting a tube into their tracheas. The current method of training at the time was to use cats, and my colleague, the veterinarian Lynne Kesel, had, in fact, done such training of physicians. The doctors and nurses hated handling and harming the cats. We devised a model that would mimic tracheal function, but I was skeptical about whether it could replicate the pressure and sense of urgency of a real situation. When I mentioned this to United, the executives laughed and invited me to visit the flight simulator at Denver's Stapleton International Airport. There I climbed into the simulated cockpit with the airline's chief test pilot, to whom I explained my concerns. An engaging man, he smiled and nodded and said we would go through a simulated flight and that I should buckle up. There was a kinesthetic sense of motion, a screen simulating a window, and the correct sounds. We "cruised" over Stapleton, with me fully aware that I was only five feet above the ground in a building. Suddenly a Klaxon horn sounded, accompanied by a voice screaming something like "Emergency, emergency, crash imminent" in a robotic voice. The cabin began to shudder and veer. By the time we landed. I had been terrified into becoming a believer in the ease of simulating urgency.

We sent out questionnaires to emergency-room personnel and got an unprecedented 70 percent positive rate of return saying they welcomed an alternative to practicing intubation on cats. I thought, "Mission accomplished." Unfortunately, United decided it could not make enough money on the device and scrubbed the project, despite the goodwill it would have engendered.

Hill's Pet Nutrition

In 2007, tragedy struck the pet food industry when wheat gluten adulterated with melamine from China poisoned thousands of dogs and cats. One of the companies affected was Hill's Pet Nutrition, a high-end maker of pet food that historically has been committed to improving animals' health and veterinary medicine. Mary Beth Leininger, the first female president of the American Veterinary Medical Association, is a senior manager at Hill's, and another friend, Clayton McKay, was then a vice-president in the company's Canadian division. Both are among the most progressive veterinarians I know in terms of ethics and welfare, and both requested I fly to the company's headquarters in Topeka to help its staff deal with the crisis.

The company's most serious problem was the staff of veterinarians who handled the phone lines to provide nutritional advice to practicing veterinarians. When contaminated Hill's foods ended up sickening and killing animals, the veterinarians were under considerable pressure. Working inhuman numbers of hours, they fielded calls from distraught practitioners who personalized their grief: "I trusted you, and you let me down." The callers were sometimes in tears, which were bullets into the hearts of the Hill's veterinarians. I read the situation as one of moral stress (discussed earlier) and flew to Topeka.

I asked the company for an open-ended session with the veterinarians. I also asked that no management personnel attend so that the people could talk freely. Finally, I indicated to management and to the vets that I would take no compensation unless I helped them climb out of the stress they were under. After an emotional meeting in which people were very grateful for the session, I made recommendations to the management team. I have been told I did some good. I hope so, as the veterinarians were in significant emotional pain.

Religion and Animals

Probably the most unexpected and bizarre excursus in my career was into religion. To say that I am not a religious person is an understatement analogous to calling the Korean War a "police action" or the Great Andromeda Nebula "cute." Although I went to a Jewish religious school, a yeshiva, for twelve long years, it was largely to provide day care while my mother worked, my father having left the family when I was five. The education crammed into a nine-hour day was very intense: College seemed easy in comparison. But the school's approach of beating you into Orthodoxy did not sit well or lead me to believe any of it. In retrospect, what I learned best was how to use logic and humor to fight those in power over me.

We read the Bible over and over again in Hebrew. In the fifth grade, angry at the teacher for some now forgotten offense against me (most likely being hit for not going to the synagogue), I plotted revenge. We came to the portion of the Bible where the Jews are wandering in the desert for forty years after the Exodus from Egypt. We were taught that the Jews ate the manna that miraculously appeared every morning. In my most sincere, childlike voice, I raised my hand. "Rabbi," I said. "Wouldn't it be tedious to eat the same thing, however good it might be, three times a day for forty years?" The rabbi beamed and put a hand on my shoulder. "Ah, Rollin, the rabbis have addressed this very question. . . . They figured out [?] that the manna could taste like whatever you wanted it to taste like. If you wanted fish, it tasted like fish. If you wanted chicken, it tasted like chicken." I smiled, about to spring the trap. "Oh, Rabbi. Hallelujah. Hosanna," I said. "What a wondrous miracle. But I have one question: Could it taste like bacon?" I was suspended for insubordination for a week—not a bad result. I resolved to become a philosopher, seeing the power of reason to disturb.

Nor am I what those who are trendy call "spiritual." I have written a book attacking alternative medicine. I do not meditate. I don't see intrinsic value in nature or even understand what it means. I have never had a religious experience, never felt at one with the universe, never been drawn to Eastern religions. I am singularly unimpressed with the injunction to "listen to the sound of one hand clapping." I don't arrange my furniture in tune with feng shui. I know of the millions of innocents tortured and murdered in the name of religion or heaven. Nonetheless, I have an interest in the phenomenon of religiosity and in studying comparative religion, if only for religion's enormous impact. And I have always harbored the desire to preach a fire-and-brimstone Baptist-type sermon. It seems like fun.

Ironically, I have preached many times in Congregational, Unitarian, and Presbyterian churches and thoroughly enjoyed it. On the first occasion, the minister was the husband of a dear friend, Elizabeth Atwood Lawrence, a professor at Tufts Veterinary School who is now, regrettably, deceased. Betty has written some of the best work ever done on human–animal interactions. *Rodeo: An Anthropologist Looks at the Wild and the Tame* (Lawrence 1982) is a brilliant analysis of rodeo; her other books are also classics and must-reads for anyone interested in animals. In any event, Betty's husband, the Reverend Robert Lawrence, is a force of nature. The minister of the Congregational cathedral in Fall River, Massachusetts, he had won every award for civic work and social justice imaginable. He is a formidable man with a deep voice and a shock of white hair—central casting for a charismatic churchman. Open and warm, Bob once heard me express my desire to give a Baptist sermon. "I can't get you that," he said, "but you can preach for me on the day we have every spring for blessing the animals." I have done so on three occasions and relate well to the parishioners.

These sermons brought home to me that religion can be a powerful force for good and for ethics, as occurred with civil rights. So I resolved in the 1990s to write an article on the incompatibility of factory farming with biblical teachings on husbandry. I published that paper, and some others, in *Christian Century,* the intellectual voice of liberal Protestantism. Much to my amazement, the article received a great deal of attention. (One minister posted it on his Web site and got seventeen thousand hits. He referred to me as "an itinerant preacher teaching the Gospel of kindness to animals." I have been called far worse and cherish the description.) One day, I received a phone call inviting me to serve as "theologian in residence" for the annual meeting of the Presbyterian Synod of Lakes and Prairies at Bethel College in Storm Lake, Iowa. I protested that I was not a Presbyterian or a Protestant or even a theist. No problem, I was assured. "We just want to expose our people to your work on animals and on biotechnology." I was asked to live and eat with the participants, speak every morning to the whole group for an hour, and then be available to meet with interested people from seven to nine in the evening. I was assured that it was rare to get more than twenty people for longer than forty minutes. I was also asked to moderate my cussing. It turned out that I garnered the best audiences in the seventy-five year history of the meetings. I never had fewer than a hundred people at the sessions, and we often went on until eleven o'clock. I was informed that the people, who were wonderful, had never been exposed to these sorts of issues and committed to adopting policies on factory farming. On my last day there, I drove into a cornfield, stopped the car, and cussed for twenty minutes to make up for the lost time.

Equine Abuse

Probably the most serious area of animal abuse that has escaped public notice consists of a variety of practices in the equine industry. Given the unique place of the horse in American history in terms of winning the West and the codification of that status in characters such as the Lone Ranger's horse Silver and Roy Rogers's Trigger and in countless books such as *Black Beauty* and the more recent *Seabiscuit,* it is amazing that these abuses have not surfaced. In veterinary medicine, too, given the increasing status of horses as companion animals, many outrageous practices have endured. For example, analgesia use in equine practice lagged well behind its development for dogs (though cat analgesia also failed to emerge and was not stressed until well into the twenty-first century). One commonly found the practice of horse castration performed with paralytic drugs, not anesthetics, and in another English-speaking country I even encountered the "euthanasia" of racehorses on the track with such drugs so that the animals suffocated because it "looked better to the public than a gunshot."

A definite atmosphere of macho brutality has existed in equine veterinary practice, particularly among surgeons. I knew one paradigmatic case at CSU and found at least one similar figure at most veterinary schools. One such faculty member at a major school told me, "You have to beat a horse to show him who's boss." Since, as recounted earlier, I became quite involved with horses in my private life, I knew this to be egregiously false. Indeed, macho behavior toward horses elicits fear in them and a significant reaction, thereby buttressing the redneck predilection to use more force, in an ever increasing spiral. As the so-called horse whisperers teach, a patient, gentle approach to working with the animal, not trying to break its will, works best.

Happily, horse veterinarians not cut from the macho cloth began to make their presence known to me. One in particular was Jay Merriam, a veterinarian in Massachusetts who was devoid of macho problems and was well aware of the societal change in animal ethics. As president of the American Association of Equine Practitioners (AAEP), Jay was committed to creating awareness of animal-welfare issues in his membership and asked me to give a keynote speech to the AAEP in the early 1990s. Thanks to my equine science students, I was well prepared in all areas of animal use. What they taught me was eye-opening and depressing.

My approach was what one might expect. At the beginning of the speech, I laid out the emerging social ethics for animals. I first asked the audience members whether they thought my reconstruction was fair and accurate. Most tended to agree. I then described certain equine practices prevalent in the industry, practices I asked that they judge according to the emerging ethic. In this way, I stay true to the Socratic dictum that, when dealing with ethics and adults, one should not teach but, rather, *remind.* Interestingly, people tended to be ignorant of atrocities outside their own particular area of the equine industry and to disbelieve some of what I relayed. Fortunately, at the AAEP, there were some people from virtually every area of equine use who were able to confirm what I described. I have found this phenomenon to be ubiquitous in the equine world: People are ignorant of areas of equine practice outside their own.

What are some of the abuses to which I call attention? I first point out that horses are a favored animal, close to dogs in emotional appeal. The California law forbidding the slaughter of horses and its federal version, which never passed but led to the closing of U.S. horse slaughterhouses, attest to this. (Ironically, horses are now being shipped to Mexico, where slaughter is legal and where the slaughterhouses are atrocious.) At the same time, most people do not keep horses, make a living from them, go to racetracks, engage in endurance riding, or participate in showing horses, so they do not derive any benefit from hurting these animals. Social tolerance for suffering brought about by equine use is going to be considerably less than for that growing out of research or agriculture. If society is willing to risk the threat of endangering human health by legislating proper treatment of laboratory animals, it will surely not cavil at shutting down morally objectionable aspects of an industry from which it receives no benefit. In fact, far too many practices in the equine area, if carefully scrutinized, would very likely be rejected today not only as abuse but as downright cruelty, a word, as I have stressed, I do not use lightly or loosely.

For example, the soring of horses is a practice so objectionable to society that it evoked federal legislation before the new ethic had even taken hold. For those who are not familiar with this atrocity, it is mainly an issue in the Tennessee Walking Horse industry. Tennessee Walkers are lovely animals with a unique gait that is very smooth (i.e., not bouncy) but covers a great deal of ground quickly. Some years ago, I am told, a farrier trimmed a Walking Horse's hooves too close, impinging on an innervated area and causing the horse to walk gingerly, because it hurt to put its weight down. The judges thought the resulting gait was very aesthetic, and soon most owners began to trim too close, as well as to drive nails into the sensitive part of the hoof and otherwise hurt the hooves to achieve the desirable gait. Today, people will drive nails in, remove them, and introduce capsaicin (the active ingredient in hot pepper) or other irritants for the same purpose. For years, the southern redneck lobby blocked appropriations for the U.S. Department of Agriculture, which is responsible for enforcing the federal law banning the practice; an inspector told me that at his first show, he tried to enforce the law and was literally chased out by rednecks with tire irons. So widespread are these practices that there is actually a group called Friends of the Sound Horse who are committed to holding shows without cheating. Given that soring is still done, albeit in more ingenious ways, though, I doubt that one could find a citizen (including many owners of Tennessee Walking Horses) who would be unwilling to support a referendum abolishing it, since it is evident that regulation has not worked.

As another example, consider the chain saw bit (or mule bit) made of saw chain that one can legally buy from widely distributed catalogues of horse equipment. Most horse people are horrified when I show them one, yet in sectors of the industry they are used openly, with one trainer remarking to one of my veterinary students, "So what? The worst that happens is we cut a few tongues off." Most ordinary citizens and most horse owners, I think, would share my view of this device: Any horse that can't be ridden without it should be euthanized; any rider who refuses to ride without it should be euthanized.

Many other training methods are equally socially and ethically unacceptable. Consider "tarping," a breaking method whereby a horse is thrown on the ground, covered with a tarpaulin, and beaten with a whip or hose; or blindfolding a horse, running him down an alley into a wall, and yelling, "Whoa"; or beating a horse with cable or a hose filled with lead; or tying a horse's head to his tail and turning him back in his pen, leaving him all day without water or the ability to straighten his head, a tactic usually used when the horse refuses to give his head (submit) to the rider. Severe bits and lip chains should also be included in this list. The key point is that there are widely known alternative training methods that do not hurt horses. For example, there are all the well-publicized "natural horse" approaches based on an understanding of the horse and its nature. Given this knowledge, persisting in abusive approaches would surely count as cruelty.

The same point can be made about the show ring and the abusive shortcuts many people take, using firecrackers, whipping, electroshock, and anal irritants to excite animals for some show uses, and bleeding, hanging, taping nostrils, and even breaking ribs to make them look relaxed for other uses.

"Tail breaking," in which the depressor tendon is cut to force the tail up for appearance, is another good example.

Even veterinary medicine is vulnerable to such criticisms. Given the total absence of scientific evidence supporting any benefit to firing (burning a horse's leg along the tendon sheath) or freeze firing with liquid nitrogen, and given the pain these practices cause, do they not count as cruelty in today's moral milieu? The same can be said of practitioners who continue to use paralytic drugs when castrating horses or euthanizing them. I spoke to one equine association outside the United States that openly admits using succinylcholine to euthanize horses at racetracks. And what about drugs used to mask pain while allowing horses to continue to run and thus to injure themselves?

Long-term tethering of horses to produce pregnant-mare urine, used in hormone replacement therapy for women, provides a clear example of something that can violate the horse's nature or *telos.* So does the solitary confinement of racehorses in small stalls for twenty-three hours a day. This must be a source of suffering to herd animals that are bred to run and whose nature is to graze. In addition, it is likely that it predisposes animals to injury when they do run. A third example is the racing of young horses before they are biologically prepared. Even if the public accepts racing, it will not accept racing at an age that promotes injury.

My work in the equine area has been considerable, speaking at the Houston Livestock Show, at local horse associations, to specialty groups like the reining horse governing board, to rodeo and horse show people. Two occasions are worth mentioning. I once spoke to the Thoroughbred (racehorse) trainers of Ocala, Florida. During the question period, the trainers, some of whom use horrific and brutal methods, became so agitated that the forum's organizers asked me to cut it short and leave. "No," I said. "I'm not going to be intimidated by these dumb rednecks." Nonetheless, I was hustled out, with only a minute to point out that I had been thrown out of far better places. On the second occasion, I received a call from Dan Rosenberg, manager of the major racehorse operation Three Chimneys in Lexington, Kentucky. He was upset that, when an important racehorse had been injured and could no longer race, his owner, an oil sheik, was selling him at auction for slaughter. The meat was to be exported to Europe. Rosenberg is a large, powerful man with a booming voice and a real respect and affection for the animals. Having heard about the sale, he made it a point to attend. When the magnificent animal was at the auction block, slated to bring about six hundred dollars, Rosenberg jumped up and boomed, "If the sheik needs the money that much, I'll write him a check." Having gotten the attention of the stable managers, Dan invited me to lecture to them.

These racehorses are like house pets: They have been handled a great deal and will follow you around and nuzzle you. I pointed out that, aside from the immorality of selling them for a few hundred dollars, doing so is idiotic in that if it were widely known, it would turn society against racing. They listened and now some have established retirement homes and placement programs for former racehorses.

Thus far, horse abusers have led a charmed life. I hope that ends soon.

Students

Over the years, I have been blessed with innumerable wonderful students with whom I have maintained friendships and who have achieved great accomplishments in many fields. Nancy Cunningham Butler helped expose the open-heart surgery done on infants in the 1980s with no anesthesia; Steve Hillard won a major lawsuit against the U.S. government on behalf of the indigenous Alaskan people for compensation for the land on which Anchorage is built; Tom Edling, chief veterinarian at multibillion-dollar pet store chain Petco, called me in to consult on animal welfare; Charmaine Foltz, senior veterinarian at the National Institutes of Health (NIH), invited me there and goaded me to write opposing a proposed change in policy that would crowd mice in small cages. My lectures have inspired concern about animals' pain and suffering and animal welfare in thousands of veterinarians at CSU and elsewhere, hundreds of people who hold doctorates in science and philosophy, hundreds of ranchers and farmers in whom I helped recall the husbandry ethic. I could easily write another book chronicling their achievements.

One such student was Fred Allison, who took my animal science class more than twenty years ago. It was Fred who introduced me to issues in livestock shows and candidly recounted the abuses he had witnessed as a competitor. Some years after Fred graduated, he became a manager at the Excel slaughterhouse and packing plant in Fort Morgan in eastern Colorado. He invited me there to lecture on animal ethics. I drove out and was met by Fred at the entrance to the facility. He had changed his mind, he said, because "some of the workers said they were going to 'get you.'" "Physically or intellectually?" I asked. "Because if it is intellectually, I'm not worried. And if it's physically, tell them I'll meet them outside after the talk, one at a time. In any case, I'm not turning tail and running home." When I spoke, the room was full, and people listened. Many commented that they did not do the actual killing, and would not. The killers, I was told, tend to keep to themselves and were "creepy." Many were paroled murderers, complete with teardrop tattoos near their eyes—one for each victim. Needless to say, they did not come to hear my talk. One manager in charge of the kill floor told me that he hated killing animals and spent as little time on the kill floor as possible. Ironically, managerial supervision is essential to ensuring that things are done smoothly and humanely. I was there for three hours. It was a fine experience, and no one took me on physically or intellectually. I may be the only person in history to lecture on animal rights at a packing plant.

As I mentioned, one of my best veterinary students, Tom Edling, became the chief veterinarian for Petco. Strongly committed to the effort, Tom almost single-handedly helped the company gain an admirable reputation in animal welfare. Through his good offices, I became a member of Petco's Animal Advisory Committee. We have done much good for the animals.

Temple Grandin

Some twenty years ago, I received a call from Temple Grandin, the world-renowned expert on animal handling and facility design whose books *Thinking in Pictures* and *Animals in Translation* have been bestsellers. Temple announced that she wanted a job teaching at CSU. "Why?" I asked. "Because it's nice country, you're there, it's cattle country, and the school is interested in welfare." I sputtered and said, "It's hard to get academic jobs. A department needs to request a position; the administration must approve it . . . and . . ." she cut me short. "I don't care what you pay me. I have my own consulting business." "Temple," I replied, "you just said the magic words." I was able to arrange a part-time appointment for Temple shared between the Department of Veterinary Medicine and the Department of Animal Sciences. Temple is a great teacher and has brought much credit to CSU. Although we don't usually work collaboratively, we have done so on occasion, and our work is very complementary. As a high-functioning autistic, Temple has also advanced our knowledge of autism. The media loves to exaggerate Temple's "strangeness," as the neurologist Oliver Sacks did in *An Anthropologist on Mars.* As I once told *People* magazine: "There are far stranger people in any philosophy department in the United States."

Speeches

Many of my speaking commitments—I have done more than fifteen hundred talks in thirty-plus countries—had interesting twists worth recounting. One such engagement was an invitation to speak at the National Barrow Show in Austin, Minnesota, an annual event showcasing swine genetics and sponsored by Hormel. The company executives who invited me asked me to explain the emerging social ethic for animals to the farmers in attendance but specifically requested that I not mention sow stalls.

Austin, Minnesota, is a small agricultural community, differentiated from others by the presence of Hormel, its national headquarters, and the Spam Museum. (I'm not kidding—it is a fascinating place.) On the day of my talk, I put on a suit, as I usually do, out of respect for my audience. I was escorted to a livestock pavilion where the pigs were being shown. "Where's the lecture room?" I asked. "This is it," I was told. This was, in fact, the second time I had lectured in the middle of a pig pen, and the presence of the pigs was actually inspirational, especially when they oinked and snorted enthusiastically at the right times (or so it seemed to me). As is usually the case, the farmers were open and appreciative. The only sour note came from a group of older farmers who had a highly appropriate query: "Why the heck didn't you talk about sow stalls?"

Another interesting trip came as a result of an invitation from the U.S. Soybean Association to lecture in Borneo. I was perplexed, as my readers doubtless must be. How did my area relate to soybeans? And why Borneo? (My father-in-law, incidentally, spoke very little to me, and when he did, he took potshots at my hair by saying I resembled "the wild man of Borneo.")

Actually, it made sense. A great deal of U.S. soybeans were sold to Asia as livestock feed. The livestock producers knew nothing of animal welfare and felt they needed to learn. My audience consisted of about 250 such producers from Asia, Australia, and New Zealand, and I could not have asked for a friendlier, more attentive group. Why Borneo? Because the city where the meeting was held, Kota Kinabolu, housed a number of five-star resorts where rooms could be had at bargain rates. I have never been to a nicer resort. The staff was friendly, warm, open, and English-speaking. The only oddity about the soybean gig was that I was compelled to sign a contract promising never to badmouth soybeans. I have kept that promise.

South Africa

I found similar warmth the two times I lectured in South Africa. On both occasions, I visited Kruger Park, and, the second time, my wife and I rented a car. Kruger is a wildlife preserve, thousands of square miles where the animals run free and tourists must stay in their vehicles. The camp we stayed in had air-conditioned cabins built to look like huts; the staff could not have been friendlier, and the food was exceptional.

Linda and I got to see hippos, rhinos, zebras, lions, warthogs, elephants, and many other animals, running free, and all went smoothly, with one exception. In genuine schlemazel fashion, I blew a tire. I reasoned that this was clearly an exception to the "don't leave your car" rule. I went out, retrieved the jack, and began the task when a game warden roared up: "You're not allowed out of the car, sir!" I pointed out that I could hardly change a tire from inside the car. "I see," he said, "but take great care—you're right in the midst of the lions' hunting range." "Good God," I said. "What should I do?" "Be careful," he said, unnecessarily, "and have your wife scout for the lion." (This was not reassuring. On one occasion many years earlier, I had attempted to teach my wife tennis. I lobbed a serve, the ball bounced near her, and *five seconds later* she swung the racquet. This happened more than once.) So I figured I would be eaten before she sounded the alarm. It all worked out well, though, particularly for the lone zebra standing ten feet away who seemed greatly amused.

Iceland

A few years ago, I gave the keynote speech at the annual meeting of the Iceland Veterinary Medical Association (about sixty-five vets). Iceland boasts a Viking history, a democratic parliament during the Middle Ages that governed the country between bouts of pillaging, subterranean geothermal springs that heat the country, a tiny crime rate (presumably the pillaging got it out of their systems), and some of the most beautiful and hospitable people I have ever met. My host, Gunnar, a regulatory vet, was central casting for a Viking—six feet, six inches tall, muscular, big booming voice. Thanks to him, I saw a great deal of the country and met fascinating people—for example, his nearest neighbor, who invited us for dinner. We went the five miles to the neighbor's house on Icelandic ponies—incredibly tough, agile, sweet animals—and were met by the neighbor halfway there, who was also on horseback and who sang an ancient welcome song. A few days later, we stopped for gas. Gunnar told me that the station attendant was from an ancient line of poets and was obliged to sing me a poem because I was a guest. However, the man knew virtually no English, and I knew no Icelandic. He solved the problem with a resounding "Roses are red; violets are blue; welcome to Iceland!"

After I gave my keynote speech in a remote village, a banquet was held in my honor. Amid much festivity, I was offered the Icelandic national dish: rotted shark that had been buried for months. I can't say I liked it, but the saving grace was the Icelandic brandy with which one washed it down, the most potent alcoholic beverage I have ever consumed.

Not surprisingly, Icelanders eat a great deal of fish and smoked fish. Gunnar asked me one day how I thought the fish was smoked when there is barely a two-acre patch of trees on the entire island. I had no idea. "Well," said Gunnar, "we have plenty of sheep. We smoke it in sheep shit." Of course, perpetually twelve years old, I insisted on bringing a number of vacuum packages home to my wife, introducing them as "smoked fish." As she spit out the first bite, she yelled, "This is smoked in sheep shit!" How she knew remains a mystery.

Albuquerque Zoo

I have, through my work and talks, met groups of wonderful people I would otherwise never have known existed—ostrich growers, elk breeders, llama farmers, alpaca raisers, rodeo clowns, people who travel from fair to fair with racing pigs, producers of grass-fed beef, race horse owners, zoo vets. One of my friends, Mike Richard, is a vet who runs the Albuquerque Zoo. He let me hold Sarah, a baby orangutan. In one of my most incredible experiences, Sarah traced a four inch scar on my left forearm, moved to my right forearm, tapped it, and looked at me without a doubt wanting an explanation. With the exception of the Thoroughbred horse trainers I mentioned earlier, all the people I have met have been the salt of the earth, very open to "recollecting" moral concern for animals. I am blessed.

Dumb Responses

I was going to devote a whole chapter to imbecilic responses my work has garnered from the very beginning. I actually had a large file of such responses, reaching back to the 1970s. However, the hand of God intervened when my office was flooded and that file was destroyed, and the reader is thus spared many of the grim details. I have already recounted being called a Nazi and a lab trasher by the *New England Journal of Medicine* and a "sellout for accepting the reality of science" by the animal-rights magazine *Agenda.* I can't top those. But there are other good ones. For example, in the 1990s, I was invited to address the Society of Biology Editors, comprising the editors of the major biomedical journals. It was one of the brightest, most interested groups I ever addressed. Indeed, so moved were they by what I said about research that Albert Koltveit, then the editor of the *Journal of the American Veterinary Medical Association,* stood up and exhorted all of the editors to reject manuscripts that represented research not in accord with the letter and spirit of the laboratory animal laws. "If we won't publish such papers," said Koltveit, "they won't do them." He was exemplary in living up to his dictum. I even did some ethical reviews for *Journal of the American Veterinary Medical Association* when there was suspicion that animal care and use was questionable. The group also asked whether I would allow my paper to be published in their journal. I happily obliged.

Enter our idiot, an M.D. and Ph.D. who was editor-in-chief of that journal. He attacked me and my ideas from his editorial vantage point even though he had not heard me, met me, or even read my paper. The managing editor sent me a copy of her boss's scurrilous missive, asking whether I wished to reply. Of course, I said, after reading it. After attacking my animal ethics in an ad hominem way, he concluded with "What do you expect from someone who wrote a book entitled *The Unheeded Cry*?" I reminded him in my reply that at least I had been taught as a child not to judge a book by its cover—and certainly not by its title. After reading my letter, he offered to withdraw his if I would do the same. I was not disposed to do so, recalling the adage "Fuck with the bull and get the horn." His managing editor showed great courage by going ahead and printing the two letters, even though she said it might cost her her job.

Another noteworthy instance involved an invitation by students and animal-activist faculty to lecture at Stanford University. At the time, Stanford's medical school was a particularly strident voice for unrestricted freedom in animal research, and I had witnessed one of its surgeons doing a hatchet job on animal advocacy on *60 Minutes.* I called Stanford and made the following offer: "Instead of just giving a talk, why could I not debate one of the people attacking concern for animals? It would be much more interesting and entertaining." Someone called back and said that only one of Stanford's people would debate me: a female neurosurgeon (who later achieved some notoriety for blowing the whistle on male colleagues who pinched her butt during surgeries). The good doctor explained that she would debate me but that she "might need to do surgery that evening." I thought it highly suspicious that she could not control her calendar, but we set the date. That evening a party was held before the debate. She was not there. *Fifteen minutes* before the debate she phoned and indicated that she needed to be in surgery.

So there I was, all dressed up and full of adrenaline with no one to debate in front of an audience of 150 people. I had an inspiration: I told the audience that, in my opponent's absence, I would present both sides as well as I could, and the audience could augment my remarks. It worked beautifully and was a wonderful event. The researchers later told me that I had done a better job defending their position than she would have done.

Harley-Davidsons and Real Philosophy

Some of the readers of this book may know me through a book I edited titled *Harley-Davidson and Philosophy* (Rollin et al. 2006), published in Open Court Press's *Philosophy and Popular Culture* series. Undertaking this project was another example of "God does not punish with a stick." On one of my lecture trips prior to 2006, I had visited a bookstore that showcased the series. The response I tendered to my wife when I returned home was "What a crock. *The Simpsons and Philosophy. The Matrix and Philosophy.* What kind of idiot would do such a book? And what pandering to the students who are unwilling to do real philosophy." I railed loudly and incessantly that evening against the slippage of standards, the decline of students' ability and willingness to work, whoring academics.

The same week, I received a call from an editor at Open Court asking me to edit *Harley-Davidson and Philosophy.* My initial reaction was "No way!" But as we talked, I thawed. The very persuasive carrot dangled by the editor was a promise to print any photo I wanted as the book's frontispiece. My mind wandered back to a picture of me, shirtless, next to my Harley-Davidson. I devilishly asked the editor if she would reprint *that* photo, and she immediately agreed. And so that photo does appear at the beginning of the book.

In a final gesture of crow eating, I acknowledge that the contributors to the Harley book did a splendid job, and the book has been uniformly well reviewed. In addition to the preliminary material, I wrote two substantial chapters. One deals with the aesthetics of motorcycles, explaining why the Guggenheim's exhibit of bikes was the most popular show in the museum's history. The second, not so subtly titled "It's My Own Damn Head," deals with the ethics of helmet laws.

The Morris Animal Foundation

I have already stressed my debt to my CSU colleagues in many fields. One particularly interesting relationship is the one I have enjoyed with Patricia Olson, a veterinarian and small-animal clinician who held a doctorate in reproductive physiology when I started in veterinary medicine. Soon after we met, Patty expressed interest in ethics and animal welfare. She was increasingly uncomfortable in academe, as she put it, because she was required to do invasive research to teach young veterinarians to care for animals, and she resigned from the university. She then completed a master's degree in bioethics and was hired as scientific director of the American Humane Association and, later, as veterinary director of Guide Dogs for the Blind. While at Guide Dogs, she faced numerous animal-welfare issues and asked me to lecture for the organization's personnel. I did and then helped Guide Dogs form an Institutional Animal Care and Use Committee (IACUC) to provide a formal mechanism for ongoing handling of such issues. I also agreed to chair the committee until it developed its own momentum.

I worked with wonderful people at Guide Dogs, beginning with Patty herself. Patty has a unique trait: She never changes. She has been a hundred-pound dynamo for the thirty years I have known her. Even more unusual, she never ages. Almost everyone at Guide Dogs was absolutely committed to the animals, and the organization spent a fortune on medical care even when the dogs were not under their direct control. The organization's campus, in downtown San Rafael, California, is breathtakingly beautiful.

One of the most interesting people I met at Guide Dogs was Ariel Gilbert, who had been blinded many years before when an evil lunatic put acid into bottles of eye drops. She was devastated by losing her sight at a young age and grew despondent. As she recounts, what saved her was her relationship with her guide dog. When I worked with her, her dog was a beautiful Belgian Shepherd named Hedda Steam, who was so good at guiding her that I struggled to keep up with them. Among other things, Ariel competes internationally in rowing and wins. I also met a blind man working at Guide Dogs who was in the World Trade Center's twin towers during 9/11. He and his dog guided dozens of people to safety.

Patty moved from Guide Dogs to become president and chief executive of the Morris Animal Foundation. Contrary to popular belief, the foundation is the creation not of Morris the Cat but, rather, of the veterinarian and nutritionist Mark Morris and his son, Mark Morris Jr., who developed Hill's pet food. The foundation funds a considerable amount of research into pet and wildlife health and is highly respected internationally. Shortly after she took that job, Patty asked me if I thought it would be viable for the foundation to fund only non-invasive research that benefits animals. "Sure," I said. "There are plenty of people funding the invasive work." She then asked me to make the ethical case for doing so to the elder Dr. Morris and some board members and staff.

Patty and I drove to a meeting at Mark Morris's home in the Colorado mountains, where I spoke for ninety minutes on societal animal ethics and how fitting it was for the foundation to sponsor only non-invasive work. Dr. Morris listened astutely as few people do. After asking very smart questions, he said, "You're right, and if the scientists we work with object, I'll invoke the 'Golden Rule': He who has the gold rules." In vindication of this landmark decision, the foundation received a million-dollar donation from Hill's Pet Nutrition based specifically on the cessation of its previous funding of invasive work, except in the case of national emergencies, such as the sudden appearance of a new parvovirus.

I have continued to work with Patty on numerous issues. One day she called me with a problem. People for the Ethical Treatment of Animals (PETA) had received complaints from a "whistleblower" about the care of animals and animals' suffering in the context of a study at a veterinary school sponsored by the Morris Animal Foundation. Although the study, which involved transplanting kidneys in dogs, had considerably predated both Patty's tenure at the foundation and the new policy, she dealt with it head-on. Fortunately, the PETA representative charged with the investigation was Laura Yanne. I had an excellent relationship with Laura, and with a number of people at PETA, so I phoned her and asked her to trust Patty to deal with the issue before PETA publicized it. She agreed, and Patty asked my advice. I suggested that she assemble a team that would visit the research laboratory in question, talk to everyone involved, and look at records.

My suggestion to head the team was Lynne Kesel. She is so multitalented and so much her own person that she had no fear of professional retribution. To help her put the team together, I contacted Leon Thacker, pathologist extraordinaire, head of the Pathology Department at Purdue University, and director of Indiana's State Diagnostic Laboratory. He was as devoid of fear and as morally righteous as Lynne. Leon, in turn, suggested Dennis Chew, a kidney specialist at Ohio State University, who is also fearless. After a thorough investigation, the team reported back to Patty, verifying many of the whistleblower's complaints. Patty, in turn, demanded reform on pain of stopping additional funding to the institution. The remaining dogs were adopted out, and I enjoyed a number of creative conversations with the dean. PETA was so impressed with the process that Laura wrote a eulogistic thank-you letter to Patty, and the Morris Animal Foundation has adopted site visits as routine procedure for monitoring the welfare of the animals used in research they fund.

ILAR

In 2004, I went to the International Congress on Alternatives to Animal Testing in Berlin to receive the Spira Award (see Chapter 14). While there, Linda and I met up with an old friend, Joanne Zurlo, a morally sophisticated scientist who heads the Institute of Laboratory Animal Research (ILAR) at the National Academy of Sciences. She also convenes and administers the ILAR Council. Joanne had mentioned the opportunity of serving on the ILAR Council a year earlier when I gave the keynote to the annual meeting of Public Responsibility in Medicine and Research, a group headed by Joan Rachlin that does much good work in educating scientists to the nuances of ethical issues in research and trains Institutional Animal Care and Use Committees and Institutional Review Boards. In Berlin, we finalized my service on the ILAR Council.

I reflected on the irony of espousing the same ideas as I had when the *New England Journal of Medicine* called me a Nazi and a lab trasher in 1982 and now being invited to serve on the ILAR Council. The most significant issue I was party to as a member of the council concerned the NIH's *Guide to the Care and Use of Laboratory Animals* that, as I mentioned earlier, is regarded as the Bible for animal care in research. The *Guide,* issued since the early 1960s, has been frequently revised. I had been an external evaluator for the edition published in 1996 and was responsible for the document's giving some emphasis to environmental enrichment. But that edition is now outdated, particularly since so much current biomedical research is dominated by work with transgenic animals, and the *Guide* is silent on the creation and treatment of such animals. Though there was a great deal of demand for a new edition, the NIH, having suffered major budget cuts under President George W. Bush, had refused to undertake producing it. The ILAR Council met with senior people at the NIH for a full afternoon and seemed to persuade them of the need for a revised *Guide.* The selection of the authorial committee was completed, and the new *Guide* was released in June 2010.

Exemplary Colleagues

In the past decade, my work at CSU has been enhanced immeasurably by the acquisition of two new allies who are deeply concerned about animal welfare. Terry Engle, is an associate professor of animal sciences and, along with Bill Wailes, chairman of the Department of Animal Sciences, he is my strongest ally in agricultural-animal welfare. I have known Terry since he was an undergraduate at CSU; we used to lift weights together when he was captain of the football team. Those who consider me stocky have never seen Terry. He stands about six feet, four inches tall and weighs about 275 pounds. He has a huge a heart to match. Terry chairs our IACUC and signs the letters I write when PETA or Mercy for Animals sends me atrocious videos of agricultural atrocities, as does Bill Wailes, his department chairman.

Another close colleague is Wade Troxell, professor of mechanical engineering and associate dean of engineering. Wade, too, was a football player and team captain at CSU with whom I worked out. He is the person who gave me the doctoral students to work on alternatives to hot-iron branding of cattle.

Many years ago, I became concerned about the euthanizing of small rodents. According to the federal laws of 1985, the euthanizing of research animals must meet the stipulations of guidelines prepared by the American Veterinary Medical Association's Panel on Euthanasia. This is a good idea in principle, as various methods of killing animals have been deployed in research and at humane societies, pounds, and slaughterhouses that are less than humane. They include drowning, use of paralytic drugs that cause death through paralysis of the diaphragmatic respiratory muscles that leads to asphyxia, direct injection of barbiturates into the heart, clubbing, cervical dislocation, decapitation, gassing with automobile exhaust, and crushing of the chest. Larry Carbone, the eminent laboratory-animal veterinarian and animal ethicist, is very concerned with proper euthanasia. He did graduate work on subtle aspects of the 1985 laws and called my attention to the fact that some of the Panel on Euthanasia's recommendations were political compromises, with the veterinary panel subjected to strong pressure from the research community. In particular, the scientists needed an easy and convenient method to kill large numbers of rats and mice in a manner that did not affect various scientifically relevant physiological parameters. The method of choice has been the use of carbon dioxide, which, at a certain level, can function as an anesthetic but kills by suffocation.

The situation is rather complex. Ideally, one wishes to create hypoxia—that is, the lack of oxygen to the brain—thereby killing brain cells. Carbon dioxide does this, but by suffocation, or what is called asphyxia. Recall as a young person being held under water or having someone put a pillow over your face or having an asthma attack. Although we think we are suffering from lack of oxygen in such situations, what is really going on is the inability to exhale carbon dioxide. Humans breathe oxygen to live, and when it is used in the body, it creates carbon dioxide, which we excrete through the lungs. It is carbon dioxide that triggers the feeling of gasping and not being able to breathe. As scientists say, the accumulation of carbon dioxide drives respiration.

Clearly, then, to kill via an overdose of carbon dioxide is to create some period of subjective distress from feeling "unable to breathe." If the reader wishes to get a sense of what it feels like, he or she should take a whiff of dry ice, which is frozen carbon dioxide. This is quite aversive; it "takes your breath away." When carbon dioxide is used for euthanasia, the animal eventually loses consciousness but clearly not before a period of gasping for breath. The issue, more an ethical than a scientific one, is whether this truly counts as a "good death." Some people say, "It is only, at most, thirty seconds of gasping." Others say, "My God, it can be a full thirty seconds of distress from gasping." I fall into the latter group: Those twenty to forty seconds of gasping do not constitute a good death. Many veterinarians and researchers agree, even people who created the AVMA's euthanasia guidelines, but have been unable to find a more humane alternative.

What was needed, I realized, was to induce unconsciousness and brain-cell death without asphyxia—in other words, to create hypoxic unconsciousness without a sense of suffocation. If this could be done, one could create true euthanasia (good death) without distress or suffering. I resolved to try. After all, 90 percent of the animals used in research are rats and mice. Even if the experimental procedures were painless and did not induce distress, death by carbon dioxide surely did.

Historically, before about 1980, many shelter animals were killed in "high-altitude chambers." This method was replaced by pentobarbital injection, in which the animals "go to sleep" (recall the discussion of the "euthanasia school"). The principle behind high-altitude chambers may be familiar to many readers. As one ascends in altitude in mountain climbing or in a balloon, the air gets "thinner" (i.e., contains less oxygen). If one goes high enough (twelve thousand feet), one gets lightheaded and woozy. At high altitudes, as the brain is deprived of oxygen, humans feel intoxicated to a degree equivalent to that of consuming six ounces of alcohol. All pilots must experience this in training to be familiar with it, and they report that the feeling is not unpleasant. In the eighteenth century, French hot-air balloonists kept diaries of the ascent and recorded their feelings of euphoria. Indeed, the experience was so pleasant that some continued to ascend, eventually succumbing to hypoxia, as people on the ground discovered when the balloons and diaries and corpses returned to Earth. I recall seeing World War II movies as a child in which pilots flew too high without ancillary oxygen and blacked out.

In principle, then, one could generate hypoxia without asphyxia in euthanasia chambers for rodents. Unfortunately, the vacuum chambers were imperfectly sealed and would re-pressurize, causing the animals to regain consciousness. Even worse, animals were elevated to high-altitude conditions too quickly, before they could equilibrate, and this could cause painful ear pressure (ear popping is a mild example of this). Animals with ear or nose infections could suffer a great deal of pain and even bleed through ears, nose, or eyes. This is why pentobarbital replaced these chambers.

I discussed this with Terry and Wade. Wade found two bright graduate students in mechanical engineering, Carl Kaiser and Ross McGregor, who were eager to work on this problem and who quickly, under a grant from Petco (whose mouse suppliers hated carbon dioxide) developed a leak-proof, computer-controlled chamber in which a high-altitude ascent could be precisely and predictably controlled. With the help of Lynne Kesel and the veterinary physiologist Ray Whalen, we tried the device on a small number of mice and rats that otherwise would have been killed using carbon dioxide. As we had hoped, unlike animals in carbon dioxide chambers, the test animals showed no signs of distress or struggle to escape or gasping for air. They simply stumbled a bit, lay down, and went to sleep.

My colleagues, who had witnessed thousands of mice killed using carbon dioxide, were unanimous in praising this method because it did not appear to cause distress or a struggle to breathe. The next step was to do physiological measurement on the animals to validate the phenomenological belief that there was no discomfort. Although I am very uncomfortable about doing such experiments, I am driven by the desire to eliminate death by suffocation for millions of small animals. Our approach has implications beyond laboratory animals. Currently, pigs being slaughtered are "stunned" (i.e., rendered unconscious using carbon dioxide before being exsanguinated and processed into meat). Sick babies are also suffocated. Everyone who has seen the carbon-dioxide procedure in use finds it abhorrent, even people in the industry.

A Life's Work

I have now done more than fiften hundred talks in more than thirty countries. Many of the speaking commitments have separated me from my family. Heeding Harry Chapin's message in the song "Cat's in the Cradle," I found ways to spend a large amount of time with my son during the years he was growing up, often taking him with me to talks on the Harley. When I needed to be gone, I always brought back a gift, starting in 1979 with a stuffed alligator from the University of Florida. I continue this tradition. (The stuff I have given him fills a room in his apartment, and occasionally he says, "Enough already. I'm thirty-one.") Partner in dialogue, companion, helper in numerous projects, Michael David Hume Rollin has been my closest male friend while living intellectually up to his name. He is a graduate of Stanford and of the University of Colorado Medical School and is now a child psychiatrist in Denver. While he had intended to be a pediatric oncologist, he told me one day, "Cancer kids are cured or dead in five years. Psychiatric children suffer their whole lives." He is so good at what he does that when he was working at the Veterans Administration hospital on a two-week rotation and had to move on, a patient who was a Vietnam War vet went to the administrator to demand that the "good doctor come back." It has been pointed out to me that he advocates for children as I do for animals, yet neither of us could stand the heartbreak of the other's job.

When I developed life-threatening cellulitis ("blood poisoning") in my leg in 1996 and required a week of hospitalization after running a 106-degree fever and requiring intravenous antibiotics, Mikey and Linda never left my bedside. Mikey carried me to the shower when I could not walk. A year later, when CSU experienced twelve inches of rain in a few hours and my office was under water, Mikey, then seventeen, willingly cut short our vacation to New Zealand to help save my books and papers and worked tirelessly for a week hauling and drying them. When the university tried to stop me from entering the building and saving my stuff, Mikey stood with me and faced down the moron campus policeman who tried to arrest us for trespassing. No one has ever had a better son—or a better wife. If I were religious, I would call their presence compensation for my lack of a father. Without them, I surely would have broken under the pressures of what I have chosen to combat.

I have many other projects for the future. For example, just as the Colorado agriculture law was signed, I was approached by the organizers of three western rodeos to help them harmonize rodeo with the emerging social ethics for animals I have described. I am often asked, "When will you retire?" My reply is "When they carry me out." As long as I'm physically and mentally healthy (some may doubt the latter even now), I will continue my battle for what Gandhi called the "most disenfranchised members of society." I have been blessed to have the opportunity to work in this area and would not have chosen any other path. I have seen many hideous and evil things, but in the end, I have seen more than enough good to balance it out. I hope in some way this book inspires other people to undertake this battle.

Acknowledgments

Family and More

My mother, **Yetta Rollin**, who taught me compassion
My wife, **Linda**, and son, **Mike**, for love, friendship, and criticism
Dr. Arthur Danto, mentor and friend
Dr. Harold Breen, pathologist, who created my interest in veterinary ethics
Dr. Bill Tietz, dean, who gave me the chance to teach it
Dr. Bob Phemister, dean, who supported me through critical years
Dr. James Voss, dean and friend
Dr. Harry Gorman, co-teacher and friend
Dr. Dennis McCurnin, co-teacher of veterinary ethics and friend
Dr. Tony Knight, co-teacher of veterinary ethics and force for change
Dr. Lynne Kesel, longtime student, teacher, colleague, and collaborator
Dr. Glenn Severin, colleague and friend
Dr. Cleon Kimberling, colleague and friend
Dr. Steve Withrow, colleague and friend
Dr. Wayne Mcllwraith, colleague and friend
Dr. Jim Wilson, veterinarian, lawyer, colleague, and friend
Dr. Tim Blackwell, editor of my *Canadian Veterinary Journal* ethics column, friend, and colleague
Dr. Terry Engle, colleague and friend
Drs. Doug Hare and **Carlton Gyles**, editors, *Canadian Veterinary Journal*

Rev. Dr. Robert Lawrence and the late **Dr. Betty Lawrence**, fast friends
Dr. Jay Merriam, colleague and friend
Drs. Patty and **Jerry Olson**, colleagues and friends
Kent Deitemeyer, colleague and close friend
Drs. Bruce Golden and **Ralph Switzer**, business partners and friends
Dr. Ray Whalen, colleague and friend
Drs. Walt Weirich, **Mimi Arighi**, and **Alan Beck**, friends and mentors at Purdue University
Drs. Brian Forsgren and **Barry Kipperman**, practitioners extraordinaire and friends
Gretchen Van Houten and **David Rosenbaum**, friends and editors at Iowa State Press/Blackwell
Drs. Wade Troxell, **Carl Kaiser**, and **Ross McGregor**, colleagues and friends

Animal Ethics

Dr. Steve Sapontzis, colleague and friend
Dr. Evelyn Pluhar, colleague and friend
Dr. Michael Fox, colleague and friend
Dr. Andrew Rowan, colleague and friend
Dr. Franklin Loew, colleague and friend
Dr. Earl Dixon, colleague and friend
Dr. Paul Waldau, former head of the master's program in Animals and Public Policy, Tufts University
Steve Mitchell, editor at Prometheus
Dr. Dick Kitchener and my Department of Philosophy colleagues at Colorado State University
Dr. Marc Bekoff, scientist, philosopher, ally, and friend

Animal Research

Dr. David Neil, laboratory-animal veterinarian and coauthor of the U.S. laws
Bob Welborn, lawyer and coauthor of the U.S. laws
Dr. Gordan Niswender, orchestrator of CSU's IACU in 1980
Dr. David Robertshaw, physiologist and colleague
Dr. Ralph Christofferson, president of CSU, who gave me the university's endorsement when I testified before Congress
U.S. Senator **Bob Dole** and U.S. Representative **Pat Schroeder**, who carried the laws
Dr. Lloyd Faulkner for his trust in giving me a position in physiology

Drs. Ed Hoover, **Gerry Callahan**, **Dick Bowen**, **Colin Clay, Alan Tucker**, **George Seidel**, **Terry Nett**, and **Skip Bartol** for much dialogue on these issues
Dr. Sue Vanderwoude, colleague and friend
Dr. Bruce Wunder, colleague and friend
Dr. Alan Goldberg, colleague and friend
Dr. Tom Wolfle, colleague and friend
Dr. Charmaine Foltz, colleague and friend
Dr. Harry Rowsell, colleague and friend
Dr. Larry Carbone, colleague and friend
All of the authors who contributed to the two volumes of *The Experimental Animal in Biomedical Research*

Agriculture

Dr. Glen Rask, colleague and friend
Dr. Ed Pexton, who first gave me the chance to teach in animal sciences
Dr. John Edwards, colleague and friend
Dr. Bill Wailes, colleague and friend
Dr. David Ames, colleague and friend
Dr. James Heird, colleague and friend
Steve Levalley, colleague and friend
Garth Boyd, colleague and friend
Animal Science Association
The fifteen thousand ranchers I have addressed
Robbie Hoffman and **Dennis Treacy**, executives at Smithfield Foods
Dr. John Benson, coeditor of *The Well-Being of Farm Animals: Challenges and Solutions*
My colleagues on the Pew Commission, as discussed in the text
My thousands of students in veterinary medicine, agriculture, and philosophy, particularly **Nancy Cunningham Butler** and **Steve Hillard**—the best!
Dr. Murray Nabors, co-teacher of biology for twenty-five years
Dr. Tony Frank, president of CSU
Thousands of veterinarians and scientists who have welcomed me as a colleague
My weight-room friends
Dr. George Davie, great teacher and role model
Colorado State University, the most supportive institution possible
Chuck Sylvester, **Barney Casher**, and **Leon Vick**, friends in the rodeo and show industries

As Well As

My animal friends: **Queenie**, **Blackie**, **Helga**, **Mao**, **Maw**, **Moo**, **Julius**, **Judy**, **Allergen**, **Stephen**, **Wild Oscar**, **Punks**, **Brandy**, **Blitz**, **Dillinger**, **Parvo**, **Gizmo**, **Colonel**, **Xander**, **Kiwi**, **Walter**, **Tootsie**, **Fritz**, **Molly**, **King**, **Raszam**, **Edward R.**, **Lisa**, **Farkie**, **Tuna**, and **Fin**, whom I thank for their unqualified love and to whom I hope I was, in small measure, as good a friend as they were to me

Last, but Not Least

Brittnee Merritt and **Joycebeth Emanuel**, typists extraordinaire, for turning handwritten gibberish into intelligible typescript

References

Anand, K.J.S., and K. D. Craig. 1996. "New Perspectives on the Definition of Pain." *Pain* 67:3–6.

Anand, K.J.S., and P. R. Hickey. 1987. "Pain and Its Effects in the Human Neonate and Fetus." *New England Journal of Medicine* 317, no. 21 (November 19): 1321–1329.

———. 1992. "Halothane–Morphine Compared with High-Dose Sufentanil for Anesthesia and Post-operative Analgesia in Neonatal Cardiac Surgery." *New England Journal of Medicine* 326, no. 1 (January 2): 1–9.

Ayer, Alfred J. 1936. *Language, Truth, and Logic.* London: V. Gollancz.

Beggs, S. 2003. "Postnatal Development of Pain Pathways and Consequences of Early Injury." Paper presented at the Eighth World Congress of Veterinary Anesthesia, Knoxville, Tennessee.

Benson, G. John, and Bernard E. Rollin, eds. 2004. *The Well-Being of Farm Animals: Challenges and Solutions.* Ames, Iowa: Blackwell.

Bentham, Jeremy. 1789. *An Introduction to the Principles of Morals and Legislation.* London: Payne.

Boring, Edwin G. 1950. *A History of Experimental Psychology.* 2nd ed. Englewood Cliffs, N.J.: Prentice-Hall.

Braybrooke, David. 1967. "Ideology." In *The Encyclopedia of Philosophy.* Vol. 4. New York: Macmillan, 124–127.

Clanton. C. 1990. "Animal Welfare: Lessons from Europe." *National Hog Farmer* (December 15).

Council for Agricultural Science and Technology (CAST). 1981. *Scientific Aspects of the Welfare of Food Animals.* Report no. 91, November.

Crawford, M. 1987. "Religious Groups Join Animal Patent Battle." *Science* 237:480–481

Darwin, Charles. 1872. *The Expression of the Emotions in Man and Animals.* London: John Murray.

———. 1886. *The Formation of Vegetable Mould through the Action of Worms with Observations on Their Habits.* London: John Murray.

———. [1871] 1971. *The Descent of Man, and Selection in Relation to Sex.* New York: Modern American Library.

Davis, Lloyd E. 1983. "Species Differences in Drug Disposition as Factors in Alleviation of Pain." In *Animal Pain: Perception and Alleviation.* Ed. R. L. Kitchell and H. H. Erickson. Bethesda, Md.: American Physiological Society, 161–178.

Evans, Edward P. 1898. *Evolutional Ethics and Animal Psychology.* New York: D. Appleton.

Ferrell, B. R., and M. Rhiner. 1991. "High-Tech Comfort: Ethical Issues in Cancer Pain Management for the 1990s." *Journal of Clinical Ethics* 2:108–112.

Feyerabend, Paul. 1975. *Against Method: Outline of an Anarchistic Theory of Knowledge.* Atlantic Highlands, N.J.: Humanities Press.

Finsen, Lawrence, and Susan Finsen. 1994. *The Animal Rights Movement in America: From Compassion to Respect.* New York: Twayne.

Fraser, Andrew F., and Donald M. Broom. 1990. *Farm Animal Welfare and Behaviour.* Wallingford, U.K.: CAB International.

Gärtner, K., D. Buttner, R. Döhler, J. Friedel, J. Lindena, and I. Trautschold. 1980. "Stress Response of Rats to Handling and Isolation on Some Physiological Variables, Skin Function, and Experimental Procedures." *Laboratory Animals* 14:267–274.

Gaskell, George, J. Durant, W. Wagner, H. Torgerson, E. Einsiedel, E. Jelsoe, H. Fredrickson, et al. 1997. "Europe Ambivalent on Biotechnology." *Nature* 387:845–847.

Glut, Donald F. 1984. *The Frankenstein Catalogue: Being a Comprehensive History of Novels, Translations, Adaptations, Stories, Critical Works, Popular Articles, Series, Verse, Stage Plays, Films, Cartoons, Puppetry, Radio and Television Programs, Comics, Satire and Humor, Spoken Musical Recordings, Tapes and Sheet Music Featuring Frankenstein's Monster and/or Descended from Mary Shelley's Novels.* Jefferson, N.C.: McFarland.

Goldhagen, Daniel J. 1996. *Hitler's Willing Executioners: Ordinary Germans and the Holocaust.* New York: Alfred A. Knopf.

Gonyou, H. W., P. H. Hemsworth, and J. L. Barnett. 1986. "Effects of Frequent Interactions with Humans on Growing Pigs." *Applied Animal Behavior Science* 16:269–278.

Gould, James L., and William T. Keeton, eds. 1986. *Biological Science.* New York: W. W. Norton.

Grandin, Temple. 1991. "Handling Problems Caused by Excitable Pigs." In *Proceedings of the 37th International Congress of Meat Science and Technology.* Vol. 1. Kulmbach, Germany: Federal Centre for Meat Research, 249–251.

———. 1995. *Thinking in Pictures: And Other Reports from My Life with Autism.* New York: Doubleday.

Grandin, Temple, with Catherine Johnson. 2005. *Animals in Translation: Using the Mysteries of Autism to Decode Animal Behavior.* New York: Scribner.

Gray, Elizabeth. 1999. "Do Respiratory Patients Receive Adequate Analgesia?" *Nursing Standard* 13 (47): 32–35.

Harrison, Ruth. 1964. *Animal Machines: The New Factory Farming Industry.* London: V. Stuart.

Hemsworth, P. H., J. L. Barnett, and C. Hansen. 1986. "The Influence of Handling by Humans on the Behavior, Reproduction, and Cortico Steroids of Male and Female Pigs." *Applied Animal Behaviour Science* 15 (July): 303–314.

Hofstadter, Richard. 1963. *Anti-intellectualism in American Life.* New York: Knopf.

Hume, David. [1739] 1896. *A Treatise of Human Nature.* Ed. Lewis A. Selby-Bigge. Oxford: Clarendon Press.

Johnstone, Robert E. 1973. "A Ketamine Trip" (letter to the editor). *Anesthesiology* 39, no. 4 (October): 460–461.

Kilgour, Ronald, and Clive Dalton. 1984. *Livestock Behaviour: A Practical Guide.* Boulder, Colo.: Westview Press.

Kitchell, Ralph L., and Howard H. Erickson, eds. 1983. *Animal Pain: Perception and Alleviation.* Bethesda, Md.: American Physiological Society.

Lawrence, Elizabeth Atwood. 1982. *Rodeo: An Anthropologist Looks at the Wild and the Tame.* Knoxville: University of Tennessee Press.

LeBaron, Charles. 1981. *Gentle Vengeance: An Account of the First Year at Harvard Medical School.* New York: R. Marek.

Lee, B. Howard. 2002. "Managing Pain in Human Neonates: Applications for Animals." *Journal of the American Veterinary Medical Association* 221, no. 2 (July): 233–237.

Legislative History of the Animal Wefare Act. 2007. AWIC Resource Series No. 41. Available at www.nal.usda.gov/awic/pubs/AWA2007/awa.shtml.

Liebeskind, John C., and Ronald Melzack. 1987. "The International Pain Foundation: Meeting a Need for Education in Pain Management." *Pain* 30, no. 1 (July): 1–2.

Lumb, W. V. 1963. *Small Animal Anesthesia.* Philadelphia: Lea and Febiger.

Lumb, W. V., and E. W. Jones. 1973. *Veterinary Anesthesia.* Philadelphia: Lea and Febiger.

Mader, Sylvia S. 1987. *Biology: Evolution, Diversity, and the Environment.* 2nd ed. Dubuque, Iowa: W. C. Brown.

Marks, Richard M., and Edward J. Sachar. 1973. "Undertreatment of Medical Inpatients with Narcotic Analgesics." *Annals of Internal Medicine* 78, no. 2 (February): 173–181.

Marx, Melvin H., and William A. Hillix. 1963. *Systems and Theories in Psychology.* New York: McGraw-Hill.

Merillat, Louis A. 1906. *Veterinary Surgery.* Chicago: A. Eger.

Merksey, Harold. 1996. "Response to Editorial: New Perspectives on the Definition of Pain." *Pain* 60:209.

Milgram, Stanley. 1975. *Obedience to Authority: An Experimental View.* New York: Harper and Row.

Mill, John Stuart. 1852. *Principles of Political Economy.* Vol. 2. 3rd ed. London: John W. Parker and Son.

Morgan, Conway Lloyd. [1904] 2000. *An Introduction to Comparative Psychology.* Repr. ed. Boston: Adamant Media.

Nerein, R. M., M. J. Levesque, and J. F. Cornhill. 1980. "Social Environment as a Factor in Diet-Induced Atherosclerosis." *Science* 208 (4451): 1475–1476.

Pernick, Martin S. 1985. *A Calculus of Suffering: Pain, Professionalism, and Anesthesia in Nineteenth-Century America.* New York: Columbia University Press.

Pursel, Vernon G., Carl A. Pinkert, Kurt F. Miller, Douglas J. Bolt, Roger G. Campbell, Richard D. Palmiter, Ralph L. Brinster, and Robert E. Hammer. 1989. "Genetic Engineering of Livestock." *Science* 244 (June 16): 1281–1288.

Regan, Tom. 1983. *The Case for Animal Rights.* Berkeley: University of California Press.

Rifkin, Jeremy. 1895. *Declaration of a Heretic.* Boston: Routledge and Kegan Paul.

Rollin, Bernard E. 1976. *Natural and Conventional Meaning: An Examination of the Distinction.* The Hague: Mouton.

———. 1981. *Animal Rights and Human Morality.* Buffalo, N.Y.: Prometheus Books [2nd ed., 1992; 3rd ed., 2006].

———. 1989. *The Unheeded Cry: Animal Consciousness, Animal Pain, and Science.* Oxford: Oxford University Press.

———. 1995a. *Farm Animal Welfare: Social, Bioethical, and Research Issues.* Ames: Iowa State University Press.

———. 1995b. *The Frankenstein Syndrome: Ethical and Social Issues in the Genetic Engineering of Animals.* Cambridge: Cambridge University Press.

———. 1999. "Some Conceptual and Ethical Concerns about Current Views of Pain." *Pain Forum* 8 (2): 78–83.

———. 2001. "Ethics, Science, and Antimicrobial Resistance." *Journal of Agricultural and Environmental Ethics* 14 (1): 29–37

———. 2004. "Annual Meeting Keynote Address: Animal Agriculture and Emerging Social Ethics for Animals." *Journal of Animal Science* 82:955–964.

———. [1981] 2006. *Animal Rights and Human Morality.* 3rd ed. Amherst, N.Y.: Prometheus Books.

———. 2006a. *An Introduction to Veterinary Ethics: Theory and Cases.* 3rd ed. Ames, Iowa: Blackwell.

———. 2006b. "'It's My Own Damn Head': Ethics, Freedom, and Helmet Laws." In *Harley-Davidson and Philosophy: Full-Throttle Aristotle.* Ed. Bernard E. Rollin, Carolyn M. Gray, Kerri Mommer, and Cynthia Pineo. Chicago: Open Court, 133–144.

———. 2006c. *Science and Ethics.* Cambridge: Cambridge University Press.

———. 2007a. "Animal Research: A Moral Science," *EMBO Reports* 8 (6): 521–525.

———. 2007b. "Overcoming Ideology: Why It Is Necessary to Create a Culture in Which the Ethical Review of Protocols Can Flourish?" *ILAR Journal* 48 (1): 47–53.

Rollin, Bernard E., Carolyn M. Gray, Kerri Mommer, and Cynthia Pineo, eds. 2006. *Harley-Davidson and Philosophy: Full-Throttle Aristotle.* Chicago: Open Court.

Rollin, Bernard E., and M. Lynne Kesel. 1989–1995. *The Experimental Animal in Biomedical Research.* 2 vols. Boca Raton, Fla.: CRC Press.

Romanes, George J. 1883. *Animal Intelligence.* New York: D. Appleton.

———. 1884. *Mental Evolution in Animals.* New York: D. Appleton.

Russell, Bertrand. 1912. *The Problems of Philosophy.* Cambridge: Williams and Norgate.

Russell, W.M.S., and R. L. Burch 1959. *The Principles of Humane Experimental Technique.* London: Methuen.

Sacks, Oliver W. 1995. *An Anthropologist on Mars: Seven Paradoxical Tales.* New York: Knopf.

Salt, Henry S. 1892. *Animal Rights Considered in Relation to Social Progress.* London: George Bell and Sons.

Sapontzis, Steve F. 1987. *Morals, Reason, and Animals.* Philadelphia: Temple University Press.

Schiller, Claire H., ed. and trans. 1957. *Instinctive Behavior: The Development of a Modern Concept.* New York: International Universities Press.

Seabrook, M. F. 1980. "The Psychological Relationship between Diary Cows and Dairymen and Its Implication for Animal Welfare." *Journal for the Study of Animal Problems* 1:295–298

Singer, Peter. 1975. *Animal Liberation: A New Ethics for Our Treatment of Animals.* New York: Random House.

State v. Bogardus. 1877. 4 Mo. App. 215.

Stolba, Alex, and David Wood-Gush. 1981. "Behaviour of Pigs and the Design of a New Housing System." *Applied Animal Ethology* 8 (6): 583–584.

Stookey, J. M., and J. F. Patience. 1991. "High Technology in Pork Production and Its Welfare Implications." In *High Technology and Animal Welfare.* Ed. Jerome Martin. Edmonton: University of Alberta Press, 61–79.

Taylor, Robert E. 1992. *Scientific Farm Animal Production: An Introduction to Animal Science.* 4th ed. New York: Macmillan.

Walco, Gary A., Robert C. Cassidy, and Neil L. Schechter. 1994. "Pain, Hurt, and Harm: The Ethics of Pain Control in Infants and Children." *New England Journal of Medicine* 331, no. 8 (August 25): 541–544.

Waters v. the People. 1896. 23 Colo. 33.

Watson, John B. 1913. "Psychology as the Behaviorist Views It." *Psychological Review* 20:158–177.

Wittgenstein, Ludwig. 1965. "A Lecture on Ethics." *Philosophical Review* 74:3–12.

Wood-Gush, David G. M. 1983. *Elements of Ethnology: A Textbook for Agricultural and Veterinary Students.* London: Chapman and Hall.

Index

Bernard E. Rollin is Colorado State University Distinguished Professor of Philosophy and University Bioethicist. He is the author of more than five hundred articles and seventeen books, the most recent of which is the book *Science and Ethics*. In 2005 he received the Henry Spira Award from the Johns Hopkins University Center for Alternatives to Animal Testing.